HELL IS UPON US

HELL IS UPON US

D-Day in the Pacific
June–August 1944

VICTOR BROOKS

DA CAPO PRESS
A Member of the Perseus Books Group

Library of Congress Cataloging-in-Publication Data
Brooks, Victor.
    Hell is upon us: D-Day in the Pacific—
June-August 1944 / Victor Brooks.
        p.   cm.
    Includes bibliographical references and index.
    HC: ISBN-13: 978-0-306-81369-6; ISBN-10: 0-306-81369-6
    PBK: ISBN-13: 978-0-306-81549-2; ISBN-10: 0-306-81549-4
    1. World War, 1939-1945—Campaigns—Mariana Islands.
I. Title.
D767.99.M27B76 2005
940.54'26—dc22

                                        2005022090

Book Design by Cynthia Young

First Da Capo Press paperback edition 2007
First Da Capo Press edition 2005
A Member of the Perseus Books Group
http://www.dacapopress.com

Da Capo Press books are available at special discounts for bulk
purchases in the U.S. by corporations, institutions, and other
organizations. For more information, please contact the Special
Markets Department at the Perseus Books Group, 11 Cambridge
Center, Cambridge, MA 02142, or call (800)255-1514 or
(617)252-5298, or e-mail special.markets@perseusbooks.com

CONTENTS

MAPS

PREFACE

FOR AMERICANS the war with Japan was, in many respects, a three-part drama that rivaled the war described in Homer's *Iliad* in its rapid shifts along the emotional spectrum. During the course of four years, the people of the United States experienced a range of emotions—from the utter shock and outrage at the news of the attack on Pearl Harbor to the ultimate relief and satisfaction of an unconditional Nipponese surrender at the end of the conflict. The story of the epic conflict in the Pacific can be told as a trilogy: The opening episode would chronicle the account from Pearl Harbor to the first American offensive at Guadalcanal, and the concluding episode would describe the period from Douglas MacArthur's return to the Philippines to the Japanese surrender on the battleship *Missouri*. However, the middle period of the Pacific War, which extends roughly from early 1943 to late summer of 1944, tends to receive proportionately far less attention in films, documentaries, and books. Yet it was during this period that the fate of Japan was sealed: The tide of war swung irrevocably in favor of the United States.

This book focuses on the most important battle in the middle period of the Pacific War—the struggle by the United States and Japan to control the land, seas, and skies in and around the Marianas Islands, which the senior officer in the United States Navy, Admiral Ernest King, insisted was the key to the ultimate American victory.

I entered the intriguing world of Operation Forager and the rest of the Central Pacific campaign somewhat through the side door. As I worked on a previous book about the Normandy campaign, I came to appreciate the ability of the United States to conduct two of the most massive invasions in history within just nine days, and the enormity of the task involved in America's attempt to breach, almost simultaneously, both Adolf Hitler's Atlantic Wall and Hideki Tojo's Absolute Defense Line. As I investigated the interaction between

Overlord and Forager, I realized that a book-length treatment of the Pacific campaign surrounding "the other D-Day" would be an appealing and worthwhile project.

This book is an attempt to chronicle the Marianas campaign, not only from the experiences of the men who planned the battles and fought in them but also from a broader perspective in overall American military history. I have not hesitated to chronicle this campaign in the broader context of the strategy to defeat the Axis as a whole, which was the central consideration of all American planning during World War II.

Writing this book was a project that benefited enormously from numerous relationships in several environments. At my publishing home of the Perseus Group, Robert Pigeon, senior editor at DaCapo, encouraged me to pursue this topic from the day it was suggested. At my academic home, Villanova University, Dr. John Johannes, Vice-President of Academic Affairs, the Reverend Kail Ellis, O.S.A., Dean of the College of Arts and Sciences, and Dr. Connie Titone, Chairperson of the Department of Education and Human Services, provided reduced teaching loads and travel funds for my research. Jessica Kirwan, Liz Elsas, and Anne Feldman have assisted immeasurably in developing the successive drafts of the book.

Colonel Bruce Hulick, USMC, Chair of the NROTC Program at Villanova, opened an invaluable portal to armed services archives.

At my real home, my sons, Matthew, Gregory, and Stephen Brooks, helped me keep at least one eye on the outside world while I researched the events of 1944. Finally, a special acknowledgement must go to the surviving members of the U.S. Army, Navy, and Marine Corps units who engaged a brave and deadly enemy in that long-ago summer and left their own unique imprint on a world that is much better for their heroic sacrifices.

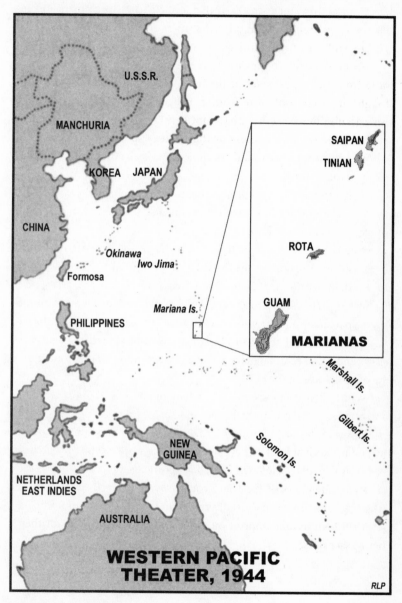

SAIPAN

TINIAN

ROTA

GUAM

MARIANAS

U.S.S.R.

MANCHURIA

KOREA JAPAN

CHINA

Okinawa

Iwo Jima

Formosa

PHILIPPINES

Mariana Is.

Marshall Is.

Gilbert Is.

NEW
GUINEA

Solomon Is.

NETHERLANDS
EAST INDIES

AUSTRALIA

WESTERN PACIFIC
THEATER, 1944

RLP

Western Pacific Theater

PROLOGUE

THE FIRST HINT of the tropical dawn on Monday, December 8, 1941, found Captain George McMillen, USN, preparing for two notable events on the island for which he was both governor and garrison commander. First, the Pan American Airlines flying boat *Philippine Clipper* was just taking off from Wake Island, 1,300 miles to the east, and would land on Guam later in the day as one leg of its journey from California to the Orient. The arrival of the *Clipper* was usually a festive occasion because the passenger list was filled with movie stars, major corporate executives, and other celebrities who could afford the fare that was the equivalent of two years wages for an average American factory worker. However, today the arrival of the *Clipper* coincided with an equally festive event, the celebration of the feast of the Immaculate Conception with its mix of liturgical and social pageantry. The 25,000 natives of Guam had enthusiastically supported their ties with the United States over the past four decades, but the Catholicism brought by the Spanish missionaries in an earlier time still dominated the spiritual lives of the Chamorro people.

As Captain McMillen and his staff waited for word of the arrival time of the *Clipper* from Wake Island, more than one serviceman probably compared his tour of duty on Guam with the conditions of his comrades in arms 1,300 miles to the east. Guam had more than a hundred times the land mass of Wake and featured towns with movies, restaurants, and bars peopled by an enormously pro-American population that was already enjoying many of the benefits of United States citizenship. On the other hand, Wake's population of hermit crabs, birds, and oversized rats offered little distraction for the bored sailors and Marines deployed on the island.

This was late autumn, 1941, and Captain McMillen knew that in the increasingly imminent showdown with the Japanese Empire the bored garrison on Wake was far more likely to defend itself successfully than his own meager forces. During the past few months, Wake had begun to emerge as a major linchpin in the American presence in the Pacific Ocean; already four hundred Marines, batteries of 5-inch naval guns and 3-inch antiaircraft guns, and a squadron of Wildcat fighter planes had arrived, and a steady stream of men, tanks, and planes was expected in the near future. Guam had initially been on the same priority list as Wake, but the island's relative proximity to Japan and Imperial control of the rest of the Marianas chain had induced more pacifistic members of Congress to limit the American presence to a token force.

Guam was not totally defenseless. McMillen could deploy an understrength company of 153 Marines equipped with perhaps 120 rifles, a dozen World War I Lewis machine guns, and a few Browning automatic rifles. However, the rest of the garrison of 266 naval personnel, five navy nurses, and eighty native Insular Force Guards was armed only with a motley collection of .45 pistols and a few rifles dating from the initial American landing four decades earlier. The naval captain also commanded a "fleet" of two unarmed patrol boats: a decommissioned oiler, USS *Barnes,* and a "flagship," USS *Penguin,* which was a slightly larger patrol boat that boasted a pair of 50-caliber machine guns, the heaviest firepower on the island. This small, underarmed force was only 34 miles from the southern tip of the Japanese-occupied Marianas that bristled with naval bases, airfields, and encampments for several thousand Imperial troops. Although a powerfully fortified Guam could have been an outer bastion of the Philippines and a springboard for American submarines and air attacks on any southward Japanese offensive, McMillen and his tiny garrison were little more than prisoners of war in waiting the moment the expansionist Nipponese decided to challenge the United States for control of the Pacific.

At 5:45 a.m. on Monday morning in Hawaii, Captain McMillen received the startling news from Asiatic Fleet headquarters near Manila that Pearl Harbor had been attacked, the *Clipper* had been recalled to Wake, and the Japanese could be expected to bomb Guam at any minute. The small number of Japanese subjects were duly rounded up and imprisoned, the few available machine guns were fully manned, and the *Penguin* prepared to move from Apra Harbor to the open sea. Twenty minutes earlier, the commander of Japanese air units on Saipan, 100 miles north, had received word that war with America had begun and he was to "begin attacks on Guam immediately." Less than three hours later, the battle for the Marianas began.

At just past 8:30 a.m., lookouts on Guam sighted neat V-formations of Japanese planes glide out of a brilliant blue sky and begin their work of destruction. *Barnes* was still moored to a dock in Apra Harbor and pummeled by a string of bombs. *Penguin* was just leaving the harbor when the first strafing run cut through several crew members. A few minutes later, a stick of bombs sent the tiny vessel to the bottom as its captain and other survivors began to swim for shore. Other Japanese squadrons hit cable and wireless stations, bombed the Marine barracks on Orote Peninsula, and pounded the handful of machine guns that challenged their control of the air.

The next day, Tuesday, December 9, while Franklin Roosevelt was delivering his famous "day of infamy" speech in Congress, the planes returned to further demolish American defenses while a powerful invasion force maneuvered toward the island. To defeat an American garrison of less than five hundred men with fewer than two hundred rifles among them, the Japanese senior commanders had dispatched two invasion forces, either one of which could easily have captured Guam on its own. The navy contributed a special naval infantry landing force of seven hundred men and an invasion fleet that included four destroyers, a seaplane tender, and a mine layer, all covered by more than a hundred attack planes. In turn, not to be outdone, the army contributed the South Seas Detachment, a contingent of 5,500 soldiers that had been assembled in the Bonin Islands in November. Either the Japanese high command believed that the Americans had cleverly concealed several thousand troops in the jungle portions of Guam or this was one battle that the Imperial forces had no intention of losing under any circumstances.

At 4:00 a.m. on Wednesday, December 10, landing boats carrying four hundred Japanese naval troops maneuvered offshore from the main recreational beach just north of Guam's capital city of Agana and the first troops splashed into waist-deep water and streamed ashore. As the lead units pushed down the shore road toward the outskirts of Agana, a single machine gun manned by Insular Guards opened fire and brought the advance to a temporary halt. The defenders were now fully warned of the threat. Marine Lieutenant Charles Todd stormed out of Government House, the seat of government on Guam, and pulled together a makeshift defense force of about twenty Marines and sailors and nearly sixty Insular Guards and deployed them in the buildings surrounding Agana's main plaza. Although outnumbered five-to-one, the lightly armed defenders used cover and concealment to maximum advantage and twice launched successful counterattacks to drive the invaders out of the plaza. However, as the battle evolved into a house-to-house shootout, the majority of leathernecks and blue jackets were killed or wounded and the Insular Guards were rapidly running out of ammunition for their antiquated weapons.

At this point, the fighting spilled onto the grounds of Government House just as Captain McMillen was receiving reports of an even larger landing attempt to the south of Orote Peninsula and the Marine barracks. "The situation was simply hopeless," McMillen related, and the governor envisioned the already one-sided battle degenerating into a massacre of civilians. At a few minutes past 5:30, an auto horn sounded three times and Commander D. T. Giles walked out of the palace to parley with Commander Hiromu Hayashi, who insisted that immediate surrender would guarantee the civil rights of the natives and decent treatment for the garrison.

At 5:45 a.m., exactly forty-eight hours after he received Admiral Thomas Hart's war warning, Captain McMillen signed the articles of surrender and the Stars and Stripes were lowered from Government House, where they had flown for more than forty-two years. A few hours later, as Japanese army personnel marched out onto Orote Peninsula and into the Marine encampment, the colors were lowered from the Marine barracks in the first American military surrender of World War II. As American sailors and Marines were herded into prison camps for transfer to the harshness of captivity in Japan, nearly 25,000 residents of Guam settled into an uncertain existence as new subjects of the Japanese Empire, a life that would enter an increasing world of horror during the next thirty months.

However, neither the surrendered garrison nor the native population of Guam ever doubted that the Americans would return and, just over a year later, events were set in motion by which not only Guam but also the key Japanese-mandated islands of Saipan and Tinian would become the objectives in one of the largest amphibious invasions in history.

1

RENDEZVOUS
AT CASABLANCA

As people throughout the Unites States celebrated their farewells to 1942 and prepared to welcome the new year of 1943, a small but lively gathering of six couples was finishing dinner in the White House. Franklin and Eleanor Roosevelt were hosting the crown prince and princess of German-occupied Norway and a group of close friends and advisors, including Harry Hopkins. After a leisurely, convivial meal, the president directed his guests to his intimate, plush theater, where he informed the small gathering that he had obtained an advance copy of a film that would almost certainly become one of the biggest hits of the coming year. A few minutes later, the members sat spellbound as they watched black-and-white images of Humphrey Bogart and Ingrid Bergman reignite a long-dormant love affair set against the background of exotic French North Africa. The dominant theme of sacrificing personal romantic desires for the greater cause of democracy and freedom would thrill movie audiences a few weeks later when the film was released to theaters and would create a bond with its audience that far transcended the World War II era.[1]

A week or so after this private film screening, Franklin Roosevelt was transported to a special railroad siding under the Bureau of

Engineering and Printing and was ushered aboard a special twelve-car train that included a presidential coach equipped with a card room and kitchen and fitted with windows designed to deflect machine-gun bullets. At 10:30 on a cold Saturday night, the train lurched into motion and sped southward toward Miami, the first stop in a 6,000-mile odyssey for the commander in chief. As the train glided through the frosty fields and small towns of the Virginia countryside, the president most likely spent some time savoring the excitement of becoming the first chief executive since Abraham Lincoln to visit an active war front and the first American leader in history to leave the country in wartime.[2]

It is also reasonable to expect that Roosevelt's thoughts shifted for at least a moment to the irony of this journey in relation to the film he had enjoyed a few days earlier. The title of the movie was *Casablanca,* and now the president was traveling to the real city of that name for his first meeting with the British prime minister Winston Churchill since the dark days of December 1941.

Although few people realized it at the time, this conference, set against the spectacular backdrop of the Mediterranean Sea, would initiate one of the greatest combined air, sea, and land confrontations of World War II. It would be the beginning of the end for Japanese hopes of emerging from the conflict anything short of total defeat.

Franklin Delano Roosevelt had not traveled in an airplane since his dramatic flight from Albany to Chicago to accept his party's nomination for the 1932 presidential election. Roosevelt's boyish sense of adventure made the series of noisy, jolting, bumpy flights more tolerable for the president than for his staff, who simply wanted this aerial purgatory to end as soon as possible. As the plane droned toward the German-dominated continent of Europe, the commander in chief peered out of his window at the American fighter planes flying close cover and perhaps wondered more than once whether he would see them engage warplanes that featured the markings of the still-potent Luftwaffe. However, the presidential plane reached the snowcapped Atlas Mountains without incident and landed near Casablanca; as the olive-drab aircraft taxied, a plump, cigar-puffing colleague strode towards it.

Winston Spencer Churchill had completed an equally uncomfortable, though shorter, journey from England two days earlier and now he effusively welcomed his American counterpart and pointed out the impressive sights as the official motorcade carried them from newly liberated Casablanca to the resort town of Anfa, just outside the main city. This location featured a large hotel for conference meetings and a cluster of comfortable villas for the accommodation of Churchill, Roosevelt, and their senior advisors. The members of both parties noted the stunning contrast of purple flowers, white buildings, red soil, and blue sea, but the ocean was far from tranquil as Churchill insisted that "wonderful waves were rolling in with enormous clouds of foam. Waves 15 feet high were roaring up terrible rocks."[3]

The restless power and fury of the sea took on human form around the conference site. Churchill's advisor, the future prime minister Harold Macmillan, noted the imposing sight of "buildings ringed by a wire fence of immense strength and guarded by dozens of American soldiers" under the overall command of the omnipresent General George Patton. Macmillan said that he had "never seen so many soldiers around with such terrifying weapons"[4] but insisted that the presence of dozens of suspected Axis agents and sympathizers in the area necessitated the strictest security possible.

This summit by the sea, codenamed Symbol, was an opportunity for the president, the prime minister, and their respective military advisors to confer about strategic options that had altered dramatically since the dark days of thirteen months earlier. As senior British and American officers sat down at a glistening mahogany table in the Anfa Hotel's conference room on the morning of January 14, 1943, there was general agreement that the tide of battle was turning in favor of the Allies.[5]

During the past ten weeks, the texture of the European war had turned violently against the Axis. Germany's most publicized hero, Field Marshal Erwin Rommel, had been sent reeling from a dusty railroad depot at El Alamein after his lines were punctured by the awesome firepower of British Eighth Army under General Bernard Montgomery. Then a brilliant Allied amphibious landing in North Africa had not only threatened the Desert Fox's rear but also liberated the very city in which this conference was being held. Meanwhile, the quarter of a million crack troops of the German Sixth Army were being pulverized by the Red Army in the snow-covered skeletons that had once been the factories and department stores of the Volga River city of Stalingrad. The 90,000 emaciated survivors were now only days away from their final march into the enemy's prisoner of war camps. Few would ever emerge. On the other side of the globe, a Japanese high command that had lost four irreplaceable aircraft carriers in the tropical waters near Midway Island was now in the process of authorizing a humiliating evacuation of the island of Guadalcanal, in the Southern Solomons, as all attempts to expel an American invasion force had failed.

Thus, although some of the bloodiest battles of World War II remained to be fought, there was increasing agreement among the Anglo-American commanders that because the Axis had failed to win the war in 1942, the odds were shifting towards an eventual Allied victory. Roosevelt and Churchill were now so optimistic about the Allied prospects that they sat together in the almost blindingly bright North African sunshine and sternly informed reporters that they had just scuttled notions of a negotiated peace and would accept only unconditional surrender from their adversaries. Although British and American military leaders inwardly winced at political sloganeering that might push the enemy forces into a corner from which they would make a mutually bloody last stand, they also admitted that, for the first time, the totalitarian foes might actually collapse in the relatively imminent future. Unfortunately for the Allied cause, that was about the last point on which British and American officers could reach unreserved agreement with one another.

The Anglo-Americans formed one of the most impressive alliances in the annals of warfare. Winston Churchill paid glowing tributes to the beneficial partnership of these two dominant players in the

English-speaking "family of nations." However, the British and Americans were cousins, not identical twins, and the conference at Casablanca exposed some of the rifts within this extended "family." The British were fighting a war not only to prevent the enemy occupation of their homeland but to maintain an empire that contained millions of less-than-enthusiastic colonials. Churchill encouraged his commanders to develop strategies that would recover lost territories, such as Burma, Singapore, and Hong Kong; protect threatened ones, such as India; and regain control of the key imperial thoroughfare, the Mediterranean Sea.

However, by early 1943, Britain had mobilized about as many military units as the nation was capable of sustaining; Churchill and his commanders knew that as casualty lists lengthened there would not be enough replacements to keep regiments and divisions at full strength. On the other hand, the United States was nowhere near the peak of its military strength and would probably field far more divisions than the British if the war lasted much longer. Therefore, as Britain gradually slipped toward junior partner status, the nation's leaders designed two related strategies: one for their enemies, the other for their allies.

The strategy for dealing with the Axis would fall back on the traditional and proven technique of confronting the enemy around the periphery, thereby softening the opponent until a more decisive confrontation had a high probability of success. For the British leaders at Casablanca, this translated into a series of offensives in the Mediterranean to knock Italy out of the war, the postponement of a cross-Channel invasion of northwestern Europe until the Germans were somewhat less formidable, and a largely defensive posture against Japan until Hitler was defeated.[6]

This agenda would in turn be sold to the Americans by displaying more unified leadership, acquiring better intelligence-gathering capabilities, and utilizing far more personnel to develop these plans than the Americans would deploy for their similar tasks.

The American strategic vision revolved around far different theories and realities. The most important historical precedent to American commanders was the Civil War, in which Ulysses S. Grant and William T. Sherman had used concentrations of awesome military power to bludgeon the rebels into submission in bloody, but eventually decisive, battles. The Mediterranean would look surprisingly like a sideshow; the real action would be somewhere in the French countryside, where American tanks and soldiers would duel their German counterparts until the invaders thrust their forces deep inside Hitler's lair and forced a twentieth-century equivalent of Appomattox on the enemy. As the debate surged back and forth across that rich mahogany conference table, one senior American commander dramatically used the impending stalemate to shift the focus of the war thousands of miles from the Mediterranean or Europe.

Admiral Ernest J. King arrived at Casablanca as commander of a service that was expanding to become the largest navy in the history of warfare. He was convinced that most of his colleagues in the Hotel Anfa conference room were so focused on defeating Hitler that they were ignoring the far more imminent threat of Japanese aggression along an extended line that stretched all the way from Australia to Alaska. King's British parentage did not prevent him from deeply mistrusting the notions of Churchill and his commanders in developing proposed strategies, and he was convinced that Franklin Roosevelt, General George Marshall, and General Henry "Hap" Arnold were far from immune to British influence.

Ernest King's personal résumé was hardly an example of how to win friends and influence people. He was a heavy drinker, a notorious womanizer, and a highly opinionated mariner who was also foulmouthed, ill-tempered, and distant. He was also consistently loyal and gracious to junior officers on his staff, he exuded a bluff demeanor that often resonated with enlisted men, and he offered a blunt honesty that gained increasing favor with the commander in chief. Because the admiral had emerged as an excellent commander of the Atlantic Fleet during the twilight war with Germany in 1941, he was promoted to commander in chief, United States Fleet, a week after Pearl Harbor. He set up shop in a bare, dusty office, initially furnished with only a broken table and two chairs, on the third floor of the Navy Department building on Constitution Avenue. As papers piled up and his in-box overflowed, the Ohioan set in motion the plans to recover from Pearl Harbor, check the German submarine menace, and begin the long road back across the Pacific to recapture lost territories and eventually force Japan into submission. Now King sat at a conference table with his British and American counterparts and attempted to shift deliberations back from Europe to the Pacific. While British General Alan Brooke insisted of King that "the European war was just a great nuisance that kept him from waging his Pacific war undisturbed,"[7] the American admiral ignored neither the German naval threat to Allied communications nor the general policy of making the defeat of Hitler the highest priority. However, he vigorously opposed the British concept of war against Japan and attempted to discourage his American colleagues from jumping on this bandwagon.

The British view of the Pacific War in January 1943 was one that essentially accepted a stalemate until Germany was defeated. Churchill and his military commanders were certainly deeply concerned about the humiliating defeats in Hong Kong, Singapore, and Burma, and were probably as determined as their American counterparts to pound Japan into submission. However, at the moment, a huge German army was still poised only 20 miles from the shops and homes of Dover, London was under continued threat from the Luftwaffe, and the Nazi banner flew over most of the capitals of Europe. Hong Kong and Singapore were alien cities thousands of miles away; their liberation could wait until the main war was over. Therefore, the British strategy in the Pacific was to establish a defensive line to protect Australia, New Zealand, and Hawaii, and to smash enemy attempts to penetrate those positions. Then, after Hitler was defeated, those territories would be the springboard to an Allied offensive complemented by a drive from India toward Japanese positions in Burma and China.

King believed this strategy was a recipe for disaster.[8]

The admiral insisted that it was ridiculous to assume that the Japanese would simply halt operations at a line arbitrarily fixed by the Allies, probe up and down the long line of communication until they detected a weak spot, and then concentrate powerful forces to pierce the position and throw the Anglo-American strategy into chaos. The American naval commander argued that the enemy had to be kept off balance through a series of Allied offensives at places of their own choosing until the defeat of Germany released the overwhelming forces that would pound the enemy into submission.

King further pressed his argument for a more ambitious agenda towards Japan by revealing a complex set of computations suggesting that only 15 percent of all Allied resources in money, manpower, and weapons were directed toward the Pacific War and 85 percent were directed toward the European members of the Axis. An increase to even a modest 30 percent of all resources would support a series of campaigns that would keep the Japanese off balance and reduce the possibility of an enemy surprise offensive comparable in shock value to the attack on Pearl Harbor.[9]

This salty, opinionated sailor was essentially playing a high-stakes poker game with his British and American counterparts, but he quickly realized that he was gradually constructing a fairly solid hand. He then parlayed the complex interaction of the remaining five members of the Combined Chiefs of Staff into tacit approval for a Central Pacific offensive that would ultimately feature a massive Japanese-American showdown in the Marianas Islands.

The three British members of the Combined Chiefs, Field Marshal Sir Alan Brooke, Admiral Sir Dudley Pound, and Air Chief Marshal Sir Charles Portal, had used their far larger staffs and far better information-gathering facilities to shift the direction of the conference away from the American proposals of launching a cross-Channel invasion during 1943 and towards an enhanced Mediterranean offensive once the Germans were pushed out of North Africa. As their relentless offensive began to emerge victorious, they were willing to sweeten this tactical defeat for their American counterparts by proposing a statement for "maintaining pressure on Japan, retaining the initiative and attaining a position of readiness for a full scale offensive against Japan by the United Nations as soon as Germany is defeated."[10]

Although the directive did not envision a massive reallocation of resources from Europe to the Pacific, it did give King the authorization to initiate planning for his coveted operation, a drive across the Central Pacific. Once the British Chiefs had given their tacit approval for opening a new offensive against Japan, King shifted his attention to the commander of the United States Army to gain more tangible support for the projected thrust outward from Hawaii.

Although George C. Marshall was King's counterpart as chief of staff of the U.S. Army, the four-star general shared few personality traits with the outspoken admiral. The Virginia Military Institute graduate from Uniontown, Pennsylvania, seldom exhibited bursts of anger, enjoyed pre-dinner walks with his wife, Katherine, and rationed himself to minimal amounts of alcohol. His calm, sometimes icy, formality discouraged his commander in chief, who called virtually all service officers by their first names, from calling Marshall anything but General. However, by early 1943, Marshall and King, despite a wide range of differing viewpoints, were developing a high level of army-navy teamwork that the admiral was not hesitant to utilize.

King already commanded a formidable land force in the Marine Corps, which was currently expanding toward six combat divisions. This force, if fully concentrated, could probably outnumber the Japanese garrison of almost any targeted island between Hawaii and the inner defenses of the Nipponese homeland, but there were two significant complications to this calculus. First, the Marine units were not concentrated but were spread out throughout the Pacific and in other duty stations and training bases throughout the United States. For the foreseeable future, it was unlikely that more than two or three divisions would be available in a unified force for Central Pacific operations. Second, as each enemy island was captured, a fairly significant garrison would have to be deployed to discourage an enemy counterattack. As this process continued, the potential assault force for the next objective would become progressively smaller. Therefore, the army, which was expanding toward nearly ninety divisions, would emerge as a significant partner in King's offensive plans.

Events at the Casablanca meetings began to convince Marshall that Roosevelt was moving toward Churchill's plan to focus on the Mediterranean and postpone the chief of staff's plan for a cross-Channel invasion for at least a year. The general barely concealed his anger and disappointment with the British hijacking of his most important objective: He made less than subtle suggestions that if American soldiers were not going to be used in combat against Hitler in 1943, they might as well be used against Emperor Hirohito.[11]

Marshall's increasing enthusiasm for using more army resources to push the enemy back towards their home islands did not necessarily mean that those forces would be available for King's planned offensive. A brilliant, egocentric leader by the name of Douglas MacArthur had very different ideas on how to get to Japan; but as British and American leaders shared a final drink at Casablanca and headed back to their respective headquarters, the first, crucial steps toward the Marianas campaign had been taken.

2.

THE BALANCE OF FORCES

WHILE ERNEST KING was enjoying the bracing air and spectacular scenery of Casablanca, his Japanese counterpart was spending his waking hours in a hot, airless cabin in the mind-numbing humidity of the Imperial naval base on Truk Island. Admiral Isoroku Yamamoto, the son of peasants, had sought escape from a dull agrarian routine by enrolling in the Japanese naval academy and had subsequently prospered in a maritime career. Yamamoto was progressive and cosmopolitan, an officer who spoke English, avidly read *Life* and *Time* magazines, and preferred poker to the more nuanced games of his native land. An academic career at Harvard and a subsequent posting as a naval attaché in Washington impressed upon the future admiral the almost limitless productive capacity of the United States; thus Yamamoto leaned toward the senior officials who believed that war with America would be the greatest mistake in the nation's history. As the former peasant rose to the rank of senior command, he became increasingly identified with those army and navy officers who viewed the revolutionary, atheistic Soviet Union not only as Japan's primary enemy but the antithesis of everything the culturally conservative Japanese Empire valued.

Yamamoto watched the unraveling of relations between Japan and the United States with a degree of dread, but he was immensely proud of the powerful fleet of aircraft carriers he had developed, a force that by 1941 was actually slightly superior to its American counterpart. Thus, when General Hideki Tojo seized the positions of both war minister and prime minister and determined to attack the United States if the diplomatic stalemate continued, the admiral could confidently promise a devastating first blow against the enemy fleet anchored at Pearl Harbor. However, although Yamamoto assured the government leaders that he could "give America hell" for perhaps six months to a year, he insisted ominously that if Japan could not bring the United States to the peace table soon after, the empire would face terrible retribution from what the mariner called "a sleeping giant" that was America.

Yamamoto scored a spectacular, though incomplete, victory at Pearl Harbor and then proceeded to "give the Americans hell" for the six months he had predicted. However, now it was early 1943 and the other part of the admiral's prediction was also coming painfully true. A titanic showdown between an outnumbered American fleet and an overconfident Imperial force off the coast of Midway Island had reduced Japan's dominance in carriers to mere parity in that vital weapon. A surprise American counteroffensive in the Solomon Islands had pushed the Japanese forces back to their final lines of defense on Guadalcanal and prompted serious talk of evacuation. American shipyards and aircraft factories were working twenty-four hours a day as newspapers and political leaders called for the treacherous Japanese to be pulverized back into the Stone Age. The negotiated peace that the admiral had insisted was the only reasonable hope of Japanese success in its desperate gamble was highly unlikely in an American environment in which only total war was acceptable.

Now, in January 1943, Yamamoto gazed across the bustling harbor here in the Caroline Islands and assessed the capabilities of Imperial and American forces in the coming year. The year had begun somewhat less than auspiciously when the traditional New Year's ceremonies were marred by stale rice cakes that were almost inedible, Ozoni Soup so watery that it was tasteless, and ceremonial fish served with heads and tails pointed away from their normal "good luck" positions.[1]

But despite these ominous portents, Yamamoto tried to put a positive spin on the Japanese strategic position thirteen months after Pearl Harbor.

The last significant Imperial victory had occurred the previous May when the Stars and Stripes were hauled down from the flagstaffs on Corregidor Island at the entrance to Manila Harbor. The surrender of the survivors of the Bataan Garrison set in motion a flurry of negotiations in which General Jonathan Wainwright ordered the cessation of all American resistance in the Philippine Islands and removed the last potential internal military resistance in the newly organized Greater East Asia Co-Prosperity Sphere. Japan now had a secure hold on Hong Kong, Singapore, Malaya, the Dutch East Indies, the Philippines, and most of Burma, along with a list of island chains, large and small, throughout the Pacific. The empire had ready access to huge supplies of tin, rubber, oil, and other resources, all notably absent in the homeland. However, problems arose when Japan attempted to launch its "second phase offensive" in the wake of its initial run of victories.

The empire now possessed all the resource-rich territories it needed, but there was still a danger that the Americans would counterattack from the still substantial areas remaining in Allied hands. The surprise April bombing raid on Japan led by Colonel James Doolittle was a strategic pinprick by sixteen medium bombers, but the attack showed that the Americans were a threat as long as they held bases in the Pacific. Thus the new offensive was designed to capture or neutralize bases in such widely scattered areas as Alaska, Hawaii, and Australia; American forces would then essentially be thrown back to the West Coast of the United States, the Pacific Ocean becoming a Japanese lake. However, a series of offensives in the Coral Sea, in New Guinea, and toward the Hawaiian outpost of Midway had produced a series of reverses that crippled much of the power of the Imperial Navy and shifted the strategic initiative to the Americans.

The impact of those early summer battles became apparent throughout the later months of 1942 when the little-known island of

Guadalcanal became the focal point for Japanese and American tenacity and will to victory. The shoestring American landings on Guadalcanal would have been annihilated by an Imperial Navy that was at is peak strength. However, Coral Sea and Midway had effectively removed six irreplaceable carriers from the chessboard of war and left the two opponents evenly matched in the waters that would soon be called Ironbottom Sound. Each side could gain only temporary advantage in a see-saw contest that decimated both navies but produced few decisive results. The air and water of the Solomons was largely American by sunlight and Japanese by moonlight, but the invaders gained an almost imperceptibly increasing advantage in the closing weeks of 1942 while Japanese ground commanders frittered away many of their best units in costly, though emotionally satisfying, banzai charges. By early December, the slowly advancing American lines were becoming almost impervious to a serious breakthrough and the Japanese garrison was now in mortal danger.

On January 1, 1943, as Yamamoto noted the grim portent of his ceremonial New Year's meal, other senior Japanese leaders were meeting at the Imperial Palace to consider the mounting crisis in the Solomons.[2]

Army commanders argued that their men could hardly be expected to defeat American ground forces if the navy failed to provide food, ammunition, and reinforcements. Naval officers insisted that they were being compelled to use proud warships as virtual passenger ferries and cargo ships to replace men and supplies squandered in the ill-advised strategy employed on Guadalcanal, and, as a result, they were unable to concentrate the fleet for a decisive sea engagement with the Americans. The meeting took a shocking turn when the usually silent Emperor Hirohito admitted that the Americans seemed to be winning the battle through their growing air superiority and, in a rare gesture of barely disguised anger, raised his voice as he ordered total evacuation of Guadalcanal. Two weeks later, a staff officer was sent ashore to inform General Harukichi Hyakutake that his surviving healthy soldiers were to be removed by ship; the wounded defenders were expected to form a final defense line and then kill themselves along with as many Americans as they could take with them.

On January 24, frontline troops began crawling from their foxholes toward the beach as 50,000 American soldiers pushed continuously forward through the steamy, insect-ridden jungle. At dusk on February 1, American planes sighted a fleet of Japanese destroyers approaching the coast on an apparent reinforcement mission. Several squadrons of Japanese fighters fended off the inevitable American air attacks while a covering force of surface ships dueled with American PT boats. During the night, 5,000 troops were ferried to fourteen circling destroyers while two more rescue flotillas waited their turn to move toward shore and ferry an additional 8,000 Imperial soldiers to safety. Meanwhile, hundreds of wounded comrades either made individual and group last stands or merely killed themselves with grenades.

Thirteen thousand of His Majesty's soldiers lived to fight in future battles, but 25,000 Imperial warriors had died in the fetid jungle along with 1,600 of their American counterparts. Not only had the Japanese failed for the first time to hold a territory they had captured but even the most optimistic Japanese leader was forced to admit that the innate spiritual superiority of Imperial soldiers could not counterbalance a loss of twenty men for every American killed in battle. Admiral Watome Ugaki, Yamamoto's chief of staff, saw the evacuation of Guadalcanal as the possible first step down from the height of victory secured only months earlier: "How splendid the first stage of our operations was! But how unsuccessfully we have fought since the defeat of Midway. Our strategy aimed at invasion of Hawaii, Fiji and Samoa and North Caledonia as well as domination over India is disappearing like a dream. I cannot stem my feeling of mortification. The desperate trials of our officers and men are now too numerous to mention."[3]

Ugaki's comments were a startling about-face from the once optimistic "victory disease" that had affected so many Japanese leaders in the months following Pearl Harbor. However, in the early months of 1943, the Pacific War was teetering in a balance: Either side could win or lose the war. The discouraging retreat by the United States and its allies was now over, but the Japanese Empire still held the vast majority of territories it had conquered in 1942. Each side enjoyed certain advantages and was challenged by certain liabilities that in the short term tended to cancel each other out. Only some combination of superior strategy, improved weaponry, and plain luck could tilt the balance in a decisive direction.

The Japanese war machine that was attempting to respond to the twin disasters of Midway and Guadalcanal in late January 1943 still possessed awesome power and a list of considerable advantages over its enemies. Perhaps the most tangible symbol of Imperial might in early 1943 was the Mitsubishi AGM fighter plane, better known as the Zero. This plane was the terror of the skies in the first year of the war as its speed, range, and nimble handling made it more than a match for most Allied planes in one-on-one combat. The Japanese aircraft industry would eventually produce more than 10,000 of these superb planes, which received their nickname in Japan through their introduction in 1940, which was 2600 in the traditional calendar. This plane, designated the Zeke by American Headquarters, would continue to be a fearsome sight in the Pacific skies as long as the empire could continue to deploy experienced pilots to fly it against increasingly sophisticated American challengers.

The Japanese army also enjoyed access to one of the most fabled weapons in maritime engagements, the Type 93 "Long Lance" torpedo. This 24-inch-surface ship torpedo was reliable, fast, and deadly, and it was also available in modified submarine and aerial versions. These weapons were far superior to any equivalents the Americans could employ at this point in the war and were responsible for a disturbingly long list of American vessels that were now resting in Ironbottom Sound, the deceptively calm waters off the coast of Guadalcanal. An exchange of torpedoes between American and Japanese ships would continue to favor the Imperial forces until the United States Navy could produce a weapon that would not only find its target but also explode on contact with the same reliability as their adversaries'.

As the Japanese had already conquered most of the territory they needed to make the empire largely self-sufficient in important raw materials, they would now enjoy many of the strategic advantages of being on the defensive for future campaigns. The defenders would not only be familiar with the territory they were defending and able to pick their ground to deploy their forces, they would also benefit from traditional military wisdom that insisted that the attackers needed to enjoy a three-to-one manpower advantage against their adversaries. The advantage of the defensive implied that, theoretically, the Japanese could continue to inflict massive casualties on American assault forces as they inched across the vast Pacific until the United States finally tired of the game and accepted a negotiated peace. One possible arrangement discussed in Japanese circles in 1943 was a peace treaty that would return all American territory seized by Imperial forces if the United States allowed Japan to keep the far more important British and Dutch colonies conquered in the same post–Pearl Harbor offensive.

The discussion of possible negotiated peace scenarios also underscores one of the major disadvantages of the Japanese side at the midpoint of the war. The Imperial mindset was still largely tied to earlier conflicts against China and Russia in which the emperor's forces won a series of stunning victories and then encouraged their adversary to make peace based on a compromise settlement that, although favoring Japan, did not result in complete surrender by their antagonist. The Japanese leaders were still generally convinced that the United States was a rampantly individualistic and pleasure-loving society spiritually and psychologically incapable of a fight to the finish in an obscure corner of the globe. Most Japanese civilian and military officials simply could not appreciate the firestorm of anger and desire for revenge incited by the surprise attack on Pearl Harbor. They saw the war ended by diplomats in morning suits shaking hands over plush mahogany tables; the Americans saw the ending with the emperor being marched at bayonet point from the rubble that had once been his palace as the Rising Sun was replaced on the imperial flagstaff by the Stars and Stripes. This mindset meant that although Japanese leaders were quite willing to order wounded soldiers to kill themselves and to authorize mass suicide attacks in which hundreds of Imperial troops reveled in their opportunity to die for the emperor, there was still no hard-headed, dispassionate concept of total war against the United States in purely strategic terms.

The empire still deployed massive military formations in China and Manchuria and through much of 1943 still had enough air and sea power to redeploy much of that army to the territories in the line of fire of a possible American advance. Some substantial units were ferried southward during the next few months, but the high command would not make this transfer a priority until 1944, when American planes, surface ships, and submarines marauded the Pacific and sent as many men, tanks, and cannons to the bottom of the ocean as reached their destination. The Japanese high command was still convinced that a significant pullout in China would somehow call into question the whole purpose of the original pursuit of aggressive military expansion, which was largely what forced the nation into its current multifront war in the first place. However, Japanese soldiers suppressing Chinese bandits, battling Chiang Kai Chek, or keeping a wary eye on Soviet deployment near Manchuria were of little use in countering a single-minded American war machine that was about to surge across the Pacific. Japan, much like its Axis partner Germany, was beginning to spread its combat forces too thin. The empire would spend the rest of the war deploying large units in positions from which they never fired a shot in anger; yet in other locations, their comrades were being overwhelmed by superior Allied forces.

A second liability on the Japanese war ledger in 1943 was the emerging weakness of the entire Imperial air strategy. First, although the Zero was the best fighter plane in the Pacific during the first year of the war, this single plane, with modest upgrades, was the backbone of the Japanese air defense for virtually the entire war. The superior range and speed of this terror of the skies had been obtained at a price; the lack of armor around the pilot, the absence of self-sealing fuel tanks, and the relatively modest firepower of the plane were already enabling the more rugged, durable, and heavily armed Warhawks and Wildcats to make a reasonable account of themselves in optimal combat situations. As the United States Army, Air Force, and Navy introduced second- and even third-generation war-era fighters, Japanese dominance of the skies would be seriously threatened. Another component of a possible air crisis was the training and deployment of pilots. Because the Japanese high command had expected a brief war with the United States, only a modest expansion of the number of pilots trained had been authorized during 1942. Yet the Midway and Guadalcanal campaigns had drastically reduced the number of surviving experienced pilots. As the relatively limited supply of new fliers was introduced to the swirling combat over the Pacific, the pool of replacements was even further diminished because the young, inexperienced pilots were more likely to be shot down. Also, Japanese policy was to keep the best pilots in combat until they were killed, whereas the Americans rotated their fliers back to stateside instructional posts where they could teach the next class of aviators the secrets of successful air combat. Unless drastic measures were introduced in 1943, the skies over the battle zone would become increasingly American-dominated.

A final significant flaw in the Japanese war effort in early 1943 was the concept of the disposable warrior. Although the high command had just authorized a large-scale evacuation of Guadalcanal and would permit one or two other "strategic withdrawals" later in the year, the Imperial mindset was rapidly moving toward an all-or-nothing, victory-or-death approach to the war. Even at Guadalcanal, many wounded soldiers who could have been restored to some form of active duty in Western armies were essentially ordered to kill themselves rather than become burdens to the evacuation. Similarly, parachutes were becoming less and less common in Japanese planes, already far more dangerous to their pilots than their American counterparts. Japanese commanders were becoming so obsessed with the spiritual superiority of Imperial troops that they began to dismiss the threat of a technologically superior enemy that enjoyed a larger manpower pool than their own country. Japan was about to throw away large numbers

of soldiers, sailors, and airmen through a combination of partially enforced suicide, alarmingly primitive medical care, and ill-conceived
charges that would often do the Americans' job for them. When
Union's General Ambrose Burnside squandered thousands of Federal
troops in an ill-conceived frontal assault against Robert E. Lee's superb
position behind the town of Fredericksburg, Lee's western counterpart
Joseph Johnston asked plaintively, "Why could not the Yankee army
facing me attack me under the same circumstances?" When Japanese
leaders began to squander their precious manpower resources in modern versions of Fredericksburg, American commanders frequently became the beneficiaries of this fatal obsession.

The American leaders responsible for transforming a largely defensive Pacific War into a thrust toward the Marianas and beyond faced
their own series of impediments to victory. One of the most significant
defects of the American effort in early 1943 was that the United States
Navy was close to firing blanks with its array of torpedoes. The Mark 14
torpedo, the standard submarine weapon at the beginning of the war,
used a detonator able to detect magnetic fields that had been tested in
the Atlantic Ocean and seemed reliable. However, water conditions in
the Pacific were dramatically different and the weapons consistently either went off target or failed to explode. The navy then began substituting conventional firing pins that were made of cheap metal and often bent at the critical moment. Submarine captains had to place their
boats and crews at great personal risk to achieve optimum range for
launch and then watch enemy ships escape damage as the warheads
went astray or failed to detonate. The powerful American undersea
fleet could not cut vital Japanese communication links until this problem was rectified.

A second liability in the American arsenal was the communication
relationship between air, ground, and naval forces. As American forces
shifted to the offensive, they encountered an awesome variety of
Japanese defensive fortifications. Superbly camouflaged troops entrenched in imaginatively constructed fortifications could take a large
toll on attackers unless they could be discovered and virtually blown

out of their holes. The Americans were ready to deploy powerful ships' batteries, field artillery, tanks, and ground attack planes, but until they could effectively communicate with the riflemen who were the objects of this unwanted Japanese attention, the firepower would be of only marginal value. As the Central Pacific offensive gained momentum, the attackers would have to develop the ability to deploy radios that would not only function after contact with salt water and operate in gusts of sand but also allow vulnerable riflemen to call in the aerial, naval, and ground firepower that the American war factories were producing in such quantity.

A third potential liability in the American conduct on the Pacific was the ongoing debate concerning the allocation of resources in competing theatres. The surprise attack on Pearl Harbor and the growing realization that Imperial forces were conducting a particularly brutal form of warfare tended to encourage the American public to see Japan as the primary adversary and Germany as a lesser threat to the American mainland and a less barbaric foe. However, Roosevelt and most of his senior advisors saw Hitler as the far more dangerous long-term threat, and the president's warm relationship with Winston Churchill did little to negate this outlook. By 1943, the United States was developing a powerful war machine, but the nation's resources were not infinite: Choices would have to be made and priorities determined. The nation would be forced to confront Hitler directly on one or more fronts, send massive supplies to the Soviet Union to challenge Germany on another front, and conduct operations against Japan in the China-Burma-India area and in the Pacific Ocean. Therefore, initial Japanese aversion to redeploying major units in China and Manchuria to the Pacific Ocean front would be at least partially counterbalanced by American reluctance to shift units slated to fight in Germany to active duty against Imperial forces.

This list of significant liabilities was mitigated by several promising developments in the American war effort as the conflict reached its midpoint. First, the quantity and quality of United States air units had improved markedly since the dark days in the aftermath of Pearl

Harbor. During the first stage of the war, the American air effort boasted brave pilots and little else. At Pearl Harbor, only a handful of planes ever left the ground, and two pilots accounted for nearly all the air-to-air combat victories on that infamous Sunday. Air defense of the vital Marine base at Wake Island was entrusted to a squadron of twelve marginally modern Wildcat fighters that was reduced to a pitiful four machines during the first enemy air strikes. By the end of the first day of the war, the air defense of the entire Philippines Island group was reduced to seventeen Flying Fortresses and thirty Warhawks matched against more than five hundred modern enemy planes. Filipino pilots actually dueled with Zeros in ancient P-26 fighters that featured fixed landing gear, open cockpits, and two puny 0.30-caliber machine guns that seemed more appropriate for action over the Western Front in 1917. Lack of American air power had made the capture of Wake Island, Bataan, and Corregidor far easier for the Japanese invaders; but by 1943, the balance in the air was beginning to shift.

The U.S. Army Air Force was beginning to introduce a pair of new fighters that would be far more formidable machines than the Mohawks, Warhawks, and Tomahawks that had attempted to stem the Japanese aerial onslaught in 1941–1942. The P-38 was a two-engine fighter heavily armed with 37 mm cannon and four machine guns; it could use its high speed and superior ceiling to surprise adversaries, and it could absorb more punishment than most fighters. Relative lack of maneuverability at low altitudes was more than compensated by exceptional range and excellent high-altitude capabilities. The P-47 Thunderbolt would not see action in the Pacific until the very end of 1943, but it was designed around one of the most powerful engines available, was equipped with eight machine guns, and could carry up to 3,000 pounds of bombs. The Thunderbolt could inflict heavy damage on air and ground targets alike and was enormously difficult for Japanese fighters to destroy.

The army also introduced three more medium and heavy bombers to the Pacific to supplement the already excellent B-17 Flying Fortresses. The B-24 Liberator was an extremely versatile heavy bomber that was eventually produced in significantly larger quantities than the more famous Fortress. The B-24's superior range made the plane indispensable as a long-range bomber, long-range patrol plane, and antisubmarine aircraft fitted with up to two dozen depth changes. Hundreds of Liberators were also converted to transports carrying fuel, freight, and passengers. The B-25 Mitchell was a medium bomber that first gained fame as the aircraft used by Doolittle's Tokyo raiders. By 1943, Mitchells were being fitted with forward firing 75 mm cannons and machine guns, six machine guns in other locations, and rigged with torpedoes, or more than 3,000 pounds of bombs. Sea-level attacks by these flying arsenals would become a nightmare vision for Japanese naval and merchant ship captains. The B-26 Marauder was just entering service in early 1943, although in much smaller numbers than the Mitchells. Because the B-25s were already being retrofitted into "ship killer" functions, the Marauders were deployed as conventional medium- and high-level bombers striking against ground targets. The army fighters and bombers were increasingly able to outperform their Japanese counterparts; yet just over the horizon were the planes that would take the air war from the Marianas to the Japanese homeland, the B-29 Superfortress and the P-51 Mustang.

Navy and Marine pilots had faced the first stages of the Japanese on-slaught with an array of aircraft that were no better than their army comrades were flying. Buffalo fighters and Devastator torpedo planes proved to be little better than flying coffins for their pilots and were pathetically below enemy aircraft performance. Wildcat fighters could inflict some damage on the enemy with superior pilots and optimal combat circumstances, but still could not normally destroy a Zero in one-to-one confrontations. However, a new generation of U.S. Navy and Marine planes was just beginning to make its presence known to the Japanese in the early months of 1943.

The main replacement for the stubby Wildcats was the F-6F Hellcat, a more graceful aircraft that would become more than a match for the legendary Zero. The Hellcat would eventually roll up an impressive 25:1 ratio of losses in air combat. While the Hellcats were deployed on the new carriers, Marine air wings began flying the powerful new F-4U Corsair. These gull-winged aircraft experienced just enough cockpit visibility and undercarriage wheel problems to make them less than ideal carrier planes, but they were so superior in overall combat operations that they were readily accepted by the Marines as a land-based fighter. The Corsair weighed more than six tons if fully loaded with bombs, but could still outfly most Zeros and shoot down ten enemy planes for every one lost in the melees above the Pacific atolls. The almost laughably slow Devastators, nicknamed "Wind Indicators" by their often doomed pilots, were now being replaced with the TBF Avenger, which was 50 percent faster and carried twice the payload. The versatile Avenger would soon be used both as a torpedo and a conventional bomber and eventually would be fitted with radar to expand its scouting capabilities.

This generation of army, navy, and Marine planes was already beginning to tip the scales of air power in favor of the United States by early 1943. When this formidable array of aircraft appeared over the Marianas the following year, their presence would provoke one of the most massive confrontations in aerial history. Yet the majority of these planes were relatively short-range aircraft and they would need the support of a powerful new fleet that was the second major asset in the calculus of respective power at the midpoint of the Pacific War.

The American invasion of Guadalcanal was on the verge of a successful conclusion in early 1943, but the United States Navy had suffered fearsome losses in this initial Pacific offensive. On several occasions in the autumn of 1942, the navy had been reduced to one operational carrier in the theater as a steady stream of flattops either limped into Pearl Harbor for extensive repairs or settled on the ocean floor at the bottom of Ironbottom Sound. However, by the early months of 1943, the dockyards of America were producing the first of a steady stream of new carriers that would eventually make the Marianas campaign feasible. The projection of naval air power deep into the Japanese Empire would be based on a trio of different carrier designs that produced maximum versatility for the tasks at hand.

The most glamorous of the new arrivals were the sixteen Essex-class fleet carriers that were the most technologically advanced ships of their type in World War II. They were fast, large, and bristling with far more antiaircraft batteries than their predecessors. Each vessel was capable of carrying ninety planes in a variety of fighter, torpedo plane, dive bomber, and scout plane configurations. These ships were supported by an additional nine Independence-class light carriers that were largely partially-built cruisers converted to carrier configurations at some point during construction. This task was initiated at the personal insistence of Franklin Roosevelt when nine Cleveland-class light cruisers were converted during 1942 and readied for fleet service in the early weeks of 1943. These ships were relatively cramped and uncomfortable for the crew members, but they could deploy thirty aircraft and move fast enough to keep up with the fleet carriers. The most innovative design was the escort carriers, which were largely merchant ships converted to air service. The vessels were slow and somewhat cumbersome, but they could carry an average of two dozen planes to serve in convoy escort, with supporting roles in offensive operations. The "Jeep carriers" were cheap and quick to construct, and the seventy-two vessels commissioned provided an attack platform for nearly 2,000 additional aircraft, a welcome addition when operating deep inside enemy waters. Although the very nature of the aircraft carrier made it one of the most vulnerable ships in a fleet, these vessels had now become the primary naval weapon of modern warfare. By 1943, the United States Navy was beginning to deploy new carriers far more rapidly than their Imperial adversaries, and this process deeply concerned the Japanese high command. However, although the massive new American carrier fleet could project power deep into enemy territory, a series of key territories, including the Marianas, would have to be physically wrested from the enemy before the war could be taken to the Japanese homeland. Fortunately for the American soldiers and Marines, they would be equipped with weapons that would prove to be another significant advantage over their enemies.

The Japanese war machine supplied the emperor's ground soldiers with relatively slow-firing rifles and machine guns, and only marginally better support weapons, but American forces in 1943 were deploying significantly enhanced weapons. The initial showpiece of American small-arms design was the Garand M-1 rifle, the most advanced regular issue personal weapon of World War II. The average British, German, Russian, or Japanese soldier was still using a bolt action rifle little different from the weapons of the Great War. American troops were now being equipped with a rapid-firing weapon that provided them with double or triple the firepower of their adversaries, an advantage that was already influencing the course of battles throughout the Pacific theater.

The stage was now set for a series of campaigns that would serve as the prelude to the great Central Pacific offensive and the climactic air, sea, and ground confrontations at the Marianas Islands. Because each side entered the 1943 campaign season with a finely balanced series of advantages and liabilities, the outcome of the Pacific War was far from certain. Now a series of engagements that would stretch from the green hell of New Guinea to the white hell of the Aleutians would begin to crystallize the course of the conflict and demonstrate grimly that the most advanced weapons systems available to either side were still more often than not subordinate to the sheer bravery, tenacity, and determination to sacrifice exhibited by Imperial and American warriors.

3

SECURING THE FLANKS

THE CONQUEST OF the Marianas Islands was emerging as the centerpiece of Ernest King's strategy as he strolled the dazzling white Mediterranean beaches during the closing days of the Casablanca conference. However, his plan for a powerful thrust across the Central Pacific toward the enemy homeland would become feasible only when the northern and southern flanks of this vast battleground were secured from massive, and potentially disastrous, Japanese intervention. The potential success for the proposed Central Pacific drive scheduled for 1944 was dependent on events far to the south and north in 1943.

The southern flank of the Pacific battle zone in early 1943 centered on the lush but largely inhospitable jungles of New Guinea and the northern Solomons. The two American commanders in the area, General Douglas MacArthur, senior officer in the Southwest Pacific, and Admiral William Halsey, responsible for the South Pacific, would spend the better part of the coming year focusing on one prime object of their combined attentions, the Japanese base on Rabaul, at the tip of New Britain. At Rabaul, starkly beautiful white coral reefs fronted a protected harbor large enough to anchor the entire Imperial Japanese Navy. Just beyond this invaluable harbor was a wide stretch of flat land that the Japanese had developed into five major air bases capable of supporting more than a thousand planes. An American amphibious assault would be countered by more than 100,000 combat troops backed up by powerful artillery and armored units. A fully operational Japanese naval and air base on New Britain could checkmate almost any American drive across the Pacific, and MacArthur and Halsey were under firm orders to dispose of this looming menace.

Isoroko Yamamoto was equally aware that Rabaul was one of the empire's most valuable pieces on the chessboard of war. By February 1943, the admiral had secured army cooperation in a plan for the massive reinforcement of Japanese bases on the northern coast of New Guinea, which was the portal for an American thrust across the Bismarck Sea far into New Britain and its vital base. While Yamamoto orchestrated a concentration of naval forces for the expedition, the army high command recalled two divisions from China and Korea and placed Lieutenant General Adachi Hatazo in charge of a newly designated Eighteenth Army.

On the cloud-covered evening of February 28, 1943, 6,900 soldiers and four hundred Marines were loaded onto eight army transports escorted by eight destroyers and an aerial umbrella of a hundred Zeroes. They steamed out of Rabaul and into the Bismarck Sea and headed for the Japanese base at Lae on the north shore of New Guinea. The next afternoon, an American reconnaissance plane spotted the convoy steaming around Cape Gloucester and entering a narrow body of water called Dampier Strait. Soon, almost thirty Flying Fortresses and Liberators droned overhead just as much of the Japanese air cover returned to base for refueling. The high-level attack left one transport sinking and two more reduced to pieces of floating junk, but the Japanese ordeal had just begun.

At this point, wave after wave of specially equipped B-25 medium bombers flew in just above sea level, spraying crowded decks with forward firing machine guns and dropping bombs that seldom missed their targets. A swarm of forty Zeroes flying in to the rescue was met by squadrons of new twin-engined P-38 Lightnings that held the Japanese planes at bay while the convoy was reduced to a smoking wreck. Every transport and four of the destroyers were sunk along with nearly twenty-five Imperial planes. At a cost of exactly five aircraft, the Americans had sunk twelve ships and killed 3,700 enemy soldiers, including General Adachi and virtually every member of his command staff.

The one-sided confrontation, named by the Americans as the battle of the Bismarck Sea, shocked Yamamoto into stripping his carriers of planes so that he could launch a land-based counterattack designed to destroy enemy air fields before they could launch a sequel to this first massacre. Yamamoto left his cramped ship-bound office in Turk Harbor and flew to Rabaul so that he could personally supervise Operation I-GO, a succession of attacks by three hundred Japanese aircraft on American bases on New Guinea and the southern Solomons. This was the largest concentration of Japanese air power since Pearl Harbor, and the admiral received glowing reports from the many inexperienced pilots that they had destroyed hundreds of American planes and sent dozens of enemy ships to the bottom. Because American squadrons deployed to protect their bases and nearby harbors were more interested in breaking up enemy attacks than in shooting down Japanese planes, only thirty Imperial aircraft were destroyed. However, the attackers' actual successes were extremely modest: They destroyed two Allied patrol boats, sank two small merchant vessels, and eliminated twenty-five American planes, mainly those caught on the ground.

Overeager Japanese pilots, who were shooting up more palm trees than planes, convinced Yamamoto that they had the Americans on the run, a situation that encouraged the now jubilant admiral to make a personal inspection tour of frontline airfields to decorate the new generation of the emperor's heroic warriors. This inspection tour would be the final act of perhaps the most popular war hero in Japan and the most reviled enemy commander in the United States.

The itinerary of Yamamoto's inspection tour was a model of meticulous Japanese staff planning with a precise timetable that would make Swiss railroad officials slightly envious. Unfortunately for the admiral,

American cryptographers had decoded the entire schedule and confirmed that one stop on the tour was just within the limits of American fighter range. On Sunday, April 18, 1943, exactly one year to the day after Doolittle's raid on Japan, eighteen brand-new silver P-38 Lightnings raced across the sea to ambush Yamamoto as he approached southern Bougainville Island. The two transport planes carrying the admiral and his staff were escorted by nine Zeroes, but Yamamoto and the pilots assumed they were too far inside Japanese territory to be in any real danger. As would happen frequently during the war, Japanese overconfidence was a fatal weakness; indeed, given the already demonstrated American tendency to spring surprises and the almost irreplaceable status of the admiral, a leader of Yamamoto's stature should have been escorted by at least forty or fifty fighters.

Just as the air flotilla was about to descend into the green landscape below, the Lightnings swooped down from high altitude and began engaging the outnumbered escorts. Then, four of these silver marauders broke off from the main combat and pumped machine-gun bullets and cannon shells into the two unarmed transports. One plane sputtered into the sea just off the beach, and the admiral's aide and a few other survivors were rescued. Yamamoto's plane, belching smoke and flames, crashed into the jungle; all the occupants were killed.[1]

The repercussions of less than five minutes of aerial combat were felt from Washington to Tokyo.

In a less total war in an earlier time, the deliberate killing of an enemy senior commander was often considered beyond the bounds of "civilized" warfare. However, the war between the United States and Japan was already bursting beyond the boundaries of conventional war, and Pearl Harbor and Bataan were still recent memories to Americans. Ironically, Yamamoto was probably the most pro-American military leader in Japan and seemed to have the willingness, if not the ability, to keep the conflict within some traditional limits. Yet the deaths of 3,000 persons at Pearl Harbor while America was still officially at peace and the consistent mistreatment of American prisoners on land and at sea would almost certainly have branded the admiral a war criminal if he had survived to the end of the conflict. Most Americans believed that Yamamoto's death was simply a legitimate payback for the violence and barbarism of Japan toward the United States during the previous eighteen months.

The emotional response to the admiral's death in Japan was a combination of shock, grief, and alarm. The death was kept secret for several weeks; but when Yamamoto was finally given a state funeral, the outpouring of bereaved subjects reached the hundreds of thousands. Most average citizens had been informed that both the Midway campaign and the Solomons campaign had been superb Japanese victories and had made the empire the master of much of the Pacific. There was no one even close to the Olympian stature of Yamamoto waiting in the wings; whoever commanded the Imperial fleet during the inevitable showdown with the United States Navy would be entering the climactic battle with no record of success. Mineichi Koga, an intelligent and relatively talented warrior was named the new senior naval commander, but the admiral admitted to the emperor that "there was only one Yamamoto and no one can replace him."[2]

The Japanese attempt to defend the Marianas a year later would provoke the largest carrier battle in history, but the officer who was the embodiment of the Imperial wartime spirit would be an enshrined god by then, not a line commander and strategist.

Isoroku Yamamoto may have joined the growing circle of venerated gods who had died in service to the emperor, but his tenure as Imperial fleet commander significantly influenced two evolving campaigns that would serve as preludes to the looming confrontation in the Marianas. Two major offensives, code-named Landcrab and Cartwheel, would secure the northern and southern flanks of the Pacific Ocean battleground and clear the way for Ernest King's vaunted drive across the Central Pacific toward Japan.

One of the major legacies of Admiral Yamamoto's complex plan to lure the American navy into decisive defeat after Pearl Harbor was the only aspect of the Midway campaign that was technically a Japanese victory. Yamamoto had assumed, fairly correctly, that Admiral Chester

Nimitz would be under enormous public pressure to safeguard the extensive West Coast of the United States. Because the Japanese admiral's primary target was the capture of Midway Island, the gateway to Hawaii, he knew that he could not spare enough ships or men to fight another major battle on or near the heavily populated stretch of coast from Southern California to northern Washington. However, far to the north was the vulnerable territory of Alaska. Yamamoto insisted that a combination of air attacks on mainland Alaska and amphibious landings in the adjacent Aleutian Islands would force Nimitz to divide his already outnumbered fleet just as the main elements of the Imperial Navy lunged towards Midway.

The Japanese admiral's plan was not unreasonable in theory, but Admiral Chester Nimitz had determined to concentrate his slender resources on countering the enemy threat to Midway; as far as the Texan was concerned, most of Alaska was sparsely inhabited frozen tundra that would dissipate Japanese power, and later in the war it could always be recaptured. Thus, when Vice Admiral Hosogaya Boshiro's Northern Area forces steamed northward with carriers *Ryujo* and *Junyo*, whatever success they gained in the frigid Alaskan waters could not compensate the Midway strike force for the diversion of a third of its potential strike force in the climactic battle that was about to begin.

In the predawn hours of June 3, 1942, Japanese planes bombed Dutch Harbor, Alaska, killing twenty-five soldiers and destroying an American petroleum depot. American P-40s based 100 miles away at Cold Bay roared southward to engage the raiders, but arrived only to find spectacular fires and an enemy that had vanished beyond the horizon. Four days later, nearly 3,000 Japanese ground troops were landed on the islands of Kiska and Attu to begin the first occupation of North American territory in World War II. Kiska was inhabited only by a small navy communications detachment that sent out a distress call and then started an abortive retreat into the hills, suffering one casualty in the process. The Japanese showed far more humanity to their captives here than they exhibited in the jungles far to the south. The one wounded American was immediately treated by a Japanese doctor, and the other prisoners largely escaped the brutalization so commonly inflicted on enemy captives by Imperial forces. Attu was slightly more heavily populated as it contained an Aleut village of about forty people and one mainland couple, a local teacher, Foster Jones, and his wife. Jones became the only fatality of the invasion when he was shot trying to elude capture.

The initial American and Japanese news blackouts of much of what had actually happened in the far larger confrontation around Midway pushed the northern aspect of the campaign into far greater prominence than its strategic importance merited. A grievously disappointed Yamamoto did little to discourage homeland assertions that the "real" objective of the Japanese offensive was more Alaska than Midway, with the latter island becoming the "diversion" to ensure the capture of the northern area. Thus the Japanese press trumpeted the invasion of the enemy homeland with hints that this Imperial tide would soon sweep southward toward the state of Washington and even California.

The American press, for once, tended to agree with their Japanese counterparts; indeed, reporters and columnists speculated that the landings in the Aleutians were a prelude to a southern drive that might eventually threaten Hollywood or Pasadena.[3]

An Imperial Army that had pulled off almost magical military conquests virtually without interruption for the previous six months seemed capable of almost anything once it had become firmly ensconced on the shores of North America.

A Japanese victory at Midway might have influenced the high command to view the Aleutian landings as merely the first step in a southward drive, but now four of his His Majesty's irreplaceable carriers were lying at the bottom of the Pacific and *Ryujo* and *Junyo* were desperately needed to provide air support for the still-formidable main battle fleet. On the other hand, Japanese leaders realized that the Aleutian landings had provoked enormous propaganda dividends both in the empire and in the United States, and the only territorial victory in the recent campaign should not be thrown away. The admirals and generals agreed that Attu and Kiska would be reinforced and occupied, at least through the winter, and that naval support would be provided by a modest surface fleet. Sometime in 1943 the situation would be reevaluated in the light of the empire's far-flung commitments in other regions of the Pacific.

Several thousand miles away, American strategists saw the enemy incursion into Alaska as a challenge and an opportunity. Given the shortage of men and ships available in the summer of 1942, an immediate counterattack in the Aleutians seemed impossible. However, as new units were activated in the coming year, and as upgraded naval and air weapons became available, it would become militarily possible and psychologically necessary to launch a counteroffensive in the North Pacific. The American public and government leadership would not tolerate an indefinite occupation of North American territory by a brutal and fearsome enemy. The challenge was to cobble together ground, naval, and air units that could operate in some of the most difficult weather conditions in the world and throw the Japanese out of the Aleutians. The opportunity was that the North Pacific might well emerge as a back door to the enemy homeland. Recapture of the Aleutians would, in theory, place substantial American forces tantalizingly close to the Japanese Kurile Islands, which might be a stepping stone to the northern Japanese mainland and, eventually, Tokyo.

The two men most responsible for meeting this challenge and evaluating this subsequent opportunity were energetic middle-aged officers who would eventually assume even larger responsibilities far to the south in the final year of the war. Simon Bolivar Buckner was the son of the Confederate general who had surrendered Fort Donelson to Ulysses S. Grant and, when forced to capitulate without concessions, provided the new Union hero with the catch title "Unconditional Surrender Grant." Simon, Jr., found himself in command of a rapidly expanding ground force that was charged with keeping the Japanese from pushing inland while concentrating its strength for an eventual counteroffensive against Attu and Kiska. Buckner's naval counterpart, Admiral Thomas Kinkaid, had already played important, but subsidiary, roles in the Coral Sea, Midway, and Guadalcanal campaigns; he now found himself in command of a vast naval arena with the promise of powerful fleets but with the initial reality of being significantly outnumbered by his Japanese nemesis.

Buckner and Kinkaid were energetic, capable officers who would spend much of the spring and summer of 1943 planning and implementing Operation Landcrab, an American offensive intended to secure the northern flank of the Pacific theater by recapturing the Aleutians and, possibly, the enemy rear through the Kuriles towards the Japanese main islands. However, the main battle of this campaign would produce a series of engagements that would resonate more closely with veterans of the battles of Monte Cassino or the Ardennes in Europe than any of the other Pacific battles far to the south.

After an undergunned American flotilla defeated a Japanese naval threat in the hard-fought surface engagement at the battle of the Komandorski Islands in March, Buckner and Kinkaid used the support of a significantly reinforced naval contingent to draw a gradual ring around Kiska and Attu with a growing number of ground installations and air bases on unoccupied islands of the Aleutian chain.

The American leaders decided to attack the more westerly island of Attu first, a move that would further isolate the larger garrison of Kiska from expected Japanese support based in the Kuriles. The assault on Attu would be conducted by the 7th Infantry Division, a National Guard unit with regiments recruited from New Mexico, Arizona, and Texas; the 4th Infantry Regiment, a unit of the Regular Army; a provisional Scout Battalion deployed for operations in difficult terrain; and a number of support units recruited from the hunters and trappers of the Alaskan mainland. The initial attack force of perhaps 15,000 men would be supported by the Flying Fortresses, Liberators, and Lightnings of the Eleventh Air Force, and by Kinkaid's increasingly powerful naval force, which deployed battleships *Nevada, Idaho,* and *Pennsylvania,* escort carrier *Nassau,* six cruisers, and nineteen destroyers, the largest concentration of American naval power since the invasion of Guadalcanal.[4]

The American landing force would enjoy a fairly substantial edge over Colonel Yasuyo Yamasake's 3,000 men supported by twelve anti-aircraft guns and several artillery batteries. However, the extremely rocky and often snow-covered terrain heavily favored the defenders, and the virtually unending clouds, which sprinkled snow, sleet, and rain showers, would negate much of the American air cover and naval gunfire support. Yamasake had also been assured by his superiors that once the enemy invasion began, significant reinforcements would be dispatched from the Kuriles to turn the American assault into a major disaster.[5]

On May 11, 1943, American forces splashed ashore on Attu and were met by an eerie freezing fog and an equally disconcerting total silence. Buckner's basic invasion plan was to land a Northern Force at Holtz Bay, a Southern Force at Massacre Bay, and a Scouting Force at the opposite side of the island behind the probable enemy positions. Invasion forces in most other battles of the Pacific War dealt with poisonous snakes, biting insects, and enervating heat, but these American soldiers battled trenchfoot, frostbite, and fog that seemed ironically similar to their fathers' descriptions of the Western Front in World War I.

The problem of battle in the northern Pacific became painfully apparent to the 244 men of the Scout Battalion, who landed in 27-degree temperatures and advanced from Austin Cove through deep snow that fronted a seemingly endless series of ridges leading to Jarmin Pass and the probable rear of the Japanese defense line. All hope of a rapid descent on an unsuspecting enemy evaporated as the small task force trudged through often knee-deep snow that slowed the advance to yards, rather than miles, in each hour.

Meanwhile, Colonel Frank Culin, a former mining engineer from Tucson, landed his Northern Force at Hotlz Bay and encountered a beach surrounded by steep 250-foot ridges looming in the fog and mist. Culin quickly pushed forward an advance force of Alaskan scouts; they attributed the eerie silence to the fact that they had landed in a part of the island that was one of the last places an invasion force would choose to launch an assault. However, when 7th Division commander General Albert Brown landed two regiments at Massacre Bay on the less formidable south side of the island, he encountered no more tangible enemy presence than at Holtz Bay. Colonel Yamasake knew exactly where his adversaries had landed, but he was content to keep the invaders guessing the time and place of the Japanese response.

As the American troops moved inland through mud and snow, the Japanese high command extended best wishes to Yamasake with this instruction: "[D]estroy the enemy as we hope and pray for your successful battle."[6]

Just as twilight swallowed the last feeble light of this gloomy landing day, the first Japanese shells careened through the fog and snow and smashed into the landing beaches. For the next four days, as American bombers, naval batteries, and field artillery pounded the mist-covered heights of Attu, the number of American casualties inched inexorably higher. Then just as the lead elements of the Scout Battalion trudged through the last snowdrift between themselves and Jarmin Pass, Yamasake rushed reinforcements to his threatened rear and forced the Americans into a hastily-dug trench line.

By Saturday, May 15, Japanese officers with megaphones were shouting taunts in English at the largely stalemated invaders. Southern Force ground commander Colonel Edward Earle had been killed by a sniper, and hundreds of GIs were limping back to aid stations with frostbite and trenchfoot. As the battle devolved into a modern version of the Western Front in 1917, General Brown was relieved of his command just as his troops were threatening to puncture the gradually unraveling Japanese defenses.

The new commander, Major General Eugene Landrum, insisted that he would not alter his predecessor's attack plan but a combination of an American breakthrough at Jarmin Pass and a rare stretch of clear weather that unleashed the most powerful bomber offensive of the campaign drove the defenders from the high ground into the far less defendable northeastern tip of the island. Only eight hundred Japanese troops were still capable of fighting, and Yamasake had just received word that the Imperial Navy could not penetrate the American naval cordon either to land reinforcements or to evacuate the garrison. The colonel now decided on a bold and desperate venture. He would concentrate every defender for a thrust into a relatively weak portion of the American lines, surge up enemy-held Engineers Hill, and capture the powerful artillery batteries before they could be used against him. This additional firepower would then be used to support an advance toward the lightly guarded American supply dumps in Massacre Valley. Once the supplies were captured, Yamasake would lead his men into the southern mountains and hold out until the Imperial Navy concentrated enough forces to smash through the enemy fleet and land massive reinforcements.[7]

At this point in the war, Japanese garrison commanders were still confident enough of the power of Imperial forces that what the Americans were now calling "banzai charges" were not intended primarily as suicide attacks from which no one would return alive. Yamasake saw his position as desperate but not hopeless; he was convinced that if he could succeed in this venture, aid would eventually arrive. However, the Americans could not decipher the fine points of what was or was not a suicide intent in a banzai charge, and enemy intentions hardly mattered to soldiers at the receiving end of these wild melees. Also, in a gruesome ritual that convinced the Americans that the enemy were fanatical barbarians, Yamasake ordered four hundred severely wounded men at the Japanese field hospital to be killed either by morphine injections or grenades lest they inadvertently become prisoners and therefore disgrace themselves. However, the Americans who heard the staccato popping sounds of enemy grenades exploding could not yet know that this was merely the opening act of a deadly drama that would be repeated in even more spectacular fashion a year later on Saipan.

As GIs ate their often cold, tasteless breakfasts on Saturday, May 24, shrill cries emerged from the mist as hundreds of Japanese soldiers poured through the American formed positions. A ghostly army swept through Company B of the 32nd Infantry Regiment and the enemy tide then surged onto a medical clearing station at the base of Engineers Hill. The Imperial troops savagely bayoneted every wounded

American, killed a chaplain who was ministering to them, and clambered up the slopes toward the summit. However, on the crest of the ridge, a grim-faced artilleryman, General Archibald Arnold, was forming medics, engineers, clerks, and cooks into a thin line of riflemen while gunners sprinted to their cannons and depressed their weapons as low as they would go.

Yamasake waved his sword and led his men forward just as the American artillery roared into action. The hastily assembled rear-echelon troops lobbed grenades down the hill and then engaged in a ferocious bayonet duel with the attackers. The Imperial tide crested, receded down the hill, and surged forward one last time. A handful of survivors trudged down the hill once again and, in a final defiant gesture, cursed the Americans as they pulled the pins of their grenades and held them against their chests. Nearly eight hundred Japanese bodies were sprawled around Engineers Hill, but twenty-eight Imperial troops, none higher ranking than a sergeant, were pulled from the heaps of dead and treated by medics who tried to comprehend the mindset of an enemy so brutal and alien.[8]

The fight for this snow-covered collection of ridges resulted in a little less than 3,000 Japanese deaths, a staggering 99 percent of the garrison. Although a more modest toll of 549 Americans died in the invasion, casualties from wounds, frostbite, and exposure pushed the total loss to nearly 4,000 men. Although many of the wounded or sick from battle in warmer climates eventually returned to service, an appallingly high number of Americans on Attu suffered the loss of feet, toes, and fingers in amputations that permanently removed them from the organizational tables of the units.

The American high command belatedly realized that the Aleutians provided an almost ideal terrain for a determined defender, and intelligence estimates that there were almost twice as many Japanese troops on Kiska as Attu spurred the concentration of a vast array of assault forces. The 7th Division and 4th Infantry Regiment were quickly augmented by 5,000 men of the 87th Mountain Combat Team who had trained to fight a winter campaign in Italy; a large Canadian contingent, including the Rocky Mountain Rangers, the Winnipeg Grenadiers, the Canadian Fusiliers, and 2,500 rough-and-ready fighters from the experimental Canadian American First Special Service Force, which specialized in fighting in mountain terrain.

By late July, an impressive assault force of 35,000 ground troops supported by four hundred combat planes and a powerful naval armada, was preparing to sail for Kiska and the decisive battle of the Aleutian campaign. However, the Japanese high command had now determined that although Kiska was expendable, its garrison was not; and on July 29, 1943, an Imperial flotilla slipped through the loose American blockade and evacuated all 5,183 defenders of the last Japanese foothold in North America. Two weeks later, the Allied invasion forces surged ashore to find smoldering equipment, a few stray dogs, and some taunting signs in English promising that battle would be joined again in a place more conducive to Japanese victory. The northern flank was now secure; but the agony of Attu had convinced American commanders that, unless Russia entered the Pacific War, the northern approach to the enemy homeland was a strategic dead end and the climactic confrontation would occur in climes warmer than the Aleutians or the Kuriles. Meanwhile, far to the south, another American offensive was securing the southern flank of the now increasingly imminent Central Pacific drive.

By the summer of 1943, the Japanese may have lost their foothold in North America but they were doggedly determined to maintain their southern "Bismarck Barrier" with its right flank in northern New Guinea and left flank in the northern Solomons. However, General Douglas MacArthur and Admiral William Halsey were launching the twin thrusts of Operation Cartwheel, designed to smash through the Bismarck Barrier and neutralize Rabaul as a factor in future American offensives. First, MacArthur's most powerful ground unit, the Alamo Force formed around General Walter Krueger's Sixth Army, splashed ashore on the Trobriand Islands off the northern coast of New Guinea in concert with a simultaneous landing at Nassau Bay on the mainland. These offensives isolated large Japanese garrisons in the towns of

Salamaua and Lae and provided a vital springboard for an invasion of the island of New Britain and the neutralization of its key port of Rabaul.[9]

Meanwhile, Halsey's powerful Third Fleet supported a series of complementary amphibious landings just south of the key enemy position of Bougainville in the northern Solomons. Imperial leaders responded with a massive reinforcement effort through a series of convoys designed to support the defenders of islands such as Vella Lavella and Rendova. The battle for the approaches to Bougainville would produce future political implications when, on the night of August 1, 1943, young Lieutenant John F. Kennedy's PT boat was rammed by a Japanese destroyer escorting a nocturnal convoy run. Lieutenant Kennedy towed a badly wounded seaman in a four-hour swim across the water to tiny Plum Pudding Island and then swam an even greater distance to contact a rescue party for his beleaguered survivors.[10]

Soon after the future president's adventure, five American carriers initiated the campaign to turn Rabaul's dockyards and airfields into smoking wrecks and, in the first raid alone, damaged six Imperial cruisers and four destroyers and destroyed dozens of enemy planes at a cost of only ten aircraft. As the subsequent attacks chipped steadily away at enemy naval and air power, the Japanese high command reluctantly argued to pull most of their irreplaceable capital ships back to Truk, leaving 100,000 ground troops to hold land defenses that were now no longer strategically important. Meanwhile, Halsey's forces splashed ashore on Bougainville and relentlessly pushed the defenders toward the last rung in the Solomon Islands' chain ladder. Landcrab and Cartwheel had secured the northern and southern flanks of the Pacific and provided Ernest King with a clear road for his vaunted Central Pacific offensive. However, in the last months of 1943, conference rooms from Washington to Brisbane reverberated with often acrimonious debate about which route to the homeland of the Japanese Empire would offer the best prospects for victory.

4

THE BATTLE OF THE
CONFERENCE ROOMS

O N JANUARY 30, 1943, Admiral Ernest King arrived back
in Washington from the Casablanca conference and traded the
balmy Mediterranean weather for a major snowstorm that
nearly paralyzed the wartime capital.[1]

A few days later, the admiral was flying westward to San Francisco to
confer with Admiral Chester Nimitz about the next stage of the Pacific
operation. King welcomed the just-breaking intelligence that the enemy had evacuated Guadalcanal and turned the first American offensive of the war into a victory, but he was deeply concerned that the
Japanese had merely abandoned the southern Solomons in the expectation of doing better somewhere else. The admiral suspected that the
Imperial forces were preparing a new offensive at the relatively vulnerable American base on Samoa, which was the main artery in the extended supply line to Australia, or a second thrust at Midway to re-
deem the failure of the previous summer. The senior officer of the navy
emphasized that the best way to forestall a surprise Japanese offensive
along the still less than totally secure American lines of communication was a massive strike at the enemy line of communication at their
most vulnerable point, the Marianas Islands.[2]

This was the vital initial prize of King's planned Central Pacific offensive, but the salty admiral was beginning to discover that an equally talented, determined, and influential commander had his own ideas about establishing a road to the enemy's homeland.

Although Ernest King had spent much of the last year in conference rooms attempting to convince American and British leaders that the war in the Pacific should not be relegated to a mere backburner in the rush to confront Hitler, General Douglas MacArthur had seen the initial power of the Japanese war machine at often uncomfortably close quarters. On the eve of Pearl Harbor, MacArthur was in command of the most exposed major base in the American defense chain, the Philippines Islands. The Commonwealth of the Philippines had a complex relationship with the government in Washington: Congress had decreed complete independence for 1946, and military leaders insisted that the islands were too exposed to be defended properly. Then only a few months before the outbreak of war, Army Air Force officials explained that a force of two hundred powerful new B-17 bombers could hold any enemy invasion at bay if only the airfields could be properly defended.

MacArthur now presided over a frantic reinforcement effort from Washington as tanks, antiaircraft guns, and planes began pouring into the Commonwealth. Unfortunately, the new strategy was based on the premise of peace with Japan at least through the spring of 1942, and by early December only the first thirty-five Flying Fortresses had arrived.

MacArthur and his air commanders received news of the attack on Pearl Harbor hours before the Japanese arrived in the skies over the Philippines, but the enemy bombers caught much of the American air fleet on the ground during refueling and, by the end of the day, the defense of the islands would rise or fall on eighteen modern bombers and perhaps two dozen fighters. As Japanese forces used almost total air and naval superiority to stage massive landings, much of the half-trained Filipino militia melted away from the invasion beaches; by New Year's Day, the capital city of Manila was falling into enemy hands.

The American commander had ordered a retreat into the jungle-covered Bataan Peninsula and established his headquarters on Corregidor Island two miles away. MacArthur now commanded a besieged army that was desperately short of food, medicine, and modern weapons. However, as the Japanese overran almost every other objective in the region, the "battling bastards of Bataan" hung grimly on and their commander emerged as America's most visible hero. Although commanders in Washington made vague promises of early relief, it was obvious to Roosevelt, Marshall, and others that Bataan was doomed to eventual surrender. There was little desire to make a present to the Japanese of a general who graced the cover of many American magazines. MacArthur initially resisted all orders to evacuate for Australia; but, finally, under a direct order from the president and the hint that he was to organize a relief expedition, the general made a daring escape by PT boat and airplane. However, when MacArthur arrived in Brisbane, he found that reinforcements were a mirage because there were almost no American combat troops on the entire continent.

A few days later, the final defense positions on Bataan collapsed. In the largest surrender in American history, 20,000 Americans and 60,000 Filipinos entered a brutal captivity from which only a minority would emerge alive. Four weeks later, in early May, the garrison on Corregidor was pounded into surrender and the Philippines became an unwilling member of the Japanese Greater East Asia Co-Prosperity Sphere as well as the beneficiary of its dubious benefits of brutality and pillage.

Soon after MacArthur had arrived safely in Australia, he had made an emotional radio address to the besieged soldiers and civilians of the Commonwealth; in that broadcast, he gave assurance that as surely as he had escaped the enemy net, he would return at the head of an avenging army to expel every vestige of Japanese imperialism and free every prisoner taken by the Nipponese. Soon, the promising phrase "I will return" was appearing on everything from Manila's buildings to matchbook covers as MacArthur assured the Filipinos that their plight was not forgotten in America.

By the spring of 1943, a resurgent U.S. Army had used Australia as a springboard for a massive offensive in the huge island of New Guinea. As Operation Cartwheel pushed Allied forces ever westward towards the tip of the island on the Vogelkop Peninsula, Douglas MacArthur pored over his maps and began planning the next great leap from New Guinea to the southern tip of the Philippines. Although he readily agreed with Ernest King that the war against Japan should be given a much higher priority than the Anglo-American leaders had demonstrated, MacArthur's focus was not on the capture of the Marianas but rather on the liberation of the Philippines; any rival operation that delayed his return to the islands was a mortal threat to his determination to raise the Stars and Stripes above the tropical splendor of Manila. American journalists declared 1943 to be the "Year of the Conference," and, in board rooms from North Africa to Canada, an ongoing war of words erupted between supporters of MacArthur's plans for an early liberation of the Philippines and King's insistence that the war would be won in the atolls of the Central Pacific.

On Wednesday, May 12, 1943, the conference season shifted into high gear when the giant liner *Queen Mary* glided into New York harbor and disembarked Winston Churchill and more than one hundred advisors and staff members for a series of meetings designated "Trident." The conference, which was held in Washington, formalized a series of Anglo-American compromises in which Roosevelt and his commanders agreed to operations designed to eliminate Italy from the war and approved a postponement of a British offensive in Burma in return for a firm date of spring 1944 for a cross-Channel invasion and the go ahead for expanded offensive operations in the Pacific.[3]

As the conference participants settled down to a form of ritualized horse trading, King outlined the navy's plan for the advance in the Central Pacific: It should begin with an invasion of the Marshall Islands, after which that atoll would be used as the springboard for the first anticipated climactic confrontation in the Marianas. MacArthur had already dispatched his Chief of Staff, General Richard Sutherland, with an emotional objection to King's plans, arguing that his own line of approach from New Guinea to Mindanao in the Philippines made full use of Australia's vast potential as a war base and that it could be supported by the relatively large reserves of land-based aircraft now available. The Southwest Pacific commander insisted that a Central Pacific advance would constitute a series of "hazardous amphibious frontal attacks against islands of limited value" that would have to be supported by carrier-based aircraft operating far from their sources of fuel and ammunition.[4]

MacArthur's objections to King's proposed offensive seemed to hold some merit to most members of the Combined Chiefs of Staff, but the general's initial advantage was diluted when Sutherland itemized the wish list for a fully fledged Southwest Pacific offensive. The theater commander requested thirteen new combat divisions, thirty air groups deploying nearly 2,000 planes and a significant augmentation of landing craft and naval support ships. King countered that, according to the latest Allied projections, only twenty-one American and Australian divisions would be available by the end of 1943 in the entire Pacific area; these included substantial forces needed merely to guard the extended Allied lines of communication. The latest projection of land-based air power indicated that, by December, only 1,350 combat planes would be available for offensive operations and the air defense of Australia and New Zealand combined. If progress was to be made in the Pacific War in the near future, difficult decisions would have to be made.

Trident's spirit of compromise extended to Pacific operations as King's Central Pacific offensive was formalized, but not exactly on the timetable the admiral had proposed. King envisioned an initial thrust at the Marshalls followed by a massive invasion of the Marianas. However, a leadoff Marshalls assault would seriously curtail MacArthur and Halsey's South Pacific operations because it would require the only two experienced Marine divisions and most of the amphibious vessels available. The compromise proposal suggested that Nimitz inaugurate the new offensive by seizing the closer Gilbert Islands, which would require only one of the Marine divisions and far fewer landing craft and also provide more opportunity than the more distant Marshalls for utilizing land-based air support.[5]

The simmering King-MacArthur controversy moved north of the border in August as the cast of characters reassembled in Quebec for Quadrant. During the relatively brief interlude between conferences, the Allies had captured Sicily, the Italian government had overthrown Benito Mussolini and was making overtures to leave the Axis, the Red Army had smashed a huge German armored offensive at Kursk, and American offensives in New Guinea, the Solomons, and the Aleutians were making significant progress. As British and American leaders toured the scene of James Wolfe's victory over the Marquis of Montcalm and inhaled the bracing air of the Quebec summer, Ernest King engaged his peers in his most specific arguments as to why the capture of the Marianas was the key to the Pacific War. First, the island of Saipan was not merely a newly acquired territory captured in the post–Pearl Harbor offensive; it was an intricate part of the Japanese Empire, it had a huge agricultural base, and it was home to a sizable Japanese civilian population who had relatives in the homeland. The loss of Saipan would cause a major loss of face for the current Japanese government and would also evoke official and public questioning about exactly where, or if, the American war machine could be stopped.

Second, the southern island of Guam was the first American territory captured in the Japanese offensive and it represented the first surrender of the American flag and an American garrison. The residents of Guam were seen as Americans; their liberation from Japanese brutality would be a psychological high point for the people in the United States.

Third, the Marianas lay astride the main Japanese line of communication between the home island and the vital resources of their new conquests. The oil, tin, and rubber produced in these territories were useless to the empire if they could not be transported to the homeland; therefore, disruption of this supply line would make it only a matter of time until much of the Japanese war machine ground to a halt.

Finally, King insisted that the Japanese high command was equally aware of the strategic importance of the Marianas and would probably risk the entire Combined Fleet to prevent a successful American invasion. The American admiral was confident that the powerful new carrier units entering service would provide the United States Navy with an excellent chance of mauling the Imperial fleet to the extent that the enemy would have relatively few ships remaining to defend the home islands.[6]

Ironically, while MacArthur continued to insist that the Central Pacific offensive was dangerous and unnecessary, King now defended much of his antagonist's own plan. The admiral strongly supported a continued Southwest Pacific offensive, for he believed that the two routes of advance were complementary and that both were essential. King defined the dual offensives as the "whipsaw plan": The adversaries would constantly keep guessing where the next American blow would land and be forced to move essential forces all around the chessboard that was the Pacific theatre, never quite certain which was the "real" enemy thrust.

As King explained, either the two thrusts could converge on the Philippines or the huge Japanese base on Truk could be caught in a giant pincer. In some respects, the admiral's plan was quite similar to Ulysses S. Grant's plan to defeat the Confederacy eighty years earlier. Grant, Sherman, and Lincoln all agreed that up to this point in the Civil War the lack of coordination of Union offensives allowed Confederate leaders to shuttle forces to the point of Federal attack by stripping less-threatened areas of part of their forces. Grant now proposed a multiple-front advance directed against two objectives: Lee's army covering the rebel capital of Richmond and Joseph Johnston's army covering the vital rail and communications center at Atlanta. Grant insisted that these twin thrusts would complicate the Confederate reinforcement strategy and make the enemy leaders unsure about which was the "real" Federal priority. King saw a multifront 1944 offensive in much the same context and was confident that the whipsaw approach would stretch enemy defenses to the breaking point somewhere along their line of communications. Thus, in the final irony of the Quadrant conference, while Douglas MacArthur railed at King's "ill advised" offensive, the American admiral proved to be one of his firmest advocates as the British commanders consistently suggested the abandonment of all offensive operations in the Southwest Pacific and the transfer of many of these assets to the war against Germany. King's insistence on a dual offensive would be a critical element of maintaining MacArthur's goal of liberating the Philippines.

The "year of the conference" was not necessarily an Allied monopoly. At 10:00 on the early autumn morning of September 30, 1943, Emperor Hirohito entered the Imperial Council Chambers of his most formal palace in Tokyo and nodded his acknowledgment to a circle of his advisors bowing in his divine presence. The most powerful of these individuals was Hideki Tojo, who was both premier and war minister, and who led the junta that had essentially established a military dictatorship on the eve of World War II. The other senior participants in the conference included Admiral Osami Nagano, chief of the Naval General Staff, Admiral Mineichi Koga, commander of the Imperial Combined Fleet, and Baron Yoshimichi Hara, president of the Imperial Privy Council.[7]

These leaders were in effect conducting a mirror image of the Trident and Quadrant conferences; and the events that evoked congratulatory remarks in Washington and Quebec encouraged undisguised concern on this side of the world. Although the Japanese public had been assured that every operation since Pearl Harbor had been a resounding Imperial victory and that peace terms would be dictated to the Americans in a Japanese-occupied Washington, the men in these rooms recognized the real peril the empire was beginning to face. A huge chart of the Pacific region dominated the conference room: Earlier advance lines in New Guinea, the Solomons, and the North Pacific were now moving ominously away from the high tide of war eighteen months earlier. Japanese intelligence knew that massive American ground, air, and naval reinforcements were beginning to arrive in the Pacific. Earlier expectations of a German-Japanese link up somewhere between the Middle East and India were almost laughable now that the Wermacht was in full retreat in Russia and the Mediterranean. The Japanese leaders were beginning to sense that Hitler had bitten off far more than he could chew with simultaneous conflicts with Britain, Russia, and America; there was also some murmuring that the empire might soon be without major allies.

However, despite the obvious declining momentum of the initial series of offensives, in late September 1943 Japan still controlled an enormous empire and could inflict an enormous cost on any Allied attempt to expel the Nipponese from their new Greater East Asia Co-Prosperity Sphere. The conferences agreed that, in the face of far greater-than-anticipated American responses, the borders of the empire were now too overextended to successfully defend every point on the perimeter. The huge map graphically represented this new reality. The dominant feature of the chart was a bold black line that passed east of the Shoto Islands, through the Bonines, Marianas, and Truk in the Carolines down to the Vogelkop Peninsula at the western tip of New Guinea, west to the Timor Sea, and then through Borneo, Singapore, the Philippines, and Hong Kong. This zigzagging black band represented what Tojo called the Absolute Imperial Defense Line, and anything on the far side of the boundary represented expendable territory held by equally expendable forces.

The territories within the new defense perimeter were considered vital to the Japanese ability to wage war and continue some level of economic self-sufficiency; indeed, they represented a critical mass that, if substantially lost, would place the home islands in a virtual state of siege by advancing Allied forces. However, although these regions could not be surrendered for the time being, neither could they be fully defended. The Imperial forces were short of aircraft carriers, trained pilots, modern armored units, and first-class artillery. Thus time would have to be bought until enough new weaponry could be produced to permit the innate spiritual advantage of the Nipponese warrior to triumph over the materialistic Americans.

Tojo's proposed plan was based on two premises. First, the garrisons on the Admiralty, Bismarck, Gilbert, and Marshall Islands, as well as units on much of New Guinea and all of the Solomons, would fight to the death in a series of delaying actions that would keep the enemy out of the Absolute Defense Line for another eighteen months until the carrier fleet could be massively reinforced. Second, the Japanese would use the territories inside the barrier as a series of "island bridges" between the homeland and the centers of resource productions in which the still-formidable Imperial land-based air units would shuttle back and forth over a series of stepping stones and be available for rapid concentration just in case the enemy unexpectedly managed to penetrate the lines before the carrier forces were ready to challenge them.

The emperor's advisors agreed that the climactic point in the war would probably occur sometime in the summer of 1945, when the enemy would finally pierce the defense lines and be challenged by the powerful new Imperial carrier fleet, which would, of course, annihilate the Americans and force the United States to the negotiating table for a compromise peace that would allow Japan to retain most of its post–Pearl Harbor acquisitions.

The senior members of Japan's military command structure spent most of this balmy Thursday morning and afternoon veering between reality and fantasy as they attempted to analyze the threat from the Americans to their forcibly acquired empire. The two senior naval representatives admitted that there was always some possibility that the enemy might seize the expendable areas more quickly than expected. However, they also insisted that as long as they could choose the place of greatest Imperial advantage for a showdown with the forces then available, there was an excellent chance the enemy would be defeated anyway. Tojo submitted a General Outline of the New Direction Policy, which was based on the assumption that an additional 40,000 combat planes would be available by the summer of 1945 and that shipyards would produce virtually nothing but aircraft carriers for the next eighteen months. At 5:00 p.m., the emperor, who had not spoken a word up to this point in the conference, accepted his commanders' operational plans and essentially ceded large stretches of his overseas empire to the oncoming Americans in a desperate gamble to keep the enemy away from the Imperial homeland and perhaps set the stage for a negotiated peace in which the Americans would allow the Japanese to keep much of the spoils of war acquired since Pearl Harbor.[8]

However, not only did the Americans entertain virtually no desire to negotiate with the hated Nipponese, they were in the process of launching a multipronged Pacific offensive designed to smash through the Absolute Defense Line almost as soon as it had been traced on Japanese maps. The most dramatic sustained offensive of the Pacific War was about to be initiated on a tiny coral atoll, the name of which would be etched in blood for both American and Imperial Marines. This bloody confrontation at Tarawa would emerge as the opening act in a deadly drama that would make the much larger battle for the Marianas a growing certainty even before another summer embraced the cities and countryside of the United States and Japan.

5

BAPTISM OF FIRE

THREE DAYS BEFORE the Imperial Conference in Tokyo, two middle-aged American admirals stood on a tropical beach, peered out into a rainswept ocean in the general direction of the Japanese homeland, and silently contemplated the geographic and military barriers that separated them from their ultimate objective. Ernest King and Chester Nimitz were spending this late September day on newly hallowed ground, Midway Island, which sixteen months earlier had stood sentinel as the last barrier between a rapidly advancing Japanese fleet and the invaluable American military and naval facilities of the Territory of Hawaii.[1]

Now the tide of war was clearly turning and the two admirals had left behind a Pearl Harbor crammed with newly arrived carriers, battleships, and support ships ticketed to take part in the forthcoming Central Pacific offensive designed to carry the war to Japan's doorstep.

By the time the great operation began, King would be on the new battleship *Iowa* sailing across the Atlantic with Franklin Roosevelt. The two were bound for Cairo and Tehran, where they would participate in summit conferences; later, they would accompany General Dwight Eisenhower on a sobering excursion to the site of the pitiful remains of the once proud city-state of Carthage.

However, the commander of the American navy left the Pacific with the comforting assurance that his theatre commander shared his vision for defeating Japan and would direct the upcoming offensive with intelligence and resoluteness.

The admiral who would push the mightiest fleet in history across the vast expanses of the Pacific Ocean was quite different from his superior and yet complemented him almost perfectly. Chester W. Nimitz was courteous, kindly, and humorous; yet he possessed the nerves of a riverboat gambler and demonstrated them more than once in this colossal encounter with the Nipponese Empire. A little less than two years earlier, a few days after America entered World War II, President Roosevelt had instructed the blondish, slightly balding fifty-six-year-old admiral to "get the hell out to Pearl Harbor and stay there till the war is over," and Nimitz had responded less than six months later by orchestrating one of the most decisive naval victories in history in the waters near tiny Midway Island.

Now, in the fall of 1943, Chester Nimitz directed the largest naval force in history from a comfortable, but not ostentatious, command center and personal quarters located on heights overlooking the magnificent panorama of Pearl Harbor and its adjoining land facilities. During the climactic events of the Pacific War, Nimitz shared many of the endearing personality traits of his fellow native Texan, Dwight D. Eisenhower. Like Ike, Nimitz exhibited an almost boyish charm and friendly manner that put enlisted men and junior officers alike at ease; yet he always gave careful consideration to the opinions of senior officers from all branches of service.

Eisenhower read popular Westerns and took drives in the country to relax, but Nimitz countered the tension of high command with sessions of shooting on a pistol range, intense rounds of pitching horseshoes, and informal dinners with a variety of junior and senior officers at which the admiral personally mixed drinks and played records on his phonograph player. The admiral encouraged discussion and disagreement in the planning stages of operations, including the Central Pacific campaigns, but this was no democratic council of war. Nimitz could, and did, overrule every one of his senior lieutenants when he was sure that his strategy was correct, and more than one high-ranking officer knew when to back off from an escalating argument and so avoid his commander's not totally submerged temper. On the other hand, the admiral with the title CINCPAC also had the great good fortune to have secure the extensive trust of his navy superior, King, while simultaneously developing a cordial working relationship with his army counterpart in the Pacific, Douglas MacArthur. Senior Japanese army and navy officers frequently appeared to be only one step from challenging each other to a duel during their often fractious conferences, but Nimitz and MacArthur used courtesy and compromise to keep interservice rivalry within reasonable bounds during the Pacific War. Although Nimitz was wholeheartedly committed to the Central Pacific offensive, he clearly saw the strategic importance of MacArthur's operations and was happy to divert at least some of the enemy attention away from what he knew would be a difficult series of battles as his forces attempted to pierce the inner defenses of the Japanese Empire.

The admiral's profitable relationship with his army counterpart was duplicated by his selection of the officers who would lead this new type of amphibious combat from the beginning of the offensive through the end of the Marianas campaign. Three very different personalities would form the triumvirate that led Americans into battle on the atolls and islands of the Central Pacific.

Nimitz's senior field commander when the American fleet steamed into the enemy lair was his current housemate and confidant, Admiral Raymond Spruance. Ray Spruance was thought by many colleagues to be the most intelligent senior officer in the navy; he had achieved considerable fame when he directed carriers *Enterprise* and *Hornet* to the spectacular victory at Midway after becoming a last-minute replacement for the ill Admiral William Halsey. Nimitz pulled Spruance back to Pearl Harbor to become his Chief of Staff and trusted lieutenant for most of the following year. The two admirals took long walks together, swam together, and gradually achieved a familiarity not unlike that enjoyed by Grant and Sherman or Lee and Stonewall Jackson eight decades earlier. In tense situations, Spruance was quiet, unassuming, and unruffled. However, his relatively cautious nature had encouraged some criticism after Midway when he failed to accept Yamamoto's virtual invitation to continue the battle after one American and four Imperial carriers were sunk. This was a time when discretion was the better part of valor: The prospect of a night engagement against the vastly superior Japanese surface fleet should have brought shudders to any reasonably intelligent naval officer. There is no hint that Spruance's actions merited anything but praise from Nimitz, who preferred the competent to the flashy in these new uncharted waters of the imminent offensive. Nimitz would welcome an opportunity to annihilate the Imperial Fleet, but it was far more important that the frontline commander support successful landings and deflect enemy threats to each invasion.

Spruance's force was the newly designated Fifth Fleet, the largest component of a blue water Pacific navy that also included William Halsey's Third Fleet in the South Pacific and MacArthur's Seventh Fleet, the seagoing contingent in the Southwest Pacific region. Spruance used his new status as a three-star admiral to request that Nimitz appoint two colorful officers as the fleet commander's amphibious experts. The proposed amphibious force commander who would actually direct each landing operation was fifty-eight-year-old Admiral Richmond Kelly Turner, who had played a major role in the Guadalcanal landings and had been exonerated of personal blame for the subsequent disaster off Savo Island in the early days of battle. "Terrible" Turner was irascible, opinionated, and short-tempered, but he was an accomplished "god" of amphibious battle. Once Spruance had secured a "terrible" amphibious commander, he paired him with a "mad" ground forces commander, General Holland Smith. Spruance had observed this Marine training the army's 7th Division for the Aleutians operation; the mild-mannered admiral had determined that the crusty, cantankerous leatherneck with the nickname "Howling Mad" was just the sort of person to direct ground assaults against defenders sworn to fight to the last man. Turner and Smith would spend the next several months arguing with superiors, subordinates, and each other, and the general would be one of the central players in one of the major command controversies of World War II; but Nimitz readily admitted that a special tolerance, perhaps accompanied by earplugs, could be extended to leaders who were capable of seizing the difficult objectives that confronted the Americans in the upcoming campaign.[2]

The most formidable challenge facing Nimitz and his lieutenants revolved around the realization that no one had ever orchestrated a successful amphibious landing against a modern army that enjoyed a fully defended beachfront and knew the invaders were coming. The previous American invasions of Guadalcanal and New Guinea were directed against large islands where the Imperial forces were deployed far too thinly to contest the initial landing, and the British attempt to seize a fully defended Gallipoli from the Turks in World War I had resulted in one of the most disastrous bloodbaths of the Great War. King and Nimitz envisioned the Central Pacific offensive eventually directed against Taiwan, the Philippines, and then Japan itself, but much of the fighting would take place on a succession of small- to medium-sized coral atolls packed with hostile land-defense troops and fronted by coral-encrusted lagoons that would prove difficult or impossible for conventional landing craft to negotiate.

King and Nimitz had largely agreed by the late summer of 1943 that the first opportunity for a major naval showdown in the new offensive would most likely be in the waters near the Marianas, as that was the first target in the Central Pacific that the Japanese simply could not afford to lose. However, the Marianas were heavily shielded by major Imperial installations in the Marshall Islands that focused on eight major airfields and presented a major land-based aerial threat to any fleet approaching Guam or Saipan. The nearest American-held territory was the island of Runafuti, a little less than 1,200 miles away; the latest model B-24 Liberator would just about reach the Marshalls under the right conditions. The problem was that a reconnaissance bomber devoid of fighter escort and at the extreme end of its range could do little more than count the number of enemy airfields; loitering in the area would mean certain death from enemy attack or lack of fuel. Therefore, the Marshalls were tantalizing objectives; the Americans had just enough information about them to know they were a formidable target but not enough to declare them an acceptable risk.

The outer rim of the new Japanese Empire was more than 500 miles closer to American territory and could be photographed, surveyed, and studied before an attack. The atoll was named the Gilbert Islands and, until the day after Pearl Harbor, they were British colonies where a few British administrators and coast watchers kept an eye on a series of tropical islands that seemed far removed from even a hint of war. Only hours after the Japanese attack on Hawaii, Imperial forces stormed ashore and began constructing an airfield on Tarawa and a seaplane base on Makin that would serve as the outermost defense of the Marianas and as a tripwire for an American attack on the Marshalls.

American intelligence knew that the Gilberts would be no pushover. The Japanese navy had dipped into its force of 50,000 rikusentai, a naval infantry force roughly similar to the U.S. Marines, and deployed two reinforced Special Naval Landing Forces on the Tarawa atoll island of Betio. Several additional companies were stationed to guard the seaplane base on Makin atoll. Including support troops and construction units, the Imperial high command was committing close to 5,000 men to the defense of the Gilberts, and a large percentage of these troops would be utilized to defend the beaches. On the other hand, the relative proximity of the Gilberts to American air bases meant that the invaders would at least generally know what they were up against, but the more distant Marshalls still seemed to be a risky enigma for an opening engagement in the impending offensive. Therefore, Operation Galvanic, the invasion of Tarawa and Betio, was approved as the opening objective of the Central Pacific campaign that would come to define so much of the American public awareness of the Pacific War.

The basic American battle plan was to land major elements of one army division and one Marine division on Makin and Tarawa in a furious, coordinated assault on Saturday, November 20, 1943. The operation was envisioned as a three-day contest in which the invaders would essentially secure a beachhead on the first day, capture the air bases on the second day, and eliminate the last major enemy resistance on the final day, although it was conceded that small numbers of enemy troops might continue some level of resistance afterwards. The key to victory was seen as an early version of the modern concept of "shock and awe": Massive naval bombardment and air strikes would precede the mass landing of specially designed amphibious vehicles that could sail through the coral lagoons and then lurch up onto the beach like alligators to deposit units of soldiers and Marines in direct contact with an already nearly pulverized enemy garrison.[3]

Unfortunately for the invaders, particularly the Marines, the plans that emerged from the comfortable and somewhat isolated conference rooms would begin to unravel almost as soon as Galvanic opened.

One of the unforeseen complicating factors was that although the American leaders knew about how many Imperial troops were garrisoned the Gilberts, they could not fully appreciate the ferocity of a tightly packed phalanx of fanatical defenders who fully intended to die to the last man for the glory of their emperor. Admiral Keiji Shibasaki, the forty-nine-year-old commander of the Betio island garrison, had spent four months turning a narrow, 2-mile-long island into a huge, oversized pillbox bristling with heaving artillery and machine guns that was manned by some of the most elite troops in the Japanese war machine. Shibasaki knew that this could not be a battle of maneuver because there was nowhere to maneuver; this meant that almost any weapon his men fired had an excellent chance of hitting an attacker on a densely packed battlefield that would resemble the killing fields of the American Civil War.[4]

The second major complicating factor for the invaders was that although American commanders had certainly not ignored the intensive planning for this ambitious enterprise, there were gaps in the planning process that would explode far beyond their perceived level of importance. The planners did not ignore the warnings of the few advisors with firsthand experience that the tides of Betio were more than a little eccentric, but they failed to understand how a "dodging tide" could wreak havoc on landing craft scraping their bottoms on jagged coral.[5]

They thought that a hundred of the new amphibious "alligators" could meet their needs for successive landing waves to hit the beaches on time, but did not fully appreciate the consequences if half were put out of action before the first wave had landed. They insisted that the new flamethrowers would annihilate enemy pillboxes, but did not appreciate the fact that the twenty-four allotted to the 2nd Marine Division was about one tenth the number that would have a real impact (243 per division were allocated in the Marianas campaign). All new campaigns tend to begin with large amounts of trial and error, and Galvanic provided both commodities in equal quantities.

On the morning of November 20, 1943, Japanese defenders peering from the slits of beach defense pillboxes squinted into the coral-rimmed lagoon in front of them and expressed surprise and curiosity at just under ninety strange hybrids that they would describe as "little boats on wheels." What they were witnessing was a new era in amphibious warfare: The "Amtracs" that did not explode in a fiery geyser from a direct hit crawled up onto the beach and began disembarking men clad in green fatigues and mottled camouflage helmets who stood in stark contrast to the almost blindingly white sand that rimmed Betio island.

The invaders had approached the beaches under the covering fire of the greatest bombardment of the war so far and then watched enthralled as dozens of dark blue planes dove like birds of prey and released their deadly cargoes of machine gun bullets and bombs onto the foliage below them. The young Marines, many of whom had been sitting in a high school English or history class at this time the year before, probably wanted to believe that nobody could reasonably survive the sheer firepower expended on these Nipponese defenders before the first invader ever set foot on the beach. However, as this string of landing craft, looking like "dozens of spiders" to one defender, approached Betio island, every weapon in Admiral Shibasaki's arsenal erupted in a shattering concert of noise and explosion. Formidable 8-inch guns sent shells whistling out to sea as smaller caliber guns focused on the lumbering alligators purring toward the shore at 4 knots. American guns and planes smashed much of the admiral's prized heavy battery, flattened pillboxes, and left smoldering heaps of coconut logs where machine-gun emplacements had once stood. In turn, a single Japanese gun crew knocked out four successive Amtracs as they attempted to cross the coral reef with their precious cargo of Marine tanks.

Thus, the initial American landing in the initial battle of the Central Pacific campaign began as a live equivalent of an arcade shooting gallery as each spurt of flame from a newly exploding LVT (landing vessel-tank) meant that more than twenty American Marines and sailors were quite probably dead or seriously injured. American teenagers and young adults whose only previous uniform had probably been a high school or college football jersey were now assuming the roles of red-coated soldiers approaching Bunker Hill or blue-coated men approaching Cold Harbor, places that had been nothing more than pictures in a high school textbook but were now startlingly relevant to these young warriors' first taste of war.

The person at center stage of this bloody drama was a thirty-eight-year-old Marine colonel, David Shoup. This future commandant of the Marine Corps was now commanding the 2nd Marine Regiment of the 2nd Marine Division and at the moment was one of fifteen hundred men comprising the initial assault waves of the attack on Betio Island. Shoup was a mid-level officer in a battle designed for the particular talents of mid-level officers. In this new world of amphibious landings, corps commanders and division commanders stayed on command ships until well into the battle and directed the fighting from frequently erratic radio communication with a shore-based surrogate. Much like fellow mid-level officers Brigadier Generals Teddy Roosevelt, Jr., and Norman "Dutch" Cota on Utah and Omaha Beaches six months later, Shoup would have to make crucial decisions far beyond the normal concerns of his relatively modest rank while his division commander, Major General Julian Smith, paced a deck and watched the battle from a far different prism.

Shoup and his men had emerged from the sea into a world largely dominated by one object, a 4-foot-high coconut log seawall that ringed most of the vital beachfront and was populated on the far side by Japanese defenders who were willing to use clubbed rifles, bayonets, and swords to prevent their enemies from surmounting this barrier.[6]

In many respects, the Marines had stumbled into a momentary time warp, a tropical re-creation of the infamous "Bloody Angle" that dominated the bloodstained fields of Spotsylvania Court House in Ulysses S. Grant's Overland campaign of 1864. Just as Grant could not fully employ his Federals as long as they were densely packed on the wrong side of a Confederate-built log wall, the Marines could not demonstrate their prowess if they simply stacked up behind a seawall as the enemy peppered them with bullets and shells.

Shibasaki was orchestrating a masterful defense of Tarawa as he shifted units from the less-threatened ocean side of the island to the lagoon beachfront in the north. However, the massive naval bombardment had knocked out most of his communications system beyond individual runners, and his casualties were reaching appalling proportions. Then, in the first key turn in the battle, the admiral announced that he and his staff would move to an alternate command post so that his heavily fortified headquarters could be turned into an emergency hospital. Perhaps six hours into the battle, the key members of the Japanese command sprinted through the trees, unknowingly observed by an American shore-fire control team. A hail of naval shells careened shoreward; in an instant the command structure of Betio was eliminated and the best chance for a coordinated counterattack on the beleaguered Americans disappeared.[7]

The defenders still had enough uninjured soldiers to smash through the thin American lines if the attacks were well coordinated and launched under the cover of darkness. Soon after the rapid tropical sunset, desperate Japanese charges did begin; but they were so loosely organized that they were never able to throw the still formidable weight of the garrison against a vulnerable point.[8]

The only significant advantage gained by the Imperial forces during this first night of battle was that small groups of men furtively swam out to the hulk of a partially sunken freighter and occupied firing positions throughout the vessel; at the same time, other troops crawled into the partially submerged American landing craft bobbing in the lagoon near a long pier jutting out into the water and set up shop to blaze away at the invaders at first light.

While Marines and rikusentai counted their losses and braced for the second day of battle, 100 miles to the north a parallel battle was winding down for the night. Makin Island was the main seaplane base for the Gilberts and would be a valuable asset in American hands. The Japanese did not have enough troops available to deploy the same dense concentration of manpower on Makin as Betio, but the garrison was not a token force. The core of the defense of Makin was formed around three hundred rikusentai, 150 Pioneers and Sappers, a hundred armed aviation personnel, and a hundred combat-trained construction troops aided by questionable support from some two hundred Korean conscript laborers. Essentially, 650 combat troops would be responsible for defending the island against three reinforced battalions of the 27th Division's 105th Regiment and a number of additional support units that would allow General Ralph Smith to deploy 6,500 ground troops supported by eight battleships and cruisers, thirteen destroyers, two fleet carriers, and three escort carriers.

Smith enjoyed an overwhelming advantage in troops and firepower, but the defenders would be able to deploy a formidable concentration of men and guns between twin antitank fortifications located roughly midway on the 11-mile-long island. It was obvious that the battle on Makin would unfold very differently from the one on Tarawa because the GIs would be obliged to push through several miles of easily defended foliage before they even approached the key objective on the island. Therefore, Kelly Turner, who was taking personal charge of this northern operation, and Ralph Smith agreed that three days was not an unreasonable timetable to secure the relatively large island.[9]

The first day of fighting on Makin was far less intensive than that on Betio. The Americans landed on the western end of the island and pushed through seemingly unending coconut palms, halting to reform after successive encounters with real and imagined snipers ensconced in the trees. Although the GIs held more than one third of the island by nightfall, they had yet to close with the main Japanese defense line. "Howling Mad" Smith, who had been directed to accompany Turner on the northern operation instead of staying with his own Marines near Tarawa, was determined to go ashore and push his army namesake to speed up the advance which, ironically, was roughly on schedule.

The resumption of action on Tarawa saw a steady column of Amtracs filled with reinforcements and supplies purring toward the beach. Suddenly, their rear exploded with rifle and machine-gun fire from the freighter and the abandoned landing craft; the approaching units were caught in a wicked crossfire as other defenders joined the fray from concealed positions on the land approach to the pier. However, as American fighters swooped in to deal with this unexpected enemy deployment, enough Marine units broke out of their narrow beachhead to allow Julian Smith the maneuvering room to land his divisional reserve, the 6th Marines, on the southeastern tip of the island and so threaten the defenders from a new direction. By nightfall, the colorful and combative divisional chief of staff, Colonel Merritt Edson, arrived to take overall command of the invasion force, thus freeing Colonel Shoup to focus on the four battalions that had made up his original combat team.

On Monday, November 22, while American tanks formed an armored spearhead, Marines advanced against a succession of pillboxes and blockhouses and knocked out the strong points one by one in brutal heat and even more brutal combat. The defenders had just enough troops remaining to launch a last-gasp night attack, but, by Tuesday morning, it was obvious that the end was near. By early afternoon, seventy-six hours after the initial landings, the last few dazed survivors had either killed themselves or been taken into an unwanted captivity. Betio Island was declared secured.[10]

Meanwhile, the soldiers of the 27th Division had spent the previous two days assaulting the 2-mile-apart Japanese tank traps, all the while encouraged by friendly natives but criticized for their lack of speed by Holland Smith. In a tactic all too common in later American experiences in Asia, Japanese troops drove natives toward the advancing Americans with snipers intermingled and then used terrified women and children as human shields as they picked off exasperated GIs. By the end of the third day, Makin had been secured at the remarkably light cost of 64 soldiers killed and 150 wounded, but two forms of fall-out would quickly sour the victory. "Howling Mad" Smith insisted that the army's tactics had lacked speed and aggressiveness and that his Marines would have taken Makin in a day, even though the cost might have been higher.[11]

Then to add a catastrophic exclamation point to Smith's charge, the most disastrous event of Operation Galvanic occurred just after Makin was secured.

While Combined Fleet Commander Mineichi Kugo of the Japanese Fleet insisted that he would not commit to a full naval showdown unless or until the enemy approached either Truk or Saipan, he did commit nine powerful fleet submarines to an undersea offensive. One of these boats, the I-175, approached the American carrier screen off Makin just as a Japanese plane dropped a float light to signal Imperial ships that an enemy target was near. At first light on November 24, two I-175s fired a spread of torpedoes at the escort carrier *Liscomb Bay* and a terrible explosion rocked the dawn. Bombs stormed in a hold detonated and ships a mile away were showered with fragments of metal and flesh. In little more than twenty minutes, the same length of time as it took the doomed *Lusitania* to sink twenty-eight years earlier, the carrier disappeared into the deep Pacific carrying an admiral, the captain, and 642 other men to watery graves; only 272 men were rescued, a loss rate slightly exceeding the *Lusitania* tragedy. This major naval disaster formed a somber endpoint to the equal horror endured by the Marines on land in the previous days of this bloody week.[12]

Operation Galvanic was clearly an American victory as both Makin and Tarawa were captured and their airbases quickly converted to use by the invaders. The opening engagement in the Central Pacific campaign accomplished all its objectives and virtually every enemy defender was killed or, more rarely, captured. However, most Americans believed that the appalling bloodletting that characterized the brute frontal assaults of earlier warfare, especially the Civil War, was unlikely to be repeated in a modern war of maneuver. Horribly, the fight for Betio Island looked surprisingly like a deadly battle between Yankees and Confederates.

Many of the most decisive battles of the war between the States resulted in a casualty rate of 25 to 30 percent of the participants, a figure that would turn once-proud regiments into company-sized remnants after two or three such encounters. Yet at Tarawa, with a total control of the sea and air, more advanced weapons than the enemy, and a substantial numerical advantage, 3,400 of the 12,000 men who saw action ended up as casualties, a rate alarmingly similar to that of the war between blue and gray. In fact, even with the far superior medical care available to mid-twentieth-century American soldiers, the fatal injury to nearly one third of the casualties was actually much higher than most Civil War counterparts. The sheer brutality of a battle in which Imperial soldiers did virtually anything to take an invader into death with them left hundreds of armies with graphically violent fatal wounds beyond the normal comprehension of even hard-bitten veterans. If the relatively modest garrison on Betio could inflict this much damage on the attackers, what would happen when further into the offensive the Americans clashed with far larger Imperial forces?

While General Douglas MacArthur offered lofty opinions that truly intelligent commanders won battles with minimal losses, Admirals Ernest King and Chester Nimitz were placed in a position not unlike that of Ulysses S. Grant as his mauled army stumbled out of the wilderness after a bloody and confused battle that was far more ferocious than the new Union supreme commander had expected. Grant's men emerged onto a road that lead either north back to Washington and safety or south toward Richmond with Robert E. Lee and the Army of Northern Virginia poised to contest every yard. While a succession of Grant's predecessors utilized a bloody encounter as a perfect opportunity to march northward and regroup, the new commander pointed a smoldering cigar toward the enemy capital and marched south safe in the knowledge that his president would support him in his decision.

King and Nimitz knew that the cost of seizing Tarawa had been high, but they knew also that the commander in chief held them in high regard and that the road to Tokyo lay westward, not east toward Pearl Harbor. There still remained one more battle to fight before the expected titanic confrontation over the Marianas. Both of the senior admirals and the lieutenants under them were determined to prove that the lessons learned at Tarawa were not wasted and that the inner ring of the Japanese Empire could be pierced without decimating American military forces in the process.

6

STORMING THE
OUTER WALLS

THE YEAR 1943 that had begun with a Central Pacific offensive that was little more than a personal focus for Admiral Ernest King ended with the United States in possession of the first objective of that plan, a 3-square-mile coral island that was a mere speck in the ocean on a household global map. The assault on Tarawa, which even General Holland Smith equated with the carnage of General George Pickett's charge at Gettysburg, convinced even relatively optimistic planners that the Japanese really would fight to the last man to defend each successive position, a grim portent for confrontations with much larger garrisons in future operations. The U.S. Marines did take prisoners on Tarawa, a contingent of nearly 150 stunned defenders dressed in the mustard uniforms of Imperial forces. However, preliminary interrogations quickly revealed that almost all of them were conscripted Korean laborers and not Japanese combat troops. The 3,000 rikusentai who formed the fighting core of the Betio garrison were reduced to exactly eight living survivors, all of them too badly wounded to kill themselves and none of them holding a rank higher than petty officer. A willingness of 99.7 percent of defenders to die fighting was a sobering calculus for the major battles that would follow.

On the other hand, the 2nd Marine Division would regain combat effectiveness only with a massive infusion of reinforcements. The unit needed the addition of the equivalent of four full combat battalions before there could be any thought of putting the division back in action. At a point in the war where the commanders of the upcoming invasion of Normandy had a priority call on American manpower resources, it was brutally apparent that units involved in future Central Pacific operations could not continue to lose nearly a third of their men in each successive battle and still have sufficient combat veterans to overwhelm the enemy when they finally arrived at the doorstep of the Imperial homeland. Future operations would have to be conducted with the harsh lessons of Tarawa always paramount in planning activities.

The general consensus in American headquarters was that the next logical objective in this process would be the Marshall Islands. Even before the bloodletting at Tarawa, a significant number of planners were convinced that the Gilberts should be bypassed in favor of these islands, and now this series of atolls became a virtually unanimous target. The logic of the operation that would be code-named Flintlock was simple: An assault on the inner core of the Japanese Empire could not ignore an island group bristling with enemy aircraft in its rear. The Marshalls contained eight Imperial airfields that could launch hundreds of enemy planes to play havoc with American lines of communications between friendly bases and supplies being taken to them. Also, the westernmost Marshalls atoll, Eniwetok, was in aerial striking range of Truk, Wake Island, and the Marianas, all potential American targets. The debate about this priority list would demonstrate that the usually placid Chester Nimitz could be as obstinate and ferocious as Ernest King when his views conflicted with those of his subordinates.

The first "battle of the Marshalls" was fought on the verdant heights overlooking Pearl Harbor and saw Nimitz and his chief planning officer, Admiral Forrest Sherman, ranged against virtually everybody else remotely connected with the Central Pacific campaign. Sherman, with Nimitz's full support, proposed to save time and resources by ignoring enemy bases in the eastern third of the Marshalls while striking di-

rectly at Kwajalein atoll in the center and then using that series of islands as a jump-off point for the capture of the vital harbor at
Eniwetok, located at the western fringe of the archipelago. When
Sherman's plan was broached to Spruance, Turner, and Smith for consideration, the three officers went into a joint rage of opposition and
questioned how Nimitz could possibly approve a dangerous scheme
that left the enemy in control of air bases on at least four islands to the
rear of the invasion force. The trio envisioned a nightmare scenario in
which their ships and troops would be caught in a giant aerial process
between the eastern Marshalls on one flank at Truk and the Marianas
on the opposite side.[1]

Sherman insisted that the carrier component of the newly designated Task Force 58 was now so powerful that it could annihilate all
enemy air power in the Marshalls before the invasion and then handle
any threat from Truk or Saipan during the ground battle for Kwajalein.
When "Terrible" Turner launched the first verbal broadside questioning Sherman's sanity, Nimitz continued with an icy stare and the
equally frosty invitation to the admiral to face replacement in the operation if he could not endorse the proposal.[2]

The somewhat more courteous objections voiced by Spruance were
met with a somewhat more polite assurance to the fleet commander
that Japanese air bases in the Marshalls would be pounded by a lethal
combination of shore-based and carrier aircraft in a series of missions
that would continue right up to the invasion of Kwajalein. Finally, tem-
pers cooled enough for a temporary truce, but this threatened to evap-
orate when the initial air strikes accomplished little of Nimitz's
promised annihilation of enemy air power.

The air component of Operation Flintlock got off to a disappointing
start in December 1943 when a carrier force under the direction of
Rear Admiral Charles Pownall ranged deep into enemy-held territory.
A massive raid on the airbase on Roi Island managed to knock out a
confirmed nineteen enemy aircraft, but dozens of other planes remained fully serviceable because they enjoyed excellent enemy camouflage. A subsequent attack on the port and airfield facilities on

Kwajalein sent three Nipponese freighters to the bottom of the harbor and destroyed more than a dozen aircraft; but it failed to prevent the evacuation of most of the merchant ships, all of the combat vessels, and the majority of serviceable planes.[3]

While the carrier planes and crews were being refitted and rested, Admiral John Hoover unleashed nearly 350 land-based U.S. Navy and Army Air Force planes from the recently captured fields on Makin and Tarawa. When the bombers concentrated on the most easterly Marshalls, which were close enough to allow fighter escorts, the results were moderately encouraging; but as the battle drifted westward and fighter protection diminished, Zeros began to tear into the formations and drastically reduce bombing efficiency. As the countdown to the initiation of Flintlock wound down to its final week, the defenders of the Marshalls could still count on nearly two hundred combat planes. The American high command passed the baton back to the carriers for one final attempt to nullify this threat before the battle began.

Admiral Pownall had emerged as a competent but extremely cautious commander of the carrier flotilla that would serve as the primary offensive naval weapon in the drive across the Central Pacific. Now Pownall's aversion to risk seemed to be emerging as a liability in the view of Chester Nimitz, and the senior commander in the Pacific was increasingly enamored with the talents of the feisty fifty-seven-year-old officer who had commanded Hornet during Colonel Jimmy Doolittle's spectacular raid on Tokyo in those early dark months after Pearl Harbor. Because Marc Mitscher had garnered laudatory comments as commander of the often outnumbered American carrier forces during the Gudalcanal campaign, Nimitz wondered what this salty mariner could do with a force that was actually superior to that of the enemy.[4]

The Wisconsin native was a short, slight, gruff chain smoker who peered mischievously from beneath a long-brimmed baseball cap as he perched from a high metal chair always facing the stern to shield against the nautical breeze. Just beneath the gruff exterior was a reservoir of mischief, daring, and twinkling humor that endeared him to seamen and junior officers. This almost fatherly concern for the welfare of pilots and air crew was famous throughout the navy and would produce a wave of positive feelings when he was named to replace Pownall as commander of Task Force 58. Unlike his predecessor, Mitscher fully appreciated that he had been provided with an awesome war-winning weapon and he intended to strike hard and deep into enemy territory and stay there until there were no enemy planes left to challenge him.

As D-Day for the Marshalls invasion approached, Mitscher wheeled his new command into attack formation and pushed the task forces into harm's way. The admiral decided to replace Pownall's highly predictable attack schedule with numerous raids launched on short notice and carried out when the enemy least expected the Americans to arrive over their airfields. The showpiece of the pre-invasion attacks occurred on Saturday, January 29, when hundreds of American planes swarmed over the bustling Japanese airfield on Roi Island. The airfield bristled with nearly a hundred combat planes and, as the raiders approached, dozens of Zero fighters clawed for higher altitude to provide a powerful welcome. The Zeros careened downward toward what they believed was a top-cover squadron of escorting Hellcat fighters, but never noticed that another force of Americans was circling above them, ready to pounce as soon as the Japanese planes were committed to battle. A wild melee followed; it knocked down all but two of the Zeros and opened the way for a hundred dive bombers to methodically eliminate the island's extensive antiaircraft batteries. Once the booming guns had been silenced, a low-level attack force sprayed plane revetments and landing strips with fragmentation bombs. As the raiders wheeled for home, a pall of smoke covered Roi and its twin island of Namur. Dazed repair crews stumbled through the rubble and identified exactly six Imperial planes still capable of flight. At a cost of five American planes, the back of Japanese air power in the Central Marshalls was broken and the ground assault would take place under almost exclusively friendly skies.[5]

The stage was now set for the invasion of the Marshalls, and the bloody experience of Tarawa colored almost every aspect of the new campaign. Only a week after the Gilberts were secured, Kelly Turner dispatched a plane to Pearl Harbor carrying a document titled "Lessons Learned at Tarawa." This paper was a point-by-point indictment of everything from bombardment procedures to utilization of landing craft. Turner insisted that it was reasonable to assume that islands occupied for more extended periods than the much more recent Nipponese acquisition of the Gilberts would feature even more formidable impediments to a successful amphibious landing; therefore, the invaders should be provided with every weapon that the vast and still expanding American arsenal could develop.

The first targeted improvement was the design and configuration of the vessels and craft that were expected to transport the soldiers and Marines from the fleet to dry land. The LVTs had proved to be invaluable to the capture of Tarawa and provided an unpleasant shock to the defenders, who viewed the Amtracs as virtual mechanical monsters crawling up the beach and creeping inland like a pack of carnivorous reptiles. However, the first-generation alligators used at Tarawa were still relatively undergunned and underarmored, and far too many of the strange-looking vehicles ended up as burning wrecks in the lagoon or on the invasion beach. Therefore, all future landings would revolve around the recently introduced LVT-A-2, which featured quarter-inch armor and three machine guns to enhance offensive and defensive capabilities. These new vehicles would be shepherded to the beach by another new craft, the LVT-A-1, which was essentially an amphibious weapons platform. This version of the alligator deployed a turret-mounted 37 mm cannon supported by up to five light and heavy machine guns; it also had a single mission of spraying shells and bullets all around the landing beach. While these new Amtracs were providing close-in support to the landing force, flank protection would be supplied by an ingenious new type of Higgins boat. Two dozen of these traditional ramped landing craft were altered to carry weapons instead of troops, and the finished product featured five heavy machine guns, three 40 mm cannons, two 20 mm cannons, and a final deadly surprise: 6 rocket launchers capable of firing 400 missiles as far out as 100 yards from the landing beaches.[6]

The vital naval bombardment process that had proved only a mixed success at Tarawa was now targeted for major expansion in ships and time. The navy had achieved some positive results in Galvanic because the ships nearly obliterated the enemy communications system, knocked out the most powerful Imperial shore guns, and killed the Japanese commander early in the battle. However, the majority of Nipponese defenders survived the shelling to inflict enormous casualties on the Marines, and this calculus would have to be altered in future battles.

Finally, Operation Flintlock would use far more assault troops than were available for earlier operations. The 27,000 men allocated to the invasion of Makin and Betio was now doubled to 54,000 invaders for Kwajalein. However, in a major reversal from the pattern in the Gilberts, the most veteran unit to be deployed was an army unit, the 7th Infantry Division; the primary Marine Corps participants, the men of the 4th Division, would be mainly newcomers to combat.

The target for this formidable concentration of American power was Kwajalein atoll in the center of the Marshall Islands. The atoll consisted of numerous islets and sandspits, with three predominant bodies of land: the island of Kwajalein located at the southern tip and the twin islands of Roi and Namur at the opposite end 44 miles to the north. The combined chain of ninety-seven land masses produced the largest coral atoll in the world fronting an immense lagoon of 800 square miles, almost a distinct inland sea.

The Japanese high command basically viewed the Marshalls as the outer bulwarks of the far more important Carolines and Marianas, which meant that they were to be defended as long as possible without the intervention of the irreplaceable carriers. Thus 10,000 far more expendable ground troops were ferried in to reinforce the 12,000-man garrison of the islands, but they were expected to extract a maximum toll of American casualties, not win a battle. Ironically, the Imperial leaders agreed with the insistence of Spruance, Turner, and Smith that an American thrust at the center of the Marshalls was far too risky as an opening move, and most of the reinforcements were deployed in the eastern islands that were about to be bypassed under Nimitz's orders. The Kwajalein atoll was hardly undefended as Kawajalein Island counted 4,600 men in its garrison, and Roi and Namur fielded an additional 3,600 defenders. However, the absence of an additional 10,000 men in the spot where the invasion was actually to take place was a major bonus for the American planners.

Although the invasion of the Marshalls was hardly expected to be a walkover, the very geography of the target areas gave the invaders an advantage that promised greatly to reduce the chances of another bloodbath like Tarawa. Both Roi-Namur and Kwajalein Island were in close proximity to dozens of satellite islets, and these miniature land masses could serve as ideal weapons platforms for American artillery battalions. Thus, on the morning of January 31, 1944, twenty-four hours before the main invasion was scheduled to begin, fleets of LCI rocket boats escorted Amtracs through the northern and southern tips of the lagoon and seized a series of tiny islands that became the temporary home for army and Marine Corps artillerists. The attackers now had the capabilities of unleashing a deadly hail of shells from several directions as they tightened the noose around essentially besieged Japanese garrisons.

Because the twin islands of Roi and Namur served as the center of Japanese air operations in the Marshalls, the position should have been more heavily fortified than Tarawa. Construction workers had fashioned a network of eight blockhouses and more than sixty smaller pillboxes, but the majority of heavy guns expected to be deployed in this string of strongpoints had not arrived when Flintlock began, and Mitscher's air strikes had mauled most of the batteries that were available. By the morning of February 1, the garrison commander, naval captain Seiko Arina, counted a meager force of one anti-tank gun, two medium naval guns, two 22 mm cannons, and fewer than a dozen heavy machine guns to contest the invasion. However, Arima could still deploy almost 4,000 ground troops, and he was determined to utilize the special features of the islands to gain maximum advantage for the defenders.[7]

Roi Island, the eastern half of the twin landmass, was almost completely dominated by a huge airfield that could support air operations for more than two hundred planes. This 2,500-foot-wide and 3,000-foot-long island had been stripped of nearly all vegetation by labor crews, but the numerous airstrips were bordered by relatively deep drainage ditches that provided a ready-made trench network to supplement the pillboxes and blockhouses.

The eastern side of the land maps, Namur Island, was about the same size as Roi and was linked to its twin by a narrow strand of beach at the south end and a causeway in the middle. Namur served as the administrative center for the airbase as well as a communications headquarters for the entire outer perimeter of the Japanese Empire, a status that prompted the construction of nearly three hundred buildings, many of which could be turned into strongpoints. The central and northern parts of the island were dominated by heavily wooded terrain that was ideal ground for a defensive stand. Therefore, Captain Arima envisioned a three-tiered defense of his position: The garrison would defend a first line of blockhouses, pillboxes, and drainage-ditch trenches, then fall back into the numerous buildings for a street battle, and finally retire to the woods for a glorious final stand. The Marine Corps invaders would face a bewildering succession of combat environments and, in Arima's hopeful view, suffer devastating casualties in each experience. The naval captain's theory of attrition would soon be put to the test.

At dawn on Tuesday, February 1, 1944, Admiral Richard Connolly, commander of the Northern Attack Force, gave orders for his bombardment squadron to open fire on Roi-Namur. A little more than four hours later, after seemingly interminable delays created by tropical downpours, clusters of cannon and rocket-firing Amtracs and landing craft let loose with their formidable array of weapons. Major General Harry Schmidt's untested but superbly trained Marines scrambled out of their amphibious landing vehicles just as the LVT-AI's surged forward to knock out enemy weapons positions lining the Red beaches on Roi and the Green beaches on Namur.

The leathernecks of the 23rd Regimental Combat Team had been assigned the open fields and runways of Roi and they quickly encountered an improvised trench system from which the defenders poured rifle and automatic weapons fire. However, the ground troops were soon supported by the firepower of sixteen Sherman tanks that, according to one account, used the open terrain to "roam like predatory dinosaurs."[8]

Communication between riflemen and tankers was still far too erratic for optimal mutual support, but the awesome firepower of the Shermans was able to negate much of the advantage of the trench system for the defenders. The Imperial forces soon faced a bitter choice: Either fight to eventual extinction in the ditches or filter back across the causeway to join in the defense of Namur. Each option produced a significant portion of takers and, with few actual orders being issued, part of the garrison simply seemed to fall into the final-stand mode while many of their comrades dashed to the temporary safety of the eastern twin, where they would engage in a different form of battle.

The Marines of the 24th Regimental Combat Team assigned to land on the Green beaches of Namur did not have to worry about attacking World War I–style trenches as their comrades on Roi did, but they were quickly challenged by a different kind of man-made hell. Each pillbox, blockhouse, warehouse, and administrative building was bristling with enemy rifles and machine guns, and each strongpoint had to be neutralized before the line of invaders could surge a little further forward. Then almost all control of the advance was temporarily lost when combat engineers arrived in front of the largest blockhouse on the island. After a few holes were blasted in the strongpoint's south wall, intrepid sappers hurled satchel charges through the openings and riflemen prepared to rush the building and engage the surviving defenders. The expected confrontation never happened as, instead, an awesome explosion belched from the fortress and produced a mushroom cloud of smoke that could be seen for miles. Tropical raindrops soon mixed with far more lethal concrete chunks, tree limbs, unexploded torpedo warheads, and jagged debris that ripped through the Marines like a monstrous primitive shotgun wielded by an aroused and angry giant. A carrier pilot circling overhead insisted to his superiors that the entire island had blown up. The satchel charges might have set off a cache of Japanese torpedo warheads, or the enemy might simply have rigged the blockhouse to explode; but, whatever the cause, nearly a hundred Marines were either writhing in agony or sprawled in death as a momentary silence took over that part of the battlefield.[9]

The shock of this catastrophe was soon merely a painful memory as the survivors moved northward through the debris and encountered the main concentration of Japanese buildings. Some were smoldering wrecks from air strikes and shelling, but this was a mixed blessing for the attackers because Imperial troops often found piles of debris to be even better strongpoints than more intact structures. A company of American tanks battered through rubber-laden streets while leveling their formidable firepower toward improvised Nipponese bastions. The commander of the armor, Captain James Denig, opened a small observation port to better direct the firing, but was soon confronted by a half dozen defenders swarming up the side of the tank and shoving grenades through the opening. Denig with his driver were killed instantly.[10]

By late afternoon, the light tanks had been joined by the larger Shermans clanking across the causeway from Roi; by nightfall, the armored units had formed an iron ring around the last significant wooded area on Namur. On Wednesday morning, tanks, half tracks, and riflemen launched a coordinated assault into the foliage and gradually pushed the defenders back towards a final clearing and the sea beyond. A climactic melee followed with swords, bayonets, pistols, and rifle butts prominently featured, and the commander of the 1st Battalion, Lieutenant Colonel Aquilla Dyess, falling from a fatal machine burst as he directed the vicious endgame.

The northern tip of Kwajalein atoll was now in American hands as more than 3,500 Japanese soldiers covered the twin islands in many postures of death. A small knot of Korean laborers and badly wounded

Imperial troops were processed as prisoners, but their numbers never reached the century mark. The Marines had hardly escaped unscathed, although with 195 leathernecks killed and 545 other men were wounded, the casualty list was far more modest than that of the Tarawa bloodbath. However, this victory would be meaningless unless the Marines' army counterparts could push through the dense foliage of Kwajalein Island and capture the other end of the lagoon more than 40 miles to the south.

On this occasion, the army had drawn the more difficult assignment, although the contrast between Roi-Namur and Kwajalein Island was far less dramatic than Makin and Tarawa. Rear Admiral Monzo Akiyama, the senior Japanese officer in the Marshalls, had taken personal charge of Kwajalein's defenses and deployed most of his 4,600 men in an elaborate ocean-front trench system that featured pillboxes, blockhouses, antitank batteries, and camouflaged shelters. The boomerang-shaped island was just less than 3 miles long and its heavy cover of coconut trees towered over the vast supply dumps of the major logistical center for the outer perimeter of the Imperial defense line. Prominent features included two major piers, one extending 1,600 feet into the lagoon, a concentration of more than a hundred major buildings, including hospitals, warehouses, and barracks, and a large bomber base that dominated the center of the island.

Capture of this vital target was the responsibility of General Charles Corlett's 7th Infantry Division, the unit that had been the focal point of the Aleutians campaign the previous spring. Corlett, who would go on to play a significant role as a corps commander in Operation Overlord during the coming summer, had begun preparation for the invasion of Kwajalein by conducting an extensive personal examination of nearly every square yard of the Tarawa battlefield. The general then essentially re-created the same locale on Oahu in Hawaii with mockups of seawalls, pillboxes, and blockhouses, and directed each invasion battalion to launch a simulated attack on the "enemy" stronghold. Finally, two weeks before the opening of Flintlock, the GIs linked up with the 22nd Marine Regiment for a dress rehearsal attack on Maui so that soldiers and leathernecks could profit from each other's combat techniques.

The initial assault on Kwajalein was similar to the Marine landing to the north. Several companies of troops seized several islets almost adjacent to the main island and orchestrated the deployment of a powerful array of artillery capped off by a battalion of twelve huge 155 mm guns that could reach almost any enemy strongpoint on Kwajalein.

On February 1, seven battleships poured fireballs onto Kwajalein as dozens of Amtracs clanked onto the eastern and northeastern beaches of the island. The Imperial forces leapfrogged unit by unit through the dense treeline as the Americans pressed inland toward the airfield. The defenders had ceded more than 1,000 yards of territory, but Akiyama had allowed this intrusion so that he could set up the invaders for a massive night counterattack. The Imperial forces used the cover of darkness to overrun and nearly obliterate a forward American platoon and broke through the line in several places; but daylight belonged to Corlett's men, and by the end of the second day of battle, the GIs had secured the airfield, one of the piers, and the entire central part of the island.

The third day of the battle of Kwajalein Island was punctuated by furious street fighting that often resembled a deadly game of blind man's bluff as each building and then each room became a miniature battlefield, possession of the chamber being the trophy of victory. By nightfall, the small town of military structures was in American hands and the surviving defenders prepared to make a final stand at the enormous N.O.B. pier and its adjacent warehouses. The battle for the pier became the focal point for the final day of the battle as a relatively large group of 174 survivors was found still alive in the rubble, although only forty-nine men were regular combat troops.

The capture of Kwajalein atoll was a giant step toward further offensives in the Central Pacific as the Marshalls represented the last effective barrier to an American invasion either of the immense Japanese naval base on Truk or of the linchpin in the Imperial communications network in the Marianas. Operation Flintlock had produced 1,954

American casualties, but the actual death toll was a relatively modest 372 men in both battles. The Imperial list of fallen heroes was a staggering 7,870; in addition, the more than 10,000 additional troops trapped on the eastern edge of the Marshalls had been effectively removed from Nipponese organizational tables.

The Japanese high command simply could not afford to continue trading twenty Imperial warriors for each American they killed, especially when the battle resulted in a decisive defeat and pushed the defenders dangerously close to the bold black line that represented the gateway to the heart of the Nipponese Empire. The growing American juggernaut was now ready to penetrate territory that the Japanese simply could not afford to evacuate and still maintain a war machine that could stave off total defeat. In turn, American commanders were now presented with an inviting choice of options for the next campaign in the Central Pacific, and their immediate concern was how to select a subsequent target that offered the greatest prospect of moving another giant step toward the Japanese mainland and victory.

7

AFTERMATH OF
OPERATION FLINTLOCK

THE CAPTURE OF KWAJALEIN atoll presented the American high command with an intriguing choice of opportunities for penetrating the inner core of the Japanese Empire. Operation Flintlock had eliminated the bulk of Imperial forces in the Marshalls and opened the way to the seizure of the excellent harbor facilities at Eniwetok, located at the extreme western edge of the island group. In turn, that island's stunningly beautiful inner lagoon provided port facilities only 500 miles from Wake Island, 700 miles from the principal Japanese naval bastion at Truk, and 900 miles from Guam at the southern tip of the Marianas. As distances from new American bases to the heart of the Nipponese Empire began to shrink rapidly, many servicemen who had originally envisioned "the Golden Gate in '48" now allowed themselves to utter a far more optimistic slogan: "Home alive in '45."

By late winter of 1944, there was a growing perception that the twin offensives mounted by Douglas MacArthur and Chester Nimitz were starting to gain real momentum. The Americans were forcing the enemy defenders off balance as Japanese commanders, never quite sure which American offensive was the "real" drive toward the Imperial heartland, shuttled forces back and forth across two threatened regions. However, if the Nipponese leaders were not exactly certain which United States operation represented the major threat, American commanders were equally at odds as to which offensive should become the primary assault on the empire.

Douglas MacArthur, watching events unfold in his headquarters in Brisbane, Australia, initially viewed the invasion of the Gilberts and the Marshalls as valuable adjuncts to his own operations: American landings in the Central Pacific protected his right flank and deflected at least some Japanese attention from his series of leapfrog amphibious assaults along the northern coast of New Guinea. However, although the invasion of Tarawa had provided a strategic benefit for Southwest Pacific operations, MacArthur was genuinely shocked by the bloodbath on Betio and was more than ever convinced that the only sensible approach to mainland Japan was through the Philippines. This strategy allowed for more low-risk battles of maneuver and fewer high-risk frontal assaults necessitated by the small land masses of many of the island targets in the Central Pacific operations. The senior army officer in the Pacific began to see Nimitz's offensive as a succession of replays of Tarawa, where army and Marine divisions would be bled white long before they came close to engaging the enemy near the Japanese homeland. He was now firmly convinced that if the Joint Chiefs allowed him to concentrate all available American forces in the Pacific for a single thrust towards the Philippines and beyond, he could defeat the enemy at far lower cost than that extracted by Ernest King's prized operation across the central part of the Pacific Ocean. Thus, written copies of this forceful argument accompanied Brigadier General Frederick Osborn of the War Department staff as he flew back to Washington from Brisbane. As a letter to Secretary of War Henry Stimson insisted: "[T]hese frontal assaults by the Navy at Tarawa are tragic and unnecessary massacres of American lives; the Navy fails to recognize that the first phase is an army phase to establish land based air protection so the Navy can move in." MacArthur then gave Stimson this assurance: "[I]f you give me central direction of the war in the Pacific, I will be in the Philippines in ten months." On the other hand, if the navy continued with its Central Pacific operations, the Japanese would be able to defend their inner empire for years.[1]

Ironically, as General Osborn was flying toward Washington with his controversial letter, a circle of navy officers in Pearl Harbor was seriously discussing the merits of an operational plan that largely agreed with MacArthur's reasoning. Just before the initiation of Operation Flintlock, Chester Nimitz extended an invitation to all the major players in the Pacific drama to convene in Hawaii and brainstorm American opportunities and options for the next year. MacArthur sent his chief of staff, General Richard Sutherland; his air commander, General George Kenney; and the commander of his naval support, Admiral Thomas Kinkaid. These officers were soon ensconced in a conference room with Admiral Charles McMorris, Nimitz's chief of staff; Admiral John Tower, theater air commander; and Lieutenant General Robert Richardson, senior army officer in the Pacific ocean area. Contrary to traditional army-navy rivalry between officers, these men shared a common perception that the real "adversary" in war planning was the circle of American and British commanders who placed an absolute premium on winning the war against Hitler. Pacific officers, regardless of U.S. Army, Navy, or Army Air Force affiliation, were convinced that they were receiving the short end of manpower and equipment compared to their European theatre counterparts and insisted that much of the high command in Washington and London simply failed to appreciate the power of the fanatical adversary that was the Japanese Empire. Thus, the normal inclination toward interservice rivalry common in other times and other places was often subsumed to an "us" against "them" attitude by many Pacific theatre officers of all services. The result of this attitude in January 1944 resulted in an astonishing display of interservice harmony in this conference room at Pearl Harbor as Nimitz and most of his subordinates assured General Sutherland that they generally supported MacArthur's call for a single line of advance toward the Philippines.[2]

One of the more fascinating side-plots of the entire Marianas campaign centers on the officer who was most directly responsible for implementing one of the largest operations of World War II; indeed, he was still tacitly opposed to the campaign less than five months before the first unit landed on the beaches of Saipan. The commander of the United States Navy was convinced that the invasion of the Marianas would be a turning point in the war; but the man he had delegated to direct the campaign was now strongly inclined to fight the battle anywhere but those particular islands.

Chester Nimitz began the year 1944 deeply troubled by the bloodbath at Tarawa and was beginning to suspect that future Central Pacific operations might be just as costly. He was particularly worried that the relatively large, heavily wooded, and hilly Marianas were even better defensive positions for the Japanese than Tarawa and thus an invasion could roll up huge American casualties; and the fray could even degenerate into a bloody stalemate. These reservations were enhanced by Admiral Tower's insistence that even when the Marianas were captured the new American bases would become vulnerable to air attack from powerful enemy forces on Iwo Jima and Chichi Jima. Furthermore, newly constructed airstrips on Guam or Saipan would be too far away from mainland Japan for the Liberators and Flying Fortresses to have a significant offensive effect. Tower adamantly recommended bypassing the Marianas for the Palaus group, which would serve as the springboard for the invasion of the Philippines.[3]

General Richardson added a proposal that would concentrate all Marine and army divisions in the theatre, a tactic that would accelerate the drive from New Guinea to the Philippines. The senior admirals agreed that the action would permit more opportunity for outmaneuvering the enemy than blasting ashore at each atoll that dotted the Central Pacific map. To no one's great surprise, General Sutherland, a rare smile crossing his usually scowling face, agreed enthusiastically with the wisdom of Nimitz's staff: "[I]f the Palaus are substituted for the Marianas we can take all of New Guinea in time to join you in amphibious movements to Mindanao this year."

Thus, only a few months before one of the most pivotal campaigns of the Pacific War, the operation was being dismissed as irrelevant or unnecessary by virtually all the senior commanders in the theatre in which it was to be undertaken. While British and American commanders in the United Kingdom were working around the clock to finalize the plans for Operation Overlord, that invasion's Pacific counterpart was being deconstructed by officers in Hawaii and Australia. However, at the very moment that Operation Forager was about to fade into history as one of the most prominent cancelled operations of World War II, the tide of events shifted dramatically to give new life to the massive invasion of the Marianas.

The first major factor in this alteration of events occurred because the men meeting in Pearl Harbor had neither as much rank nor as much will to cancel Forager as the officer 5,000 miles to the east, who was the primary advocate of the campaign. If Overlord was in some respects the personification of the sheer willpower of the operation's guiding figure, Dwight D. Eisenhower, the invasion of the Marianas was equally a product of the resolve of Ernest J. King. If Eisenhower could not envision the ultimate defeat of Hitler and Nazi Germany without a successful invasion of northwest Europe, King could not conceive of a Japanese surrender while the Rising Sun still flew over Saipan and Guam. The men meeting in Hawaii were open to a variety of approaches to the Imperial heartland, but the commander who outranked them all was committed to only one certainty: The United States could never win the Pacific War until the Stars and Stripes replaced the Nipponese emblem over the Marianas.

When King received Chester Nimitz's communiqué concerning the conference consensus for bypassing the Marianas, the salty reply dripped with incredulity and sarcasm. Noting that he had read the conference minutes with "indignant dismay," King lectured the Pacific air, ground, and sea chieftains as if they were somewhat marginal military academy cadets enrolled in a first-year course on tactics and strategy: "Apparently, neither those who advocated the concentration of effort in the Southwest Pacific nor those who admitted the possibility of such a procedure gave thought nor undertook to state when and if the Japanese occupation of the Marianas was to be terminated."[4]

Continuing his sarcastic tone, King "assumed" that "even the Southwest Pacific advocates will admit that sometime or other this thorn in the side of our communications in the western Pacific must be recovered, in other words, at some time or other we must take out time and forces to carry out this job" before the already formidable Imperial defenses in the Marianas border on impregnable. Abandoning the last veneer of polite diplomacy, King snarled: "[T]he idea of rolling up the Japanese along the New Guinea coast and up through the Philippines to Luzon as our major strategic concept, to the exclusion of clearing our Central Pacific line of communications to the Philippines is absurd."[5]

The senior officer in the navy concluded his angry rejoinder with a pointed insinuation that the commanders meeting in Pearl Harbor were simply over their heads in a contest for authority as he reminded these men that "further, it's not in accordance of the Joint Chiefs of Staff" that the Marianas be bypassed, an assertion that trumped any clout held by the men in Hawaii or Australia. One of the reasons that King could speak with such confidence about the attitude of the Joint Chiefs toward Forager was that the admiral had just gained an invaluable ally in his determination to make the invasion of the Marianas the focal point in the upcoming summer campaigning season. The cantankerous mariner had now acquired a new "best friend" in the Joint Chiefs' conference room, the master of the American aerial forces, General Henry "Hap" Arnold.

As commander of the most junior but also most technologically driven American service, Hap Arnold had often allied himself with his British Royal Air Force counterparts in their attempts to convince everyone from Roosevelt and Churchill on down that powerful flotillas of strategic bombers were the trump cards in the war against Germany and Japan; the main responsibility of the Allied fleets and armies, he asserted, was simply to put the air forces into a position where they could wreak havoc on the enemy war machine and will to fight and then use the two more senior services to enforce the occupation of the defeated foes. As ever larger fleets of Flying Fortresses and Liberators were thought to be on the brink of pounding the German war machine to rubble, the U.S. Army Air Force was on the verge of introducing its most costly and technologically advanced aircraft of the war, the B-29 Superfortress.

The "Superfort" was touted as a virtual flying battleship. It had a wing span of 141 feet, a gross weight of 140,000 pounds, a maximum speed of 360 miles an hour, and a range of 4,100 miles. Its crew of twelve would operate in an environment worthy of Buck Rogers or Flash Gordon as they flew in a pressurized cabin that had dispensed with bulky heated flying suits and oxygen masks, and they had access to a weapons system that featured remote-control gun turrets mounting a total of twelve heavy machine guns and a 20 mm high-velocity long-range cannon. The Superfortress weapons system was not only technologically advanced but also enormously expensive, costing about a billion dollars more to develop than the atomic bomb project, and there was every hope that this would win the war against Japan even before the Manhattan Project was fully completed.

Although there had been talk during the developmental stage that the B-29 would be used against both Germany and Japan, Arnold eventually agreed with his technical advisors that the Superfortress should be used for one purpose only: pounding the Nipponese into unconditional surrender.[6]

However, even if the new bomber exceeded the range of the B-17 and B-24, it still could not bomb the Japanese homeland from California, or even Hawaii. The initial U.S. Army Air Force plan was to operate the Superfortress from bases near the coast of China; but as the plane neared operational status, the operational plan began to unravel.

The simple and alarming reality was that the B-29 could operate effectively from China only if the planes could be launched from secure bases. The problem was that the still far from defeated Japanese army in China was regularly initiating major counteroffensives against General Chiang Kai Chek's often inept forces, and there was no guarantee that the Nationalist forces could effectively secure the invaluable bombers and their equally invaluable crews and ground staffs.[7]

Henry Arnold was now looking for ways to hedge his aerial bets in China with another series of bases that could be more effectively defended by more reliable American forces. It soon became evident to the air force chieftain that the place to hedge those bets was the Marianas Islands.

After making enormous groups of calculations and carefully factoring a wide number of variables, Army Air Force engineers and staff officers concluded that the optimal launch point from a fully secured Pacific location to the key industrial cities of Japan should center around Tinian, the generally flat, open island just across the bay from the main Japanese stronghold of Saipan. Once the Marianas were captured, Tinian would be easy to secure, difficult for the Japanese to bomb at will, and within tolerable operational range for attacks on the enemy war machine. Suddenly, Ernest King had an enthusiastic ally in his insistence on the priority of an invasion of the Marianas. This maritime-aviation axis insisted that suggestions to bypass the Marianas by subordinate commanders in Pearl Harbor or Brisbane were sheer folly and must be countered with a stern veto from the senior officers in Washington.[8]

The final key figure in the assertion that Operation Forager would be the next major campaign in the Central Pacific was, ironically, the very commander who had so recently expressed grave reservations about the venture, Chester Nimitz. Two events contributed to the turnabout in the attitude of the senior naval officer in the Pacific. First, Nimitz was genuinely shocked by the vehemence with which his superior in Washington had dismissed the recommendation of the Pearl Harbor conferees that Operation Forager be eliminated from the timetable of Pacific campaigns. King and Nimitz had developed an excellent working relationship; indeed, it was in the tradition of those enjoyed by Ulysses Grant and William Sherman, and Robert E. Lee and Stonewall Jackson eight decades earlier, and the junior admiral had developed an implicit trust in his superior's strategic judgment. Nimitz's opposition to the Marianas invasion was based more on the judgment of his own subordinates and that of MacArthur's Southwest Pacific staff rather than on the opinions of the senior admiral himself. Nimitz was also realistic enough to realize that it was quite possible for the reasoning of the senior admiral in the navy and his fellow Joint Chiefs to trump the perspective of the more parochial vision of theatre officers.

This shift towards seeing the war through King's perspective was substantially enhanced by the outcome of the Kwajalein operation. The relatively modest American casualties, with fairly rapid progress in the capture of Kwajalein and Roi-Namur, encouraged Nimitz to suspect that the bloody confrontation on Tarawa just might have been an aberration rather than a template for each successive assault across the Central Pacific. Chester Nimitz was not a puppet to be manipulated by King nor was he a yes-man who avoided disagreements with his superior. He was extremely loyal to his subordinates and he valued their opinions. If King had been less adamant in his support of the Marianas operation, and if Operation Flintlock had been as costly as Operation Galvanic, it is quite possible that Nimitz would have staked his continuation in Pacific command on a showdown designed to convince King to shift his priorities. However, events did not move in that direction. By early February 1944, Chester Nimitz was being connected into a reasonably enthusiastic advocate of one of the most massive operations of World War II. The lines of battle were now being formed and, before this month of presidential birthdays was finished, the first steps in capturing the Marianas would be moving to an exciting climax.

8

COUNTDOWN TO
OPERATION FORAGER

BY LATE WINTER of 1944, Ernest King's insistence on two mutually supporting drives toward Japan along the New Guinea and Central Pacific lines of advance was beginning to pay dividends in creating confusion among the Japanese high command. The Americans seemed to be striking at a bewildering variety of targets, actions that sorely tested the abilities of even the best Imperial intelligence officers to figure out exactly where the enemy intended to attack next. As Adolf Hitler and his generals pored over maps of northwestern Europe in an attempt to divine the location of the Allied invasion of the Continent, Nipponese officers carefully inspected charts of the Pacific and tried to discern a predictable pattern to the thrusts by Nimitz and MacArthur.

In February 1944, both Hitler and Tojo could still field large ground forces, but the problem was that each aggressor empire had overrun such vast territories that they were now forced to defend a huge perimeter that could not be equally strong at every point. Just as a German staff officer could cite justifiable reasons why the Allies might land in Norway, Pas de Calais, or Normandy during the coming year, a Japanese counterpart could provide cogent reasons why the Palaus, Carolines, or Marianas should receive primary call on reinforcements. Each defender, Germany and Japan, could mobilize powerful forces for a counterattack once the point of greatest danger had been identified without question; but once those reinforcements had been set in motion, it was vital that they arrive at the scene of battle more or less intact.

The challenge for the German commanders was to prevent the Allies from gaining such absolute control over the skies of northwestern Europe that powerful armored units could arrive sufficiently unscathed to push the invaders into the sea. The problem for their Nipponese counterparts was how to keep air and sea lanes open while additional forces were shuttled in from China, Japan, and islands not immediately threatened by the next American offensive. For both Axis powers, this effort would prove to be a daunting, and ultimately unsuccessful, task.

As Japanese leaders surveyed maps of their still largely intact Greater East Asia Co-Prosperity Sphere in the early weeks of 1944, their gaze almost invariably shifted to the massive expanse of occupied Manchuria and China. The entire initial reason for Nipponese aggression in the years preceding formal outbreak of war with the Anglo-American world was to secure the vast resources and farmlands of China for the burgeoning population of overcrowded Japan. Now dozens of combat divisions were tied up either fighting the Nationalist and Communist enemies or peering intently across the foggy, frigid border between Manchuria and the Soviet Union in an attempt to discern when or if Joseph Stalin would unleash his Red Army.

As the Americans began to drive across the Pacific far to the south of this frozen tundra, the Japanese high command was tortured by an exquisite dilemma. Should they strip huge numbers of men from a basically inactive front to transfer badly needed reinforcements to areas that were much more directly threatened and hope that Stalin was too preoccupied with fighting Hitler to really notice? Or should they write off increasingly large segments of the southern empire and so gain some assurance that the Red hordes would not sweep into the main granary of the empire? Realistically, the Japanese leaders had reached the point at which they could still perhaps concentrate enough forces for the tenacious defense of either the southern or the northern axis of their empire, but they probably could not protect both.

The Japanese high command, faced with this seemingly insoluble quandary, worked out a compromise that would produce enough reinforcements to assure a monumental struggle for the Marianas but not supply quite enough men to tip the trend of battle permanently in the Imperial direction. The agreement that was hammered out in Tokyo was typical of the complex, nuanced plans that often came back to haunt commanders in the field. The Imperial regiments facing the Red Army along the Manchurian border would remain in place under their current commanders. However, each regiment would provide one battalion to form a newly activated Thirty-first Army that would be ferried south to threatened areas such as the Palaus, Carolines, and Marianas island groups. It was hoped that Soviet intelligence services would not realize that the Imperial units facing them were now understrength and that the garrisons in the Central Pacific would gain badly needed reinforcements.

Lieutenant General Hideyoshi Obata was appointed to command this army of Manchurian border troops. It was scheduled to be augmented by drafts of newly enlisted Nipponese teenagers and young adults who, until recently, had been high school or college students. Although this amalgamation of grizzled veterans, teacher trainees, and impressionable adolescents shared a fairly high morale, relatively few of these Imperial warriors had ever been involved in a battle and had little idea of where they were going or why they were going there. However, the initial confusion and trepidation were soon to be increased many times over as the men of the Thirty-first Army began to realize that the United States Navy now controlled large stretches of the sea lanes between the northern and southern portions of the Japanese Empire.

The emerging difficulty of even getting newly designated reinforcements to the battlefield struck home in a spectacular way in mid-February as the huge transport *Sakito Maru* steamed southward toward the Marianas crammed with 4,100 infantrymen, most of an Imperial tank regiment, and dozens of heavy guns. As the *Sakito* and its escorts neared their destination, the convoy was interrupted by the USS *Trout,* which launched a spread of torpedoes at this prime target. Soon after the sickening concussion of multiple explosions had struck home, the ship plunged downward, sending every invaluable tank and cannon to the bottom of the Pacific.[1] A mere 1,700 survivors drifted in the warm water.

A short time later, the 118th Infantry Regiment was pulled from duty in China, embarked on seven transports, and sent southward. This convoy soon faced three American submarines that promptly sank five ships and left the dazed survivors to stagger toward Saipan with almost no weapons, organization, or sense of purpose.

General Obata was beginning to discover to his horror that if the Americans attempted to capture the Marianas, an action that was yet far from certain, he would be forced to defend the islands with fragments of units landed ashore on the wrong island and missing many of their most basic weapons. Tank regiments left far too many tanks on the bottom of the ocean, and artillery batteries were forced to deploy a bewildering variety of guns to make up for their extensive losses. Obata would ultimately command an army of about 65,000 men, but the army he would lead was a strange amalgamation of mixed brigades, independent regiments, provisional companies, and special defense units. More than half the officers embarked from China, Manchuria, and Japan to reinforce the Marianas died on their way to the battlefield, and many of the survivors found themselves commanding men who were simply lumped together in jury-rigged units. The Japanese high command would ultimately concentrate more men for the defense of the Marianas than for any previous operation in the Pacific War. Obata commanded a larger army than the Imperial commanders at Singapore, the Philippines, Guadalcanal, or any other battle from the Aleutians to the Solomons. However, the high command had dithered between defending Manchuria and holding the Central Pacific just long enough to permit the American navy to turn a sporadic undersea offensive into a tightening siege of much of the southern end of the empire. A more prompt and extensive willingness to risk Stalin's continuing neutrality to augment against the defense of the Central Pacific could easily have doubled the force under Obata's command and nullified much of the American manpower advantage in the upcoming campaign. But caution and compromise had triumphed, and the immense advantage given to the defender by much of the topography of the Marianas would be at least partially negated because there were not quite enough Imperial troops to hold every one of the almost impregnable positions that would become the hallmarks of Operation Forager.

General Obata would be responsible for the ground defense of the Marianas, but an officer with a much higher profile was charged with maintaining control of the waters surrounding these islands. Admiral Chuichi Nagumo had become the toast of the Japanese nation when, as commander of First Air Fleet, he assumed operational control of the attack on Pearl Harbor. He followed this spectacular success with a follow-up offensive that temporarily drove the Royal Navy from the Indian Ocean; and, by late spring of 1942, he was seen as the driving force behind the incredible initial success of the Imperial naval offensive. However, at Midway, Nagumo proved indecisive at critical moments of the battle and was substantially blamed for the loss of four irreplaceable Nipponese carriers. After being exiled to a series of desk jobs in the home islands, the admiral was partially exonerated by being assigned to command all naval forces in the Marianas in December 1943. This command proved to be a mixed blessing for an officer attempting to erase the shame of defeat at Midway. Nagumo now exercised command over the several thousand naval ground troops that would form an integrated part of the various island garrisons. He also assumed operational control over a small flotilla of submarines supplemented by patrol craft, supply and landing barges, and a few light escort vessels. Yet although Nagumo had technical command of an "area fleet" that included all naval vessels and naval ground troops in the region,[2] the one force that could actually contest an American invasion of the Marianas, the Japanese Mobile Fleet, was far from the Marianas with no prospect of being used in battle until the invaders had shown their hand. As Ernest King had constantly insisted, the Japanese high command would utilize virtually its entire fleet to challenge the Americans for control of the Marianas, but the hero of Pearl Harbor was not the person designated to direct what was expected to be the climactic naval battle of the Pacific War.

The first senior Japanese admiral who had to deal with the prospect of a relatively imminent American invasion of the Marianas was Admiral Mineichi Koga, successor to the revered Yamamoto as commander of the Imperial fleet. As expected by Ernest King, Koga was consistently perplexed about the intentions of the Americans as the "whipsaw" strategy of dual offensives by MacArthur and Nimitz exacted its toll in Japanese intelligence estimates. Finally, in a strange combination of exasperation and expectation, Koga issued a major operational directive on March 8, 1944. Virtually admitting that he had no exact idea of where the next enemy offensive would begin, he concocted Operation Z, a plan for a massive fleet counteroffensive at whatever point in the vast Philippine Sea perimeter the enemy initially penetrated.[3]

Koga assumed that at some point in the coming summer the Americans would attempt to break into a region that extended from the Marianas to the Carolines to the Palaus to the Vogelkop Peninsula of western New Guinea, but in many respects the target did not matter. Koga assumed that Nimitz would support any major invasion with the twelve to fifteen carriers known to be available to the American fleet, and the Japanese Mobile Fleet would counter with the nine flattops currently available to the Imperial forces. The senior admiral acknowledged that the enemy would probably enjoy an approximate three-to-two advantage in carrier-based planes, but the Japanese trump card was that almost anywhere the Americans struck, nearly five hundred land-based planes would be within range to support the Mobile Fleet; therefore, the numerical balance would almost certainly tilt in favor of the Japanese forces.[4]

Admiral Koga decided that the most central location to deploy the fleet and direct the expected counteroffensive was the Philippine Islands. On March 31, 1943, the admiral and his chief of staff, Shigeriu Fukudome, took off in two separate flying boats for the journey to Mindanao, in the southern Philippines. An ironic repeat of the fate that befell Koga's predecessor now began to unfold. However, this time it was natural rather than human forces that would inflict a grievous loss on the Japanese high command.

The two planes began to encounter the effects of a surging oceanic storm and the radio operators soon lost contact with one another. Fukudome's plane was buffeted by high winds and damaged so severely that it crashed just off the coast of Cebu. The chief of staff survived the impact and managed to swim ashore carrying a briefcase stuffed with the plans for Operation Z. He had the dubious luck of being almost immediately captured by a patrol of Filipino guerillas, who promptly delivered officer and briefcase to Lieutenant Colonel James Cushing, the American commander of guerilla operations on the island. When the Japanese command in the Philippines realized the nature of Fuku-dome's fate, they threatened massive reprisals against civilians unless the officer was released. Cushing, who had struck up an unlikely friendship with his prisoner, ignored MacArthur's orders to deliver the enemy officer to a submarine that was being dispatched to transport him to Australia. Although the American extended a warm handshake to the man he was about to exchange for Filipino hostages, he kept the invaluable briefcase and delivered the documents to the arriving American submarine. Thus, one outcome of this ill-fated flight was that American intelligence now effectively possessed the enemy plan for the next campaign. The Japanese had suffered another grievous loss beyond the documents. The second plane, which was carrying Koga, simply disappeared into the storm and never emerged from the other side. For the second time in less than a year, an aerial excursion by a commander of the Imperial Navy had ended in disaster.[5]

The emperor and his advisors were once again faced with the grim prospect of dipping into the pool of serving Imperial Navy officers and identifying a person who could deal with the ongoing crisis that was now the Pacific War. By all measurable standards, their choice was a good one. Soemu Toyoda was a fifty-nine-year-old former naval attaché to Great Britain who had been both a fleet commander and chief of the Technical Department before the war. Toyoda, who was brilliant, friendly, and sarcastic, was idolized by his men. He was a meticulous planner who was realistic enough to realize that Japan was in danger of losing the war but just optimistic enough to believe that the disastrous course might be reversed by hitting the enemy fleet before it consolidated control over its next targeted region. A subsequent massive victory might no longer win the war, but it might induce the Americans into accepting a negotiated peace.

The new commander of the Combined Fleet supported the general substance of Operation Z and had no intention of completely discarding Koga's plan even if the enemy had discerned Japanese intentions from their capture of Fukudome's documents. However, Toyoda was far more certain of probable American operations than his predecessor, and he remained convinced that the enemy would bypass the Marianas for the Palaus Islands.[6]

Perhaps it was wishful thinking to insist that Nimitz would attack him in exactly the place that Toyoda wanted to fight his battle; but more than one successful commander in history has enjoyed such good fortune. Once again, the curiously conflicting mindset halfway between fantasy and reality dominated Japanese strategic planning as Admiral Toyoda developed a scenario in which the annoying possibility that the enemy might actually attack a target relatively distant from many Imperial air bases was simply dismissed and a more congenial location for the battle almost willed into existence.

An American attack on Toyoda's preferred, and predicted target, the Palaus Islands, would put the enemy fleet within range of a vast array of Japanese land-based air units and allow Imperial forces to batter the invaders before the Mobile Fleet was even committed. However, a lone member of the admiral's staff kept insisting that the Americans would attack the Marianas. This solitary dissenter carried just enough influence to oblige Toyoda to acknowledge this uninviting prospect. The new commander of the Imperial Navy reasoned that if the Americans did indeed launch an unlikely invasion of the Marianas, the numerous fighter squadrons and 65,000 ground troops stationed in the islands could hold their positions while the Fifth Fleet was lured westward by small naval units, which would be sacrificed as bait; with this strategy, the enemy would be enticed farther and farther into the Philippine Sea. If the Americans could be lured to the western end of the sea, six hundred aircraft stationed on Yap, Truk, and the Palaus, five hundred planes from the southern Philippines, and almost five hundred carrier-based airplanes would rise up in an angry swarm to challenge the invaders and then engage in a mass use of shuttle bombing between ships and land bases to add even more punch to their operations.

As Toyoda insisted, "We must achieve our objective by crushing with one stroke the nucleus of the great enemy concentration of forces, thereby reversing the war situation all together with our armies shifting directly to the offensive; the decisive force must in one decisive battle determine the fate of the Empire."[7]

In other words, even if the enemy insisted on invading an island group that the admiral was sure would not be invaded, the climactic sea battle would still somehow be shifted westward to insure a decisive naval victory; this scenario would soon turn the American besiegers of the Marianas into the besieged as they lost the imperative support of Fifth Fleet. Toyoda was betting that superior numbers, enhanced combat range, and the advantage of shuttle bombing could overcome the superior survivability of American planes and the superior training of American pilots. Then, as the enemy fleet weakened under the Imperial attacks, the admiral would unleash his ultimate trump cards, the super-battleships *Yamato* and *Musashi*. These 63,000-ton behemoths deployed nine 18-inch rifles each; these largest guns in the world could sink any ship afloat with even one accurate broadside. Unleashing these ultimate surface weapons among the lightly armed and armored American carriers could produce astonishing destruction to the enemy and change the course of the war.

Unlike much of Japanese war planning in 1945, Toyoda's A-GO plan was not focused on some form of mass suicide. The state of the war in the spring of 1944 was critical, but the Japanese Empire still fielded enough conventional forces that a high degree of skill and luck could definitely turn the tide against the Americans. Japanese commanders realized that the American navy that had defeated them so soundly at Midway was now more outnumbered than the Imperial navy was two years later. Also, most American planes used in that decisive battle were clearly inferior to their Imperial counterparts, and relatively few American pilots had anything near extensive combat experience. Now, a whole new generation of American planes had proved their superiority over Imperial aircraft in many, but not all areas. The very lack of armor plating and self-sealing fuel tanks that made Imperial planes more dangerous to fly also gave them a significant range advantage over the enemy in a duel where striking the first blow often meant victory. Admiral Toyoda believed that if the American fleet either voluntarily steamed into the western Philippine Sea in the expected attack on the Palaus or could be lured into the same waters during a more unlikely invasion of the Marianas, he could employ his three aces—longer-ranged planes, heavier gunned battleships, and superior numbers of land-based aircraft— to annihilate the American fleet and change the course of the war. Despite enormous differences on almost every other issue, Ernest King and Soemu Toyoda could sense that the coming summer would produce a climactic battle that they were both eager to fight.

As Imperial intelligence officers worked far into the balmy spring nights attempting to divine the intentions of their enemies, their American counterparts were making final preparations for Operation Forager and initiating the supporting operations that would soon have the Japanese high command thoroughly mystified. While the Allies were confusing German commanders by forming a bogus army under George Patton that was poised to launch a sham invasion of Calais, the Americans in the Pacific were bewildering the Nipponese by launching so many real attacks that the defenders could not decide which one was the major threat.

The choreography of the complex series of offensives that culminated in the invasion of the Marianas began in Washington when Chester Nimitz and Douglas MacArthur were summoned to meet the president and Joint Chiefs of Staff to discuss the upcoming summer offensives. MacArthur, citing pressing matters at his Brisbane headquarters, committed a major tactical blunder by refusing to attend; but Nimitz flew immediately to Washington and was ensconced in a Navy Department office utilizing a large support team of WAVES (Women Accepted for Volunteer Emergency Service) and female Marines to prepare detailed plans for the Joint Chiefs of Staff and President Roosevelt.

The senior naval officer in the Pacific soon found himself accompanying Admirals Leahy and King to a private meeting with the president. Nimitz noted with shock the chief executive's ashen face and trembling hands, symptoms that marked his progression into the last months of his life, but noted that Roosevelt still exuded energy in discussing the upcoming American offensives, especially those concerning "his" navy. At the end of a convivial lunch in the Oval Office, the president offered the trio of admirals enormous cigars that had been left by Winston Churchill. All the mariners, like their commander in chief, were far more fond of cigarettes, and the foursome laughingly tabled the prime minister's gift and quickly enveloped the room in their own smoke.[8]

The next day, Nimitz and General Richard Sutherland, MacArthur's chief of staff, met with the Joint Chiefs to discuss possible options for Pacific offensives. The commander of Southwest Pacific forces had sent his alter ego to stage a last-ditch argument for funneling all available American forces into a drive from New Guinea to the Philippines and largely canceling the Central Pacific offensive. However, with King, Nimitz, and Arnold now in firm agreement that the Marianas must and would be taken, the acerbic chief of staff was sent back to Brisbane with orders for MacArthur to keep the enemy off-balance while the main summer offensive took place far to the north in the Marianas.[9]

Soon after Chester Nimitz returned to Pearl Harbor with his final authorization of a June 15 invasion date for Saipan, he found himself flying eastward once again for a San Francisco conference with Ernest

King. Operation Forager would involve nearly 130,000 ground troops, almost as many men as would be involved in the opening phase of Operation Overlord now scheduled for approximately the same time. These assault troops would be divided into two amphibious corps, V Amphibious Corps under Holland Smith forming Northern Attack Force of two Marine divisions and III Amphibious Corps under Roy Geiger forming Southern Attack Force of a Marine division and Marine provisional brigade. In turn, the army's 27th Infantry Division would serve as a floating reserve for both corps, and the 77th Infantry Division would remain on call in Hawaii as an army reserve that could be sent into battle as soon as the transports unloaded the initial invasion force.

This large ground force would be supported by a vast array of 535 naval vessels designated as Fifth Fleet under Raymond Spruance. Key units of this massive fleet included Marc Mitscher's Task Force 58 centered around fifteen aircraft carriers and the Joint Expeditionary Force, under Kelly Turner, which would be responsible for landing and supplying the men. This force had two components, a northern contingent personally commanded by Turner would focus on Saipan and Tinian; a southern contingent under R. L. Connolly would be tasked to capture Guam.

Now that the Pacific War was about to take a leap in the sheer size of the combat forces involved, King and Nimitz agreed that most of the principal players warranted ranks commensurate with their increased responsibilities. Thus, Spruance received a promotion from vice admiral to full admiral, and Turner and Mitscher each received a third star. Holland Smith, who would become the senior ground officer in the expedition, was promoted from major general to lieutenant general; he would outrank all Marine and army officers in Forager.

As this flurry of promotions was finalized, King and Nimitz agreed that the one person who would appear to be marginalized was the senior admiral in the Southwest Pacific, Admiral William Halsey. As the naval war shifted from the Solomons and New Guinea up to the Central Pacific, Halsey seemed to be steaming into the professional cul de sac of an admiral without a war to fight. The Southwest Pacific was now becoming a strategic backwater, but neither Nimitz nor King relished seeing one of their favorite fighting admirals reduced to largely administrative tasks. Thus huddled in conference in their hotel room, the natural fog of San Francisco harbor outside and the artificial fog of cigarette smoke inside, the two admirals concocted a fascinating plan.

Raymond Spruance would exercise command over the invasion of the Marianas in his title as commander of Fifth Fleet. However, once the campaign was over, the presumably victorious admiral would return to Pearl Harbor and confer with Nimitz in planning future operations. The fleet he had left behind would receive a new title and a new commander. This vast array of ships would now be magically transformed into Third Fleet and William Halsey would be piped aboard the flagship as its new commander. Then, when this new offensive was successfully completed, Halsey would return to Pearl Harbor to plan future campaigns while Spruance once more assumed command.

Halsey compared the innovative plan to a Wild West stagecoach system in which horses were changed in relays while drivers remained aboard the coach. Now the "horses" would remain the same and the "drivers" would be rotated. The plan was novel but an eminently practical solution to the problem of having two very talented admirals with only one major fleet to command. Bill Halsey would get his crack at the Japanese fleet soon enough, but for the moment it was Ray Spruance's show. Indeed, the quiet, studious commander was soon surrounded by hundreds of ships and thousands of fighting men as the warriors of Forager gathered along the waters and beaches of Kwajalein in preparation for their great adventure.[10] Now it was June 1944, and two of the greatest amphibious invasions in history were about to begin on opposite sides of the globe. While men of the Allied Expeditionary Force clambered aboard transports in the mists and drizzle of the southern coast of England, their counterparts checked weapons, sharpened bayonets, and gathered under the palm trees to watch the nightly movies that were one of their main links to the homeland they were defending. Their own transports were rocking gently in the warm waters of the Central Pacific, but almost every man knew that his own trial by fire was not many days in the future.

9

CLOSING THE
RING OF STEEL

ON A BALMY TROPICAL EVENING in the first week of
June 1944, American soldiers, sailors, and Marines were
sprawled across the beaches of Kwajalein atoll preparing to enjoy a brief reunion with the normal world via a silver screen and a clattering movie projector. However, this night's festivities would be a little
different. Lieutenant Robert White, the son of an Episcopal minister
from Georgia, had been sitting in a communications room monitoring
radio traffic when the stunning news of the Allied invasion of Normandy crackled over the ether. As word was relayed to the outdoor
movie locations, hundreds of men collectively stood up and let out a
huge cheer in an instinctive realization that the climactic campaign
season of World War II had now begun and that the 375,000 men con-
gregated together in this tropical paradise were about to play a major
role in ending Axis aggression.[1]

The next afternoon, a group of American officers retreated from the
almost blinding brilliance of a tropical sun and made themselves comfortable in a new two-story building that featured enormous screened-
in porches and a long, elaborately decorated bar. The gathering included Vice Admiral John McCain, Vice Admiral Marc Mitscher, and

the commander of Fifth Fleet, Admiral Raymond Spruance. After long confining weeks at sea, few people could resist an invitation to attend the grand opening of the Eniwetok Officers Clubs, especially when the invited guests included a group of navy nurses stationed aboard a nearby hospital ship. Yet these American fighting men knew that the festivities were merely an interlude before a far more serious matter intruded. The Fifth Fleet was about to sail for the Marianas and most of these officers would be in harm's way in the very near future.[2]

Several hundred miles to the northwest, two of the men responsible for putting these Americans in grave danger were conferring in the principal's office of the main elementary school in the lovely port town of Charan Kanoa, Saipan. Lieutenant General Yoshitsugo Saito and Admiral Chuichi Nagumo were each in their own way attempting to adjust to a command responsibility that they did not expect to have. General Saito was commander of the Imperial 43rd Division, which had been transferred from Japan only a few weeks earlier and assigned the task of becoming the main army unit defending Saipan. Normally, the senior army officer on the island was General Hideyoshi Obata, commander of Thirty-first Army and responsible for a vast swath of territory extending almost to the Philippine Islands. But Obata was on an inspection tour of the Carolines and, as a result of the rapidly tightening American naval blockade, was in danger of being stranded somewhere below Saipan. Thus, until his superior could arrive safely back at headquarters, Saito was "promoted" to orchestrating the army's role in the defense of Saipan.[3]

Saito was moving up in responsibility, but Admiral Nagumo was heading in the other direction. Chuichi Nagumo had become the darling of the Japanese homeland when he commanded the six Imperial carriers that had devastated Pearl Harbor; but, unfortunately, he had still been in command of four of those vessels when Raymond Spruance sent them to the bottom of the sea off Midway Island. Although the Japanese naval high command was too civilized to have the unfortunate admiral shot for losing the emperor's irreplaceable carriers, it was far too vindictive to allow him to keep his command. The compromise solution was to appoint Nagumo to lead all the naval units in the Central Pacific. Unfortunately, when Nagumo arrived at his new headquarters on Saipan, he discovered that very little of the Central Pacific Fleet actually floated in the sea. Nagumo commanded smartly dressed headquarters guards, several units of naval infantry, plenty of dockyard and construction personnel, and a handful of patrol craft sub-chasers and mine-layers; yet, despite the impressive array, Central Pacific Fleet deployed not one vessel that could properly be called a combat ship. Now the hero of Pearl Harbor found himself sitting in a schoolhouse with a mere division commander and attempting to figure out how they were going to fight a land battle for control of Saipan.

The promoted general and the demoted admiral carefully scanned their organizational tables and attempted to conjure up a brilliant victory plan against the potential invaders. The centerpiece of the defense of Saipan was Saito's own unit, the 43rd Division, which had arrived, more or less, in Tanapag Harbor—minus five transport ships—carrying a quarter of the troops, half the tanks, and three quarters of the equipment. Because far too many officers had been aboard the unlucky ships that had foundered, Saito was busily signing field promotions in which platoon commanders now found themselves leading companies and company commanders now commanded battalions.

Beyond his own division, Saito could deploy three battalions of the 47th Independent Mixed Brigade; the 7th and 16th Independent Engineer Regiments, which were responsible for most of the fortifications; the 3rd Independent Mountain Artillery Regiment, which could deploy two dozen 75 mm guns; the 25th Anti-Aircraft Regiment, which fielded several batteries of dual-purpose guns; and, finally, the surviving thirty-six medium and twelve light tanks of the 9th Tank Regiment, which represented the garrison's most powerful mobile force. The aggregate strengths of Saito's army units came to a little more than 26,000 men, which was an impressive force in this island war; but it would have been far more impressive if the 14,000 infantrymen and fifty tanks lost at sea were on Saipan instead of on the bottom of the Pacific.[4]

The loss of these forces was partially compensated by the fact that even though Nagumo could offer little sea power, he did command 6,200 naval personnel centered around the 55th Naval Guard Force, a regiment-sized unit charged with manning the island's coast defense artillery, and the 1st Special Naval Landing Force, which was a reinforced battalion of naval infantry charged with defending harbors and beaches.[5]

When Nagumo and Saito tallied their parallel personnel rolls, they concluded that they could field the equivalent of fourteen combat battalions and an understrength tank regiment that would ultimately have to confront twenty-seven enemy infantry battalions and two armored regiments. In the annals of defensive warfare, this did not constitute an overwhelming disadvantage and was hardly the equivalent of what the Spartans at Thermopylae or the Texans at the Alamo faced. Traditional military theory called for a successful attack to have a three-to-one manpower superiority over the defender; here, the odds were more like two-to-one, and Saipan's topography, especially in the northern half of the island, dramatically favored the Japanese.

General Saito had been assured by headquarters that Admiral Toyoda's A-GO plan would smash the American fleet and send reinforcements streaming into the Marianas in the unlikely event of attack; but the general preferred to concentrate on the forces he knew he had at hand and planned to throw his energies into dumping the enemy into the sea within the first twenty-four hours of an invasion. This "Rommelesque" *"Longest Day"* mentality depended on using his carefully positioned naval and army artillery to decimate the invaders on the beaches, thus setting them up for a final coup with a massed tank-infantry counterattack.

Saito's major dilemma was that he could only hazard an educated guess at the location of the enemy landings, and he had the equivalent of only forty-two rifle companies to defend the circumference of the island. Saipan may appear on a map as only a tiny speck in the vast Pacific Ocean, but, as is true of equivalent North American islands such as Nantucket or Bermuda, a person attempting to walk the entire extent of the beach finds the distance formidable. Saito had about one company of infantrymen for every mile of coast; this meant if the men were equally deployed, each defender would be about 10 yards away from his neighbor. This would leave rather wide gaps between, even for men armed with modern weapons, and therefore a way had to be found to concentrate these men in the place the enemy attempted to land.

Before he had left for his inspection tour, General Obata had attempted to deal with this quandary by trying to concentrate his forces in the most likely landing areas. Obata divided the island into four sectors with an eye to facilitating the ability to rush reinforcements to threatened points. The Northern Sector stretched from the outskirts of the northwestern coastal town of Tanapag to the upper tip of the island at Marpi Point and was entrusted to the 135th Infantry Regiment. The Western Sector extended down from Tanapag Harbor to the capital city of Garapan and inland to the most prominent elevation on the island, Mount Tapotchau. Here, Nagumo's naval units would cooperate with a battalion of the 136th Infantry Regiment to defend the coastline and the approaches to the capital. The Central Sector stretched from the southern suburbs of Garapan to the northern outskirts of the next coastal community, Charan Kanoa, and included the vital Afetna Point, which jutted into the sea and provided perfect cover for enfilading guns. Beach defense in the area was assigned to four companies of the 136th Regiment. The fourth and final area was designated the Southern Sector and included nearly half the island. This sector contained the town and harbor of Charan Kanoa, Aslito Airfield, and the eastern coastline, washed by the waters of Magicienne Bay. The 47th Independent Mixed Brigade was responsible for defending this area, with additional support provided by a carefully hoarded mobile reserve grouped of about four rifle companies and the tank regiment.

The beach defense companies were expected to receive significant support from a powerful array of naval coastal defense guns and army artillery. The core of Saipan's firepower revolved around eight 6-inch guns deployed to counter a possible landing anywhere between Tanapag Harbor and Charan Kanoa Harbor and sixty-seven smaller-caliber guns were deployed to target landing craft approaching the beaches on the east and west coasts. Thus, as the invaders would discover to their dismay on the morning of June 15, Saito had plenty of artillery and men who knew how to use it.[6]

At 1:00 p.m. on Sunday, June 11, 1944, a vast fleet not much smaller than the thousand ships of Trojan War fame closed to within 200 miles of the eastern shore of Guam as crews were called to action stations. Admiral Marc Mitscher ordered the carriers of Task Force 58 to turn into the wind and more than two hundred deep-blue Hellcat fighters soared to their rally points and flew towards the fourteen airfields that represented Japanese air power in the Marianas. Dark-green Zeros scrambled to gain altitude to challenge this aerial armada and dogfights swirled above beaches, cornfields, orchards, and water. The color of planes spiraling to the ground or the ocean was far more often green than blue, and many other Imperial aircraft became funeral pyres in their now flaming airdromes.

Meanwhile, like terrified peasants moving their carts into a neighboring castle as a marauding army of besiegers appeared on the horizon, Japanese ships unfortunate enough to be near the Marianas as the siege began steamed desperately in search of a safe haven. A convoy of twelve freighters hurriedly weighed anchor in Tanapag Harbor, intent on a run to Yokahoma with vital materials for the Imperial war effort. A motley portion of Admiral Nagumo's Fourth Fleet—ten torpedo boats, patrol craft, and sub-chasers—shepherded their charges as they steamed into the open sea. Suddenly, a swarm of flying blue predators sensed their presence and dove from the sky; within minutes, eight cargo ships and four escorts were at the bottom of the ocean.[7]

Admiral Toyoda's instincts had encouraged him to assume that the main enemy summer offensive would be directed by MacArthur against the island groups fronting to Philippines. While American carrier planes tore through fourteen airfields designed to handle the six hundred planes designated to defend the Marianas, many of those aircraft and pilots were on Truk or the Palaus Islands waiting for an attack that was actually happening far to the north.

The battle for the airfields may have been one-sided, but there were still empty seats in American ready rooms after each mission. For example, Lieutenant Commander Robert Isely's Avenger was torn to pieces by enemy antiaircraft fire as he launched a rocket attack on Aslito Airfield. Isely's plane crashed into a cornfield adjacent to the base that would be named in his honor when turned over to new American management. On a brighter note, when Commander William Martin's Avenger was shot down by enemy flak guns over Charan Kanoa, the pilot parachuted into the 4-foot-deep lagoon and made mental notes concerning enemy beach defenses while bullets whizzed past him. As Imperial patrol boats roared from their anchorage to capture the downed pilot, an American seaplane landed while covering fighters held the advancing enemy boats at bay. Less than an hour later, the somewhat dazed pilot found himself in Admiral Spruance's quarters receiving congratulations for an excellent report of the salient features of the reef and lagoon that would have to be passed by the ground forces a few days later.[8]

If the Imperial high command had fully deployed all designated squadrons on the airfields that had been constructed all around the Marianas, their numbers might have been sufficient at least to turn the American air attacks into a costly encounter for Task Force 58. But too many vital fighter squadrons had been pulled southward to meet the expected thrust toward the Philippines that Japanese intelligence had predicted, and too many available aircraft had been destroyed on the ground by endless waves of Mitscher's raiders. Now, on the eve of invasion, perhaps only a hundred Nipponese planes were combat effective, and, although this force could still shoot down American intruders, control of the skies was rapidly turning to the invaders. Just as at Normandy's beaches thousands of miles away, when the Americans splashed ashore on Saipan, the small showing of enemy planes would make the skies above far more friendly than hostile.

Now it was the turn of the battleships. Like giant sea-going catapult platforms smashing down the battlements of a medieval fortress, they trained their lethal weapons on the besieged island of Saipan.

On the morning of June 13, Admiral William "Ching" Lee's flotilla of seven new battleships was detached from the carrier force and closed to within 10 miles of Saipan. Sixty-three enormous guns elevated into firing position and unleashed their deadly cargoes. Lee's primary mission was to support the carriers in a surface engagement and provide antiaircraft cover for the relatively vulnerable flattops in an enemy carrier raid. But on this cloudy, humid morning, Lee's attention was focused shoreward toward Saito and Nagumo's numerous gun positions.

The great battleship bombardment was spectacular, dramatic, and exciting to American spectators, but terrifying to the defenders. Sergeant Takeo Yamauchi, a new college graduate drafted into the 43rd Division, was having breakfast when the enemy ships appeared on the horizon:

> I was eating a large rice ball when I heard a voice call out, "The American fleet is here!" I looked up and saw the sea completely black with them. What looked like a large city had suddenly appeared offshore. Then the naval bombardment began. The first salvo exploded along the beach and objects suddenly went sixty meters straight up! The area was pitted like the craters of the moon. We clung to the earth in our shallow trenches and were half buried. Soil filled my mouth and blinded me. The fumes and flying dirt almost choked you. The next moment I might get it.[9]

The perspective of a Japanese ground soldier was one of disbelief that anything or anyone could live through such a shattering gauntlet of fire; but when this manmade thunderstorm ended and American observation planes flew over to assess the damage, they discovered that most of Saipan's key emplacements appeared to be still largely intact. Lee's new battleships were considered far too valuable to risk in the probably mined shallows near the coast, and so the vessels stood off at a safe but unproductive distance. Also, the "fast" battleships had been designed as floating antiaircraft platforms and surface engagement vessels, not as bombardment ships; thus, the 15,000 shells they fired did far more damage to Saipan's farming industry than to its shore batteries and strongpoints. Nonetheless, help was on the way from a less-glamorous but better-prepared flotilla.

Rear Admiral Jesse Oldendorf commanded the lunch-pail, blue-collar version of Ching Lee's dreadnoughts. No one formally called these vessels the slow battleship, and in modern parlance they might be advertised as "the heritage fleet" or "battleships classic"; but in reality they were showpieces of the pre–Pearl Harbor era that had met varying fates on that Sunday morning in December 1941. While *Arizona* remained with its crew on the bottom of Pearl Harbor as a permanent memorial to a peaceful nation's rude introduction to treachery, most of its sister ships were pulled from the mud, given anything from major surgery to a face lift, and restored to active duty as bombardment specialists. Now *Maryland, Colorado, Pennsylvania, Tennessee, California, New Mexico, Mississippi* and *Idaho* were steaming toward the Marianas in a mission to prove that newer was not necessarily better in naval bombardment squadrons.

On the gray dawn of an overcast Wednesday morning, Oldendorf's ships swung around Marpi Point and began a choreography of destruction that exploded from the north point to the southern cape on Saipan. Unlike Lee's crews, the men of the "old" battleships practiced shore bombardment every day and now these innate skills began wreaking havoc on the target island. White phosphorous began to mix with the yellow smoke from burning cornfields as the flotilla concentrated on devastating Saito's communications system. Saipan was divided into six target areas, and each bombardment ship was assigned specific targets for individual attention. Some ships edged as close as 1,000 yards to the beach. Nagumo's naval guns hit *California, Tennessee,* and the destroyer *Braine,* inflicting sixty-two casualties, including twelve fatalities. In retaliation, American shells almost annihilated a powerful Imperial battery on Nafutan Point, although Saito and Nagumo purposely kept many of their guns concealed to await the actual invasion. Although the bombardment would significantly hinder Saito's ability to launch a massive coordinated counterattack on the night of the American landings, even Oldendorf's best efforts failed to knock out the majority of the artillery; indeed, it would hamper the invaders for the entire campaign.

As Japanese soldiers and sailors peered from trenches and pillboxes at the huge invasion fleet ringing the island, a small band of adventurous Americans was already penetrating sea approaches to Saipan. These amphibian buccaneers belonged to demits called Underwater Demolition Teams (U.D.T.), but they were more popularly called navy frogmen. Several months earlier, high-ranking naval officers had expressed a need for amphibian scouts who could secure information about the deployment of enemy minefields, the depth of the waters off the coast, and the distances of the coral reefs from the invasion beaches on islands targeted for invasion.

The task of organizing such a unit was assigned to Commander Draper Kauffman, the former head of the navy's bomb disposal school. Kauffman set up shop in the beachfront buildings of Fort Pierce, Florida, and trained a core group of rugged volunteers who were capable of swimming at least 2 miles; could make accurate estimates of distances; and could place and detonate explosive charges on barriers to approach lanes of landing vessels. They also had to be able to survive the hostile reaction of an aroused enemy garrison. The U.D.T. were given their baptism of fire in the waters of Roi-Namur on the night before the initiation of Operation Flintlock, but it soon became apparent that it was impossible to see underwater after dark. On the next operation, U.D.T. activities would be performed in daylight.

The advantage of daytime activities was that the frogmen could actually see what they were doing, but the disadvantage was that the Japanese could also see them, and they had guns. Therefore, the new best friends of U.D.T. were the crews of specially designed LCIs that provided cover for their exploits with an impressive array of automatic weapons. On Wednesday afternoon, June 14, the day before the Saipan invasion, two ninety-six-man frogman teams were painted with black rings at 12-inch intervals to measure water depth, equipped with fishline for measuring distances, and fitted with a stylus and piece of waterproof plastic to make notes about what they observed. Then the frogmen dropped into the water from rubber rafts attached to speeding motorboats and began their swim toward the coral reefs that fronted Saipan.

First, swimmers paired off into two-man teams; they would then split up, one man swimming toward the beach to measure distances from the reef, the other taking roundtrip of water depths. Then, just before sunset, the frogmen began planting demolition charges to blow a passage through the coral and blasted crude ramps so that the alligators could clamber over the reef into the lagoon and onto the beach beyond. However, just as medieval archers in a besieged castle fired incessant volleys of arrows at enemy scouts measuring distances for placing siege weapons and locating optimal approach paths for storming parties, Nipponese defenders engaged in a desperate shooting spree to pick off the frogmen before they could place the guide markers that would direct the assault units to the proper beach. Rifles, machine guns, and mortars engaged in a running duel with the American gunboats while the frogmen splashed in the water waiting for their pickup boats and rafts. Pools of blood began spreading in the warm water as nine frogmen were killed or wounded in the gun battle in which they were helpless spectators. Then, just as the last rays of the sun touched the horizon, the last teams finished planting their marker buoys and were brought back to the safety of the fleet for hearty congratulations.[10]

Just after midnight on a new day that would be etched in memory as D-Day on Saipan, Imperial sailors came out in their own small boats and planted worker flags between the beaches and the reef to help guide their gunners when the enemy began their inevitable invasion of the inner core of the Japanese Empire.

'10

D-DAY ON SAIPAN

THE HOURS BETWEEN SUNSET on June 14 and sunrise the next morning produced a tense atmosphere of expectation among defenders and invaders. Sergeant Takeo Yamauchi, a twenty-three-year-old squad leader, was coping with the effects of the bombardment and blast effects that had filled his mouth with dirt on several occasions and caused temporary blindness. Now, choking from fumes and flying dirt, he surveyed the ground in front of his shallow trench. The area was pitted and smoke shrouded the beaches beyond. His meager ration of rice balls had been transformed into muddy goo and no new supply of food seemed to be part of his future. Yet all thirteen of his men had survived more or less intact and his squad of mainly teenage conscripts was still eager to obey his commands. Now the balmy night moved slowly toward dawn as men peered intently toward the sun and wondered whether tomorrow would be the day that the enemy attempted to storm ashore.[1]

On the ocean side of the coral-fringed lagoon, American assault troops, if nothing else, were eating far better than Sergeant Yamauchi and his men. An emerging ritual of amphibious invasions was a 2:00 a.m. meal planned around huge portions of steak and eggs. Whether this meal was considered a very late dinner or a very early breakfast, the menu was probably not the most appropriate fare for men who would shortly be clambering aboard one of the most guaranteed sea-sickness-inducing craft ever devised by man. Callous humor about the traditionally sumptuous nature of a "last meal" for condemned men had just enough of a ring of accuracy to be digested along with the food; for even the most optimistic ground troops knew that it was unlikely that everyone would be alive for breakfast the next morning. As the meal ended, the troops joked, prayed, reflected, and shared opinions about the strength of the potential enemy resistance. Would this landing similar in intensity to that of Tarawa or Roi-Namur? Would the civilian population contest the invasion as bitterly as the Nipponese garrison? Would the Imperial Japanese Navy sortie in full strength?

As the first glimmer of dawn revealed the outline of Saipan's coastal population centers, two battleships, two cruisers, and seven destroyers steamed to within 1,000 yards of the coral reef and began bombarding the landing beaches while assault craft were winched out from the transport ships and prepared for their runs toward the coast. Thirty-four LSTs moved in unison toward their jump-off line just farther than 4,200 yards from shore. Ships opened their bow doors like the jaws of predators on the hunt and disgorged more than seven hundred amphibian tractors and tanks that began to circle around the mother ships in the choreography that was an island invasion.

The senior officers of Forager had approved an operational plan in which an initial spearhead of a hundred LVTs, seventy Amtracs, and twenty-four LCI gunboats would converge along a 4-mile stretch of Saipan's west coast. The target was the beachfront that stretched from a mile south of Garapan through Charan Kanoa and down to Agingan Point just above the southwestern tip of the island. North to south the landing points included three designated Red beaches, three Green beaches, two Blue beaches, and three Yellow beaches divided in the middle by a 500-yard gap between the Green and Blue sites.

The northern beaches would be the responsibility of the 6th and 8th Regiments of the 2nd Marine Division while the 23rd and 25th Regiments of the 4th Marine Division would be assigned to the southern sector. Each assault battalion would be responsible for ap-

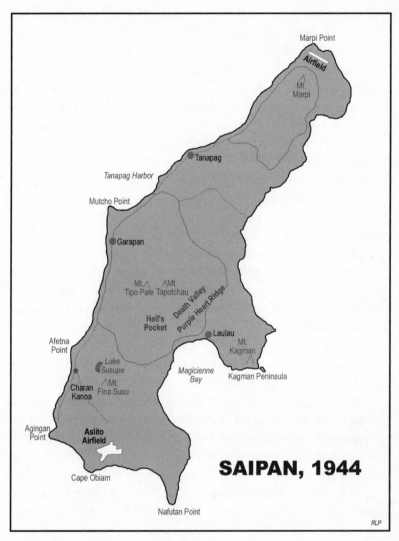

Marpi Point

Airfield

Mt.
Marpi

Tanapag

Tanapag Harbor

Mutcho Point

Garapan

Mt. ∧   ∧ Mt.
Tipo Pale Tapotchau

Death Valley

Purple Heart Ridge

Hell's
Pocket

Laulau

Mt.
Kagman

Afetna
Point

Lake
Susupe

Magicienne
Bay

Kagman Peninsula

Charan
Kanoa

∧ Mt.
Fina Susu

Agingan
Point

Aslito
Airfield

SAIPAN, 1944

Cape Obiam

Nafutan Point

RLP

Saipan, June 1944

proximately 600 yards of front, that is, the equivalent of a three-block-long stretch of beach at a typical American seashore resort. Meanwhile, to distract the defenders, the 2nd Regiment and a battalion of the 29th Regiment would conduct a landing approach toward Garapan and the southern end of Tanapag Harbor. Boats would be lowered, troops embarked, and landing craft driven to within 5,000 yards of the beaches in a diversion that would hopefully entice the defenders to maintain a strong force along a front that was not on the American list of targets.

Assuming that all went according to plan, Kelly Turner and Holland Smith would have 8,000 troops ashore in the first hour of battle and the beach line would be wide enough to begin landing the tanks and artillery that might be the keys to deflecting the expected enemy counterattack. Once the landing beaches were secured, the 2nd Division would begin to wheel in the direction of Garapan by way of the coast road and the parallel rail line while its sister division would push eastward, capture Aslito Airfield, and then advance through the farms and fields towards Magicenne Bay on the opposite side of the island. The scope and size of the battlefield would dwarf the Gilberts and Marshalls experience and offer the Pacific combat troops a taste of what their European counterparts were encountering in the battle for France. Unfortunately, much of the plan for Forager had been developed on the assumption that no more than 15,000 Imperial troops were on Saipan and thus the invaders would enjoy a substantial advantage in numbers. As American intelligence units gradually escalated the size of the enemy garrison, the prospects for a rapid victory became more daunting. The Japanese garrison on Betio had extracted a terrible price for the raising of the Stars and Stripes on that small patch of coral. Now seven times as many Nipponese were deployed on an island far better suited for defense than Tarawa's primary land mass. Operation Galvanic was sheer hell, but the ordeal ended in seventy-two bloody hours. Few people on board the ships of Fifth Fleet could have imagined that this enterprise would be decided in anything like that time frame.

As the landing craft chugged toward the line of departure, they encountered four naval patrol vessels flying color-coded identification flags to guide them to the proper approach lane. The assault troops and naval crews watched the spectacular naval bombardment come to an abrupt halt, and for a moment or two an eerie silence pervaded the humid atmosphere as the reassuring explosions ceased. Then, in a vivid assurance that the sea soldiers would not land unsupported, a formation of fighters and bombers soared just above the water, crossed the coral barrier, and unloaded their deadly cargoes on the shore. Now it seemed as if almost every object on Saipan was covered by a dark cloud of smoke. Only the general shape of the island remained visible. One war correspondent insisted that Saipan looked like a "low lying prehistoric monster whose spine rose in the center of Mount Topotchau."[2]

At just past 8:00 a.m., a flotilla of control boats raised the first of a series of colored flags and twenty-four LCIs sprinted ahead and crossed the line of departure as crewmen sprang into position around rocket batteries, machine guns, and automatic cannons. Five minutes later, companies of amphibian tanks joined the shore-bound procession while the far more numerous Amtracs jockeyed for their own place in line. The alligators were a godsend to commanders attempting to pierce the coral necklaces that stood sentinel over so many Central Pacific islands, but their maximum speed of 5 miles an hour seemed to place the entire approach operation in slow-motion. The assault troopers were approaching the beaches at little more than walking speed, and for more than half an hour men on the edge of combat remained in a limbo world between the routine of the troopships and the unknown that waited patiently on the only partially visible shore.

The first wave of attack planes had finished their tasks and were heading back for the carriers when the next hammer blow struck Saipan. This was a choreography of seaborne and airborne firepower that was unleashed only minutes before the assault began. The twenty-four LCIs veered in formation toward the shoreline and then in unison unleashed salvo after salvo of 4.5-inch rockets. A horizontal storm of machine-gun fire and cannon shells accompanied the rocket launchers and smashed into the now clearly visible treeline ashore. Then another seventy-two carrier planes buzzed over the assault craft for a last-minute strafing run that was so close to the ground that red-hot machine gun casings began falling into the landing craft like a hellish hail storm.

The Hellcats shifted their fire from the beaches to the foliage beyond and, at 8:43, the first green-denim figures pushed ashore astride their mechanical alligators. The almost surrealistic pageantry prompted even veteran Japanese soldiers to comment on the remarkable nature of the coming of the Americans. Sergeant Yamauchi had finally cleared his mouth and eyes of the dirt thrown up by the earlier naval bombardment, but he woke on the morning of June 15 exhausted and famished. Suddenly, a warning spread along the Nipponese lines: "The American army is coming!" Actually, it was the Marines, but their arrival was no less a portent of death. "I lifted my hand as they advanced like a swarm of grasshoppers. The American soldiers were all soaked. Their camouflage helmets looked black. They were so tiny wading ashore. I saw flames shooting up from American tanks hit by Japanese fire."[3]

Yamauchi had little time or inclination to consult his watch regarding the time of this first American penetration of the inner empire; but the invaders were keeping careful records and it was exactly 8:44 a.m. on Thursday, June 15, 1944, when the first of 719 Amtracs made the transition from water to dry land.

Nipponese subjects of far higher status than Sergeant Yamauchi were keenly aware of the potential disaster that awaited their nation if the enemy secured a permanent hold on Saipan and its sister islands. During a test flight over the Solomon Islands a few months earlier, a B-29 Superfortress had been shot down and the pilot captured. Incessant interrogation of the officer revealed the approximate combat range of the new super weapon, and now that it was clear that the Marianas were the next American target it required little imagination to understand what the invaders intended to do with the newly captured airfields. The divine presence of the emperor was used sparingly in encouraging Imperial warriors to battle, but now His Majesty's words, if not actual voice, crackled over the radio waves: "Because the fate of the Japanese Empire depends on the result of your operation, inspire the spirit of the officers and men and to the very end continue to destroy the enemy gallantly and persistently thus assuaging our anxiety." Saipan's radio station quickly responded with the feelings of the garrison and the island's large civilian population: "We have received your honorable imperial words and we are grateful for boundless magnanimity of the Imperial favor. By becoming the bulwark of the Pacific with 10,000 deaths, we hope to requite the Imperial favor."[4]

Unfortunately, the 85 square miles of rugged hills, cane fields, and thriving towns that constituted Saipan Island contained many more than 10,000 sons and daughters of Nippon who were now on the front lines of the Pacific War, whether or not they were thrilled by that prospect. One defender deployed in a trench not far from Sergeant Yamauchi made a final journal notation that symbolized the impact of conferring "imperial favor" on the garrison: "We are waiting with Molotov cocktails and hand grenades ready for the word to rush forward recklessly into the enemy ranks with our swords in our hands. All that worries me is what will happen to Japan after we die."[5]

This was not the mindset that was likely to lead to a negotiated surrender of the suddenly most important piece of real estate in the vast Pacific region: a fact that the men of Forager were about to learn.

Eight minutes after the first Amtrac touched the sand, there were Marines on every one of the invasion beaches, but many of them were writhing with wounds or still in death. Just as on the previous Tuesday at Normandy, events conspired to produce an operation that veered wildly between success and disaster. The demonstration attack on Garapan fooled none of the defenders, least of all General Saito, who watched the whole performance with the eye of a commander who refused to be distracted by such tricks. The curse of the right men on the wrong beach that plagued the Allies at Normandy now exhibited its Pacific counterpart. The 2nd Battalion, 8th Regiment, landed on Green Beach, but it was Green 1, not Green 2, and this was the 3rd Battalion's chosen battlefield. Battalions from the 6th Regiment jumped from their Amtracs on the wrong stretch of Red Beach, the result in both instances being congestion that was a gift for the Japanese defenders, who hardly lacked targets among the green-jacketed invaders. The Nipponese were particularly successful at identifying the officers directing the landing activities as all four battalion commanders on the left flank became casualties in the early moments of the battle.

Japanese ground troops had watched in some disappointment because the preliminary naval bombardments of the past few days had been answered by relatively few Imperial batteries. But Saito had purposely kept most of his guns concealed in depressions and caves because he knew that they could wreak far more havoc on vulnerable invasion troops than on heavily armored warships. Although much of the Nipponese communications system was a shambles, gunners had carefully marked registration points on potential invasion beaches and could now operate as independent units once the landings began. Artillerymen turned trees along the beach into deadly shrapnel and then walked their fire forward to the reef just as follow-up waves approached the coral barrier. The barrage quickly rose to such an intensity that American officers were convinced the reef had been mined. Even in those areas where the Marines were able to push the defenders off the beachfront, the enemy could strike from unexpected directions. A tragic replay of an incident on Tarawa occurred when newly landed troops surged past a "destroyed" Imperial tank. Suddenly, the dead crew came to life and swept the beach with vicious fire that paid particularly deadly attention to officers who were needed to organize the drive inland.

The 714 landing craft available for Forager managed to put 8,000 invasion troops ashore in the first twenty minutes of the battle, but the ground troops had relatively little equipment to support a drive inland. The Marines had enough men and firepower to control the ground immediately adjacent to the water, but a Japanese garrison four times their strength still held the rest of the island. Prospects for moving inland toward the heart of Saipan would not brighten significantly until some form of armored forces could be organized to cover an incursion beyond the beach. The first armored units to reach the battle were formations of specially constructed Amtracs that had been fitted out as amphibian tanks. The vehicles would hardly have been daunting to the crew of a German Panther or Tiger tank; but, at least until Saito unleashed his carefully hoarded tank regiment, the thinly armored "alligator tanks" could shepherd other Amtracs and infantry units on their forays into the world beyond the beachfront.

One mixed force of Amtrac personnel carriers and armored vehicles pushed into Charon Kanoa, giving American troops their first glimpse of a full-scale Japanese community. They were surprised to find the fragile homes of paper and wood that dominated films on Japan were conspicuously absent in this harbor town. Stores, schools, and houses were all constructed of sturdy painted concrete, not unlike those in housing developments in much of the American South and West. Familiarity and alien culture often stood side by side as Americans absorbed the paradox of an impressive baseball stadium flanked by a Buddhist temple. The assault troops certainly realized they were not home when enemy snipers appeared at the windows of the town's buildings and contested the possession of record stores, taverns, and restaurants. A new phase of the Pacific War had begun in the quaint streets of Charon Kanoa; would this phase end only in the far more extensive avenues of the Japanese capital in Tokyo?

At Japanese field headquarters near the center of the island, Yoshitsugu Saito was feeling the effects of the enemy naval bombardment on his organization of an effective response to a massive American invasion. Much of his communications network had been obliterated by Oldendorf's battleships; but during the first hours of invasion, a combination of surviving radio links and a major use of messengers gave the garrison commander a reasonably accurate picture of what was occurring. As a whole, Saito could be reasonably pleased with the situation. Columns of Amtracs and amphibious tanks had penetrated the streets of Charon Kanoa, the radio station just east of the town, and a railroad embankment 400 yards from the beach. One company of the 773rd Amphibious Tractor Battalion had even pushed as far as a rail junction 700 yards from the lagoon. But no major support units had arrived to bolster any of these incursions, and the main battle was still being fought on the beach.[6]

The invasion beaches of Saipan did not look quite as grim as Omaha Beach at the same point in the attack nine days earlier, but there were some ugly parallels. Saito's clever deployment of machine gun and mortar positions kept the early assault waves pinned to the beaches as follow-up units clambered onto an increasingly crowded battlefield. The men on foot were being squeezed between burning tractors to their rear and Japanese guns to their front. The main mobile firepower for the southern beaches, the 708th Amphibian Tank Battalion, found that access to the enemy gun positions on Fina Susu ridge was impeded by a vast inland swamp, a network of trenches, a burning gas depot, and a steep railroad embankment. The climb from the beach to the heights would be a perilous adventure that few would complete successfully.

Saito's plan to unleash calamity on the invasion forces from as many directions as possible constantly compelled the Marines to shift their attention from one threat to the next. Although Saito was retaining most of his armor in reserve for a future counterattack, small forces of Imperial tanks clanked out of wooded areas and attempted to penetrate American regimental command posts. At times, headquarters personnel were forced to assume the role of tank killers as they seized bazookas and dueled with the looming enemy vehicles. Then, just as the armored menace temporarily abated, a new battery of previously concealed guns would open up from an unexpected direction and pour fire on the crowded beachhead. The most dangerous threat came from a heavily wooded finger of land jutting into the sea just south of the right flank of the invasion force. A battery of heavy naval coastal defense guns had been concealed on Agingan Point and held out of the battle until the invaders began stocking up on the beaches just to the north.

By noon of D-Day, the assault force had won a strong presence on the invasion beaches, but there were significant gaps in the line that invited counterattack, and the casualty list was rising at an alarming rate. For example, 6th Regiment's casualties had already passed the 35 percent mark, and other units were not far behind. The battle had to be carried inland or the invasion force would soon be bled white. Ultimately, the Americans on Saipan began to understand the lesson learned by their counterparts in Normandy the previous week; remaining on the beach might very well be more dangerous than attempting to push the enemy defenders away from their front lines. Gradually, as the sun passed its zenith and began its inexorable transit toward the western horizon, Marines stirred themselves from the pockmarked shambles of beaches and pushed into the alien foliage beyond.

On the northern front of the battle, the 6th Regiment's commander, Colonel James Risely, realized that almost all his senior subordinates and most of their staff were dead or wounded. From the scant protection of his water's-edge command post, he assigned junior officers to upgraded responsibilities.[7]

While surviving officers worked out the details of their new commands, Risely received the welcome addition of a battalion of pack howitzers of the 10th Marines. At just past 2:00 p.m., the gunners had their weapons ready for action, and under this welcome covering fire the ground troops pushed forward units nearly 1,000 yards from the placid waters of the lagoon.

The other assault regiment of the 2nd Marine Division faced a more difficult task in securing their beachhead. Looming between the right flank of this unit and its sister division to the south was a protrusion of woodlands known as Afetna Point. Japanese guns on this position poured enfilading fire against northern and southern invasion forces and effectively closed the only channel through which tank landing craft and the desperately needed Shermans could reach the battlefield. The 2nd Battalion, 8th Marines, was assigned the unenviable task of neutralizing this key enemy position, and three companies of ground troops soon found themselves picking through a maze of enemy pillboxes, shrubs, and dense foliage while Imperial troops popped out from cover to offer battle. Company G of the 2nd Battalion had been issued with a generous supply of shotguns,[8] and the weapons proved their worth in a series of vicious encounters with sword-wielding Nipponese warriors contesting every foot of the American advance.

South of the enemy firebase on Afetna Point, the men of the 4th Marine Division faced their own challenges as they attempted to form a continuous line inland from the beach. The newly landed infantry units kept looking back into the lagoon to catch a glimpse of significant supporting weapons; but on this bloody invasion day, the intervention was at best a mixed blessing. The invasion of Saipan was expected to allow the Marine Corps to deploy the first truly major tank formations of the Pacific War. Each tank battalion assigned to Forager was equipped with forty-six new Shermans; these were supported by a company of light reconnaissance tanks and a platoon of specially equipped flame tanks mounting the Canadian Ronson flame gun that could spew a stream of fire up to 80 yards. This concentration of mobile firepower was essential to counter the extensive armored force the Japanese had committed to Saipan and to support the ground forces' drive beyond the beaches. The tanks would be useless until they could be put into action, however, and the defenders seemed determined to keep this weapon out of the American arsenal.

This part of the battle centered around a seemingly innocuous-looking pier extending into the lagoon from Charan Kanoa's main sugar mill. Japanese construction workers had blasted a 150-foot-wide channel alongside the pier so that freighters could anchor and load their cargoes of sugar for the home islands. When American intelligence officers saw photos of a large concrete ramp at the beach end of the pier, they designated this point the perfect landing spot for 4th Division's tank units. Unfortunately, because the powerful enemy batteries on Afetna Point were not factored into the equation, each landing craft carrying a tank became a prime target for the Japanese gunners. Enemy gunfire and increasingly heavy seas soon turned the landing process into a nightmare as some tanks sank with their landing craft, some were beached on the wrong part of the shore, and others were immobilized by deeper-than-expected water. One platoon of Shermans was rapidly shunted to the south to parry a major enemy counterattack against the 1st Battalion, 25th Marines, holding the extreme right end of the line, but the full power of American armor would not be unleashed on invasion day.

On the other hand, the 4th Marine Division began receiving formidable artillery support soon after the landing. Two battalions of 75 mm pack howitzers and three battalions of 105 mm howitzers were landed and deployed to counter the incessant enemy barrage. In the middle of this spectacular artillery duel, the commander of the 4th Division, General Harry Schmidt, arrived on the beach and, as senior officers dodged the incoming Nipponese barrage, established a primitive command post in a foxhole 50 yards from the water. Schmidt later admitted, "It was the hottest spot I was in during the war, not even excepting Iwo Jima."[9]

General Schmidt was not alone in his feelings that he had landed on someone's target shooting range, but with almost agonizingly slow progress a battle line was almost willed into existence. The last rays of the setting sun revealed a beachhead perhaps 10,000 yards long and 1,000 yards deep manned by most of the two divisions and supported by seven artillery battalions and most of two tank battalions. However, the defenders still held the two crucial fingers jutting out into the sea. As long as there were Imperial troops and artillery on Afetna Point and Agingan Point, the American position remained precarious. Now with sunset, as was so often the custom in this Pacific War, it was the Japanese army's turn to attack, and each American Marine waited in the growing darkness for the inevitable counterpunch in this unfolding slugging match.

General Saito spent the hours immediately after sunset attempting to organize the counterattack that he had already promised to his superiors in Tokyo. He gave them this optimistic message: "The Army this evening will make a night attack with all its forces and expects to annihilate the enemy at one swoop." The garrison on Saipan received specific orders: "Each unit will consolidate strategically important points and will carry out counterattacks with reserve forces and tanks against the enemy landing units and will demolish the enemy during the night at the water's edge."[10]

The newly landed American Marines dug in on a slim strand of beachfront with the sea at their backs and 32,000 hostile troops at their front would have taken this threat very seriously if they had intercepted Saito's message to his men. However, the Imperial warriors who were expected to carry out this glorious attack had their own share of problems on this tropical evening. As Sergeant Yamauchi noted glumly: "All the men in front of us were destroyed the first day. Only distance saved us. The Americans got to within 80 meters of us. We were firing at them from our trenches which were behind rocks at the top of a straight slope." A few hours earlier, Yamauchi's platoon had launched a desperate attack to push the invaders back to the beaches. "I burst forth from my hole and slid in among the small rocks in front of me. Bullets were ricocheting off the rocks in front of me. I was terrified. I fired at an American soldier who seemed practically on top of me. I suddenly felt something hot on my neck. I was too petrified to move. I couldn't even shoot anymore."[11]

What started as a formidable attack fizzled into a hasty withdrawal in which the wounded sergeant watched the man on one side of him die and the man on the other side shot in the eye.

While the daylight attacks had been sporadic and poorly coordinated, most leaders on both sides of the battle line expected the Nipponese night assault to be far more formidable. The Imperial forces were noted for their night-fighting ability and darkness would negate much of the American advantage in naval and aerial firepower. Saito certainly wanted and expected a counterattack that would be so ferocious that the Americans would be driven into the sea and the invasion ended the day it began. Then reality intruded on this dream of Samurais. The general could order an attack for tonight, but would the only partially functioning communications system allow his men to carry out his plans? What occurred was the worst of all worlds for Saito: Some units attacked the enemy lines, but never in anything approaching a unity of purpose; and other forces never even received the message of counterstrike.

At almost 10:00 p.m. on June 15, the men of the 6th Marine Regiment heard the noise of bugles, clanking swords, and clattering tanks, and suddenly their outposts were being overrun by a large enemy force sprinting southward on the coast road. Unfortunately for this endangered force, much of its artillery support was still aboard the transport ships and only one battalion of 75mm howitzers was readily available for action. However, as the Japanese assault force advanced with flags flying and swords waving, a timely call to the navy eased the plight of the Marines. A cascade of star shells sent aloft by American destroyers produced a brilliant silhouette that spelled doom for many Nipponese. Naval 5-inch guns collaborated with front-line machine guns and rifles to tear huge gaps in the enemy assault line. Then Imperial tanks entered the fray as an armored column rolled down the road and smashed into the American front lines. The tide of battle briefly shifted until a combination of American naval gunfire and the arrival of the first Shermans tipped the scales once again. The Marine medium tanks had far more armor, firepower, and speed than their Nipponese counterparts. Then an ace was thrown into the escalating confrontation. Belching fire and illumination from its weapons systems, battleship *California* began a leisurely cruise along the west coast of Saipan.

Japanese officers grudgingly called off an attack that simply did not have enough punch to push the invaders into the sea; and when they reported to headquarters, they complained bitterly about the American naval advantage. Headquarters of the Thirty-first Army admitted the potency of these marauders from the sea: "The enemy is under cover of warships nearby the coast; as soon as the night attack units go forward the enemy points out targets by using the large star shells which practically turn night into day. Thus the maneuvering of units is extremely difficult."[12]

Sergeant Yamauchi would have added his humble assent to this report of frustration as he witnessed the results from an uncomfortably close perspective. As the Imperial warrior recounted, "My 136th Regiment was strung out along the coast in front of the American forces. On it depended Japan's defense." The regimental battle flag was brought up at sunset for the initiation of the counterattack, but the sergeant's platoon was held in reserve pending the progress of the storm units. As he perched on the lip of a trench, Yamauchi noted: "We could hear men shuffling, trying to keep quiet, as they moved up. When the enemy put up their flares, it was as bright as daylight. As soon as it darkened again the men inched forward. The American forces were only a hundred meters in front of us."[13]

Yamauchi dozed as the attack force crept forward toward the enemy lines, and then suddenly night became day. "A tremendous volley from what seemed like the whole American army jolted me awake. Arrows of fire flew across the trenches. Tracers. They were beautiful." Then, "Japanese soldiers fled through our lines as they moved to our rear," and the sergeant for the first time thought the unthinkable for a Japanese warrior. Wounded, exhausted, and famished, he actually hoped that he would be captured. "I lay face down. I was going to pretend I was dead and then surrender but the Americans didn't push into the trench that night."[14]

Presumably, most Imperial troops were more insistent on giving their lives for the emperor, and on the first night of Forager, seven hundred warriors' names would be added to the roster of honored gods back in the Nipponese homeland. The American lines had held through the night and no unit was ever in real danger in being pushed into the sea. But in a scenario that would typify the increasing desperation of the Japanese and have significant consequences for the remainder of the campaign as well as future battles, some Imperial assault units used women and children to mask their approach by creating an initial impression among the Americans that they were encountering a civilian force intent on surrender. The first day of the first battle in the inner core of the Japanese Empire brought a new definition of hostilities in this already notoriously violent conflict.

Saito's first gambit had failed rather miserably, but at least he could console himself with the presumption that the next attack could be orchestrated with the full might of his still more or less intact army. Most of his formidable tank regiment was still in its lairs, Imperial artillery units were still lethal instruments, and most ground troops seemed eager to attack with the whole garrison at their side. There was plenty of time for a new and more ferocious offensive; but while the American invaders braced for the inevitable second round of the land battle, a huge storm of floating steel was gathering in mass far to the west. Virtually the entire Imperial Japanese Navy was about to enter the other end of the Philippine Sea. The largest carrier battle in history was now only hours from erupting.

11

VOYAGE TO BATTLE

THE BATTLE OF THE PHILIPPINE SEA, which is the official designation of the major naval engagement of the Marianas campaign, suffers from a form of historical identity crisis. Many of the American participants called the battle "The Great Marianas Turkey Shoot," which implies that the Japanese never stood a chance from the outset to win the engagement. Yet, although the outcome may have been one-sided, the senior Imperial admirals entered the contest with moderately optimistic feelings that the course of the Pacific War could be reversed somewhere in the waters between the Philippines and the Marianas. After the setbacks in the Gilberts and Marshalls, army and navy commanders alike understood that at whatever point the Americans penetrated the Absolute Defense Line, they would trigger a massive response from virtually every serviceable combat ship in the Imperial fleet. Now, as the Marines slogged forward on the beaches of Saipan, the tripwire had been sprung and the greatest carrier battle in history was beginning to take shape.

At 7:17 a.m. on June 15, 1944, Admiral Soemu Toyoda called Vice Admiral Jisaburo Ozawa and informed his subordinate that Operation A-GO was now in effect. Ozawa was a fifty-eight-year-old former chief of staff of the Combined Fleet who, as commander of First Naval Air Group had helped initiate the employment of carriers in an offensive role on the eve of World War II. The Miyazaki prefecture native had orchestrated the naval phase when the Japanese brilliantly captured the riches of the Dutch East Indies, Malaya, and Singapore, and was known throughout the navy as a good seaman and a first-rate innovator. When Toyoda concocted A-GO, Ozawa was commander of the Imperial Third Fleet, but the senior officer was so convinced of the vice admiral's fighting ability that he appointed him to a concurrent command of Mobile Fleet, which was essentially a euphemism for every Japanese ship above the size of a patrol boat concentrated for the new offensive.

Earlier in the spring, Ozawa had been ordered to shift his anchorage from Lingga Roads near Singapore to the former American naval base at Tawi Tawi at the southern tip of the Philippines. The new harbor was far inferior to his former base, but the American submarines were sinking dozens of oil tankers bringing fuel from the oil fields of the Dutch East Indies north to the Singapore area, and this new location was much closer to the oil wells. Yet the admiral found himself in a state of semi-siege as roaming American submarines picked off invaluable tankers and escorting destroyers almost as soon as they cleared the harbor, and the jungle covered ground offered no opportunity for the aviators to practice their skills on land. By mid-June, Ozawa had lost nearly a fourth of his vital antisubmarine screen to enemy torpedoes and he was anxious to get into the open sea and steam away from this growing death trap. Now, on this sunny June morning, Jisaburo Ozawa had received the orders he craved; virtually the entire strength of the Imperial Navy would put to sea to challenge the enemy invasion of the gates to the inner Japanese Empire.

When Admiral Ozawa received orders to implement A-GO, he commanded a fleet that in most situations would appear almost unbeatable. He would steam at the head of nine aircraft carriers carrying 430 combat planes and 50 scout planes, more aircraft than were present at either Pearl Harbor or Midway. His fleet included the two largest battleships in the world, *Yamato* and *Musashi*, armed with enormous 19-inch guns that could deliver 50,000 pounds of high explosives in one broadside, enough to sink almost any ship afloat in one salvo. The Mobile Fleet also included an impressive supporting cast of five conventional battleships, sixteen cruisers, and twenty-seven destroyers screened from a distance by twenty-five patrol submarines. Ozawa had also been assured by Toyoda that he would enjoy the support of massive land-based air cover from 598 planes stationed at airfields in a wide arc from Iwo Jima to the Palaus Islands, and he could expect an additional 400 planes to be fed into the battle if the enemy could be lured to fight relatively close to the Philippines. Because Japanese intelligence expected Fifth Fleet to deploy roughly 1,000 aircraft from its carriers, it was reasonable for Ozawa to assume that Imperial pilots would fight in conditions of anything from rough parity to a three-to-two advantage.[1]

However, this advantage could only be achieved if Raymond Spruance could somehow be enticed to sail Fifth Fleet far from the invasion beaches and toward the eastern end of the Philippine Sea.

Several hundred miles to the east, the commander of Fifth Fleet was in a position at once enviable and frustrating. Spruance had been given command of the most powerful fleet in history, a fleet that had almost five times the power of the American forces at Midway only two years earlier. His fifteen carriers could launch nearly 1,000 planes, which theoretically gave him the ability to roam the sea at will; he could even include a foray into Tokyo Bay if he could find the strategic necessity to do so. But Spruance was also an admiral on a rather short leash. He had been given explicit orders by Ernest King and Chester Nimitz to cover and protect the landing on Saipan above all other things and always to keep his fleet between the Imperial Fleet and the vulnerable invasion beaches.

Fifth Fleet had a generous supply of lethal carriers, battleships, and cruisers, but it also contained dozens of vulnerable transports, supply ships, and hospital vessels.

In some respects, Raymond Spruance shared the dilemma of Ulysses S. Grant as he prepared the Army of the Potomac for the 1864 offensive into Virginia. Grant had been given command of the largest army ever seen on the North American continent and had been given free rein by Abraham Lincoln to devise a battle plant to attack the Confederate Army. But the president had also emphasized that the Union simply could not afford to let the rebels capture the national capital and, therefore, Grant must always keep his army between Lee's forces and Washington. Just as the nightmare for Lincoln was the terror of rebel guns blasting the walls of the Capitol or the White House, terror for King and Nimitz came in the form of *Yamato* and *Musashi* sending volley after volley from their enormous guns into Saipan waters crowded with helpless ships and doomed sailors, soldiers, and Marines.

Raymond Spruance was also aware that the history of modern Japanese naval warfare was replete with incredibly complex plans filled with feints, diversions, and the division of fleets into multiple units for multiple purposes. It was probable that the enemy fleet would contest the invasion of the Marines, but, because the American admiral had to cover a wide swath of ocean, there would be numerous opportunities for a portion of the enemy fleet to slip past these extended lines and go on a rampage through the support ships. Spruance was eager to confront the Imperial Navy, but, unfortunately for Toyoda and Ozawa, until he was sure he had the enemy on the run, he would not stray far from the invasion beaches.[2]

The sailing from port of great sea vessels inspires a unique pageantry as the large ships slip their moorings, blow their signal horns, and head for open water followed by flocks of sea gulls and the cheers and waves of people watching from the docks. Now Jisburo Ozawa and the men of the Mobile Fleet were undergoing the bittersweet transition from temporary land dwellers to their more permanent home on the sea. Even the supremely loyal and obedient sailors of the emperor might have allowed a small taste of trepidation to invade their almost ritualistic exuberance at being given the opportunity to fight and die for their divine leader. Admiral Toyoda knew that his men would fight to the last man in battle; but, as added insurance, as the fleet sailed for combat, the emotional trump card was played. The ultimate reference point for a Nipponese mariner was Admiral Togo's spectacular victory over the Russian Baltic Fleet at Tsushima Strait in 1905. This was the Japanese Trafalgar, and Togo was the Nipponese Horatio Nelson exerting a nautical influence far beyond the grave. Now, as the Mobile Fleet steamed north along the Philippine coast and prepared to enter the open sea, Toyoda sent the inspirational message of Togo to his modern descendants: "The rise and fall of Imperial Japan depends on this one battle. Every man shall do his utmost."[3]

As these Nelsonian phrases reverberated through the decks and ready rooms of Mobile Fleet, Commander R. D. Risser was peering through the periscope of submarine *Flying Fish* at the entrance to San Bernardino Straits when he saw an enormous train of vessels steaming purposefully into the open sea. Minutes later, the air crackled with radio reports of the sighting to Spruance's flagship, *Indianapolis,* and the fog began to lift still more with subsequent reports from *Seahorse* and *Cavalla.*

Almost immediately, high-level conferences were initiated among Spruance, Marc Mitscher, and their staffs. A rapid-fire succession of decisions was issued. First, the invasion of Guam, scheduled for June 18, was postponed indefinitely; the troops of the 27th Division ticketed as a reserve pool for the operation would instead be landed to assist the hard-pressed Marines on Saipan. Second, a major effort would be made to offload as many supplies as possible from the support ships in the next two days before they would be ordered to retire at least 200 miles eastward to lessen their vulnerability to a Japanese end run. Oldendorf's battleships, supported by three cruisers, would form a protective screen 25 miles north of Saipan to protect the beachhead and the invasion fleet. Finally, the almost two dozen escort carriers would assume exhaustive responsibility for the close air support of ground actions and allow the main carrier fleet to concentrate on destroying Mobile Fleet.[4]

By 2:15 on the afternoon of June 17, the conferences were over, the decisions had been made, and Raymond Spruance issued his battle orders:

> Our air will first knock out enemy carriers, then will attack enemy
> battleships and cruisers to slow or divide them. Battle line will de-
> stroy enemy fleet either by fleet action, if the enemy elects to fight,
> or by sinking slowed or crippled ship if enemy retreats. Action
> against the enemy must be pushed vigorously by all hands to ensure
> complete destruction of his fleet. Destroyers running short of fuel
> may be returned to Saipan if necessary for refueling.[5]

Now, as Spruance orchestrated the strategy to annihilate the advancing enemy fleet, the tactics of the engagement would rest heavily on the
shoulders of Marc Mitscher and Willis Lee, who would be responsible
for the air and surface portions of the imminent battle. The commander of Fifth Fleet demonstrated his confidence in his lieutenants when
he issued a terse direction to Mitscher with a copy to Lee: "Desire you
proceed at your discretion selecting dispositions and movements best
calculated to meet the enemy under the most advantageous conditions.
I shall issue general directions when necessary and leave details to you
and Admiral Lee."[6]

If Marc Mitscher had grown tired of commanding ships at sea, he
could have thrived at playing a grizzled old mariner in Hollywood
films on any theme from crusty pirate to humble lobsterman. Mitscher
wasn't particularly old; he was fifty-seven in 1944, but a combination
of constant exposure to salt breeze and a heavy chain-smoking habit
gave him the appearance of a truly Ancient Mariner. The Wisconsin
native had grown up in the decidedly nonmaritime environment of
Oklahoma City, attended Annapolis, and earned the Navy Cross in
1919 for piloting a Curtiss flying boat across the Atlantic to the Azores.
He later commanded *Hornet* during Jimmy Doolittle's daring raid on
Tokyo and the subsequent battle of Midway, and became air commander on Guadalcanal during the Solomons campaign.

Now Mitscher had gone from the command of one carrier to responsibility for fifteen flattops, and this small, slight man was quickly
emerging as an authentic hero. One of the first senior command officers to wear a baseball cap on his bridge, he had become one of the

most respected and popular men in the navy; certainly aircrews and support units thought of him as a "sailor's admiral." With a twinkle in his eye that gave hints of his unruly escapades at the Naval Academy, he would share cigarettes, jokes, and laughter with men of any rank, but beneath that veneer was a keen tactical leader. Now a man who was sometimes called "Popeye" behind his back was carefully evaluating the possible avenues of approach that the enemy might use to attack the American fleet.[7]

Ozawa's first option was to approach eastward from Davao, in the Philippines, using the substantial air cover from bases in the region as a protective umbrella for a strike up from the southwest. Second, he could approach from the northwest from the general direction of Luzon. Third, he could steam directly east across the Philippine Sea and depend on the greater range of his scout planes to discover the Americans and strike a first blow before Spruance was fully able to retaliate.

Mitscher tended to downplay the thrust from the northwest because it provided the enemy with the smallest degree of land-based air cover and would make Ozawa completely dependent on his own carrier air. He was also more confident than Spruance that Oldendorf's battleships could at least temporarily counter the threat posed by a portion of the enemy fleet of hooking around the main American fleet to get among the transports. Thus, the Task Force 58 commander concentrated on meeting a thrust from the west or southwest and began his long-range searches in those directions.

On the western end of the Philippine Sea, Ozawa concentrated his fleet for final refueling and began sending out scout planes from his most easterly frontier, now 750 miles from the Saipan invasion beaches. The Mobile Fleet commander was pursuing a relatively leisurely course because he wanted to provide Admiral Kakuji Kakuta with plenty of opportunity to deploy his land-based air armada against the enemy fleet. The exuberant, optimistic Kakuta was convinced that his land-based naval air fleet headquarters on Tinian would more than make up for the fifteen-to-nine American advantage in carriers. Kakuta was under Toyoda's orders to launch a massive six-hundred-plane air assault on Fifth Fleet and eliminate at least one third of the enemy's carriers and aircraft before Ozawa's Mobile Fleet was committed to battle.

Yet, even with this promise of massive land-based air intervention, Jisaburo Ozawa was deeply troubled by an enormous handicap that would exert a major impact on the upcoming battle. If Raymond Spruance was tethered to some extent to the invasion fleet off the coast of Saipan, Ozawa was leashed to an even harsher master, namely, the unraveling fuel supply line of the Japanese Empire. Before leaving Tawi Tawi, the Mobile Fleet had filled its fuel bunkers with the volatile, unrefined petroleum directly from the East Indies oil fields. Not only did this fuel play havoc with the performance of the ship's engines but even this supply was problematic because the fleet was now short of oilers to provide additional amounts. This meant that even if Ozawa wanted to organize the complex, multipronged engagement that Spruance feared was being initiated, there was actually only enough petroleum for a single run at the enemy. Ozawa could only steam his fleet into a position that was within the range of his planes while still outside the range of the Americans and throw everything he had at the enemy in one throw of the dice. There would be no diversionary thrust, multiple approaches, or sham attacks. The future of the war in the Pacific would be determined by one action in one place. The commander of the Mobile Fleet would have to maximize the advantage provided by the aircraft designers, who gave the Imperial Navy lighter, longer-ranged planes at a cost in plane and pilot survivability. If only Ozawa could use this advantage to find Spruance first and then launch a devastating first strike, the unfavorable turn of events in the Pacific might be reversed.

Now, as the two fleets closed on one another, the burden of responsibility was placed on the shoulders of the Japanese and American naval aerial scouts. Admirals of both navies relied heavily on these unsung pilots who performed the less than glamorous but still often dangerous task of locating the enemy before the enemy located them. Naval battles in World War II were played out over an enormous stage of action on which even a massive fleet occupying dozens of square miles was a mere collection of specks in a far vaster ocean. Even when search planes were able to catch a glimpse of the opposing fleet, factors such as cloud cover, enemy antiaircraft fire, and hostile combat air patrols often limited the scouts' ability to supply usable information back to the anxious high command. Admirals had to weigh often incomplete data with a checklist of reasonable questions. Was the group of ships that was detected the entire enemy force or only a portion of its fleet? Were these ships the main attack force or part of a flanking movement? Would the ships continue their present course or veer off in another direction? The scout pilots and aircrew from both fleets shared the same emotional roller coaster of long and boring searches above a monotonous ocean punctuated by short periods of extreme excitement when an unexpected discovery was made and mixed with the danger that came with making the discovery. Sometimes, like Union or Confederate mounted scouts, who often passed one another in dense woods as they rode in opposite directions with the same purpose, American and Japanese scout planes might find themselves in the same cloud patch as they droned back and forth across the Philippine Sea hoping to catch a brief glimpse of activity on the water far below. In this part of the naval chess match that was developing in the sea, the longer-range Imperial planes had an early advantage. At 3:14 p.m. on Sunday, June 18, 1944, Search Plane 15 radioed: "Enemy task force including carriers sighted."[8]

An exultant Jisaburo Ozawa did some rapid calculations and confirmed that by the next morning he would be in range to attack Task Force 58 before the American could locate his own fleet.

The man who would match wits with Marc Mitscher now made his final preparations to initiate the most monumental carrier engagement in naval history. Ozawa ordered his captains to close the distance between the Mobile Fleet and Task Force 58 to 400 miles and hold that interval during the night in expectation of an early-morning attack on Monday, June 14. Then he broke radio silence to inform Admiral Kakuta that he should initiate a massive land-based air attack at first light to force the Americans to counter threats from several directions at once. Finally he double checked the deployment of his mobile fleet.

Ozawa confirmed that his van force under Vice Admiral Takeo Kurita maintained a constant distance of 100 miles in front of the rest of the fleet. Admiral Kurita's three carriers *Chitose, Chiyoda,* and *Zuiho* had been surrounded by most of the antiaircraft firepower of the Imperial Navy in the expectation that, as enemy air formation flew westward toward the main fleet, they would be decimated by the mass firepower of super battleships *Yamato* and *Musashi,* conventional battleships *Haruna* and *Kongo,* and cruisers *Atago, Takao, Maya,* and *Chokai.*

One hundred miles farther west, Ozawa directed the operations of two more carrier divisions from brand-new flagship *Taiho.* Carrier Division 1 deployed to the flagship along with the two remaining veterans of Pearl Harbor, *Shokaku* and *Zuikaku,* shepherded by cruisers *Myoko* and *Haguro.* Carrier Division 2, under the command of the sergeants but vaguely insubordinate, *Takro Joshima,* frontier carriers *Junyo, Hiyo,* and *Ryuho* escorted by battleship *Nagato* and cruiser *Mogami.*

If one of Ozawa's scout planes had been able to fly 400 miles eastward and had been fitted with twenty-first-century night vision equipment, that Imperial pilot would have seen the curious sight of five distinct circles of ships advancing toward the Mobile Fleet. The van of Task Force 58 had Willis Lee's powerful fast battleship flotilla with *Indiana* occupying the center of the circle followed by *Washington, North Carolina, Iowa, New Jersey, South Dakota,* and *Alabama.* This formation was essentially a floating antiaircraft platform poised to challenge enemy aircraft from almost every direction.

Roughly 6 miles to the north and east of the circle of fire was that most forward carrier formation, Task Force 58.4, commanded by rear Admiral W. K. Harrill and built around fleet carrier *Essex* and light carriers *Langley* and *Cowpens.* Six miles behind Harrill was J. M. "Jocko" Clark's Task Force 58.1 centered on fleet carriers *Hornet* and *Yorktown* and light carries *Belleau Wood* and *Bataan.* Six miles south of this wheel of ships was rear Admiral J. W. Reeves's Task Force 58.3, formed on fleet carriers *Enterprise* and *Lexington* and light carriers *San Jacinto* and *Princeton*. The same distance south of Reeves's fleet was rear Admiral A. E. Montgomery's Task Force 58.4, deploying fleet carriers *Bunker Hill* and *Wasp* and light carriers *Monterey* and *Cabot*.

Thus by dawn on June 19, a fleet of more than one hundred carriers, battleships, cruisers, and destroyers was moving in a complex unison of circular formations spread out over perhaps 60 square miles of ocean. This was a visibly moving projection of American naval power in the third year of World War II and everyone from Raymond Strudner down to a novice seaman squinting through the sights of a 20 mm antiaircraft gun was confident that this was a force that would not stop advancing until it entered Tokyo Bay. Yet Strudner knew something that the young gunner might not have as readily appreciated. Naval battles were won by more than firepower or number of ships alone. Two years earlier, a greatly outnumbered American fleet had mauled a much larger but supremely overconfident Imperial fleet off the island of Midway. The Americans generally had slower planes, inexperienced pilots, and fewer aircraft, yet they won decisively. Now the tables were turned, but the sea gods were capriciously unpredictable; Jisaburo Ozawa hoped that the intangible factors providing victory in battle would line up in favor of his experienced pilots. At 3:00 a.m. on the sultry predawn morning of June 19, 1944, the Imperial carriers began to shift into battle formation and steam into the wind for multiple takeoffs. The greatest carrier battle in history was about to commence, and few men on either side could predict its outcome.[9]

12.

DRAGONS OVER THE SEA

A T 7:30 A.M. ON JUNE 19, a single Aichi R. 13A reconnaissance floatplane, one of forty-three scout planes launched by Ozawa that morning, was just returning from its outbound search pattern when it spotted two carriers and four battleships on the water far below. The pilot reported the enemy ship as 160 miles due west of Saipan, which in turn put the enemy 380 miles from Ozawa's flagship. The admiral was ecstatic; his quarry was well within the range of his attack planes, yet he was safely beyond the operational limits of the Americans. As the Mobile Fleet commander now began the complex ritual of launching his formidable attack force toward Task Force 58, the first in a grim series of misfortunes struck Ozawa.

Ozawa could not expect to hold the enemy outside of striking range for very long, and he realized that his best chance for success was to launch a massive and coordinated initial air strike that would rip through the enemy carriers before they could fully respond. In an act of bravado and insubordination, however, Rear Admiral Sueo Obayashi, commander of the 3rd Carrier Division, followed up on the intelligence from the returning Jake and ordered his carriers *Chitose*, *Chiyoda,* and *Zuiho* to launch their attack planes before Ozawa issued a similar fleet command.[1]

Now at 8:25 a.m., sixteen Zeke fighters, forty-five Zeke fighter bombers, and eight Jill torpedo planes began lifting from their decks, unknown to the senior admiral.

These sixty-nine aircraft represented a powerful force on their own and would have been a huge threat to the relatively modest American carrier force deployed near Midway two years earlier. But now Spruance had more than a hundred warships, including fifteen carriers, that could put enough interceptors into the air to overwhelm the attackers. Ozawa had envisioned the need for at least two hundred planes in his initial punch, but now the Japanese thrust would come piecemeal. The Mobile Fleet commander waited an additional half hour to collect more information on the disposition and location of the American fleet; when no new intelligence arrived, he ordered 128 aircraft from *Taiho, Shokaku,* and *Zuikaku* into launch positions. Nearly two hundred planes were now heading eastward, but they were in two distinct formations that were at best mutually supporting. The American Combat Air Patrols orbiting over Task Force 58 had been provided with their first major advantage on this first day of the largest carrier battle in history.

At just a few minutes before 10:00 a.m., radar sets on the battleship *Alabama* picked up Obayashi's air group 140 miles out and other ships quickly verified the contact. Lookouts now peered in all approach directions as blue-clad plane handlers, green-clad catapult men and firefighters in white asbestos suits rushed to their stations. Soon, newly launched Hellcats used every ounce of horsepower to climb to ceilings of 25,000 feet and began forming a protective screen 50 miles out knowing they would have the advantage of altitude and their backs to the sun.

As the Hellcats orbited the outer periphery of the fleet, a junior grade lieutenant on *Lexington* huddled over a radio set and provided the pilots above with one of the major trump cards of the battle. Lieutenant Charles A. Sims had a rare skill for an American naval officer: He could speak perfect Japanese. Sims was now monitoring the radio of the approaching planes and passing every bit of relevant information from the Imperial pilots to the waiting adversaries.[2]

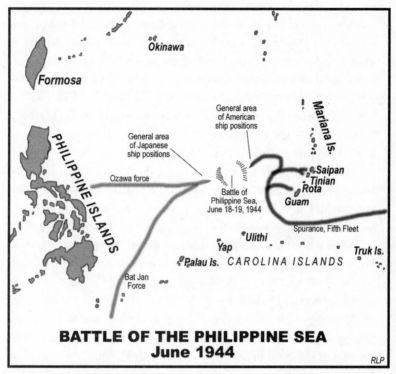

Battle of the Philippine Sea

While dozens of American fighters charged their guns and checked fuel gauges, the majority of Nimitz's formidable air fleet was essentially useless for the first stage of the battle. The hundreds of dive-bombers and torpedo planes were vital for operations against the enemy carriers but were of little value in defending against a Nipponese air attack. Therefore, Mitscher ordered every flyable attack plane to orbit well east of the fleet, relatively out of harm's way, until it was the Americans' turn to throw their first punch.

In the half hour after *Alabama*'s first radar sighting, 140 fighters had been launched from carriers to join the eighty-two Hellcats already on combat air patrol station. Now 222 dark-blue planes circled high over on an equally dark-blue ocean waiting for the first sign that the enemy had finally arrived. At first, the American pilots were perplexed; at the speed with which the Japanese were approaching, the battle should have begun, but not one hostile plane had been sighted. The reason for the delay was simple, and yet it was a profound clue to why Japan was losing the war. The approaching Nipponese formation was dominated by newly trained pilots who were brave and eager but possessed only minimal knowledge about how to launch an air attack on a huge enemy fleet. Now Japanese squadron commanders had to utilize valuable time and fuel in forming rendezvous points and giving their charges instructions and exhortations, and they only sluggishly transformed their formations from observers to attackers. For more than a quarter of an hour, time seemed to stand still as dozens of Imperial planes virtually halted 70 miles from Task Force 58 and awaited the final order to attack. Twenty miles away, incredulous Hellcat pilots marked time as they listened to Lieutenant Sims's translation of enemy orders and battle cries. Then, in a moment of pure cinematic drama, the Imperial planes gave a final waggle of their wings to commanders and began their final run in toward the dozens of ships steaming far below.[3]

Sixty-nine planes represented an impressive concentration of air power, but only sixteen of them were functioning as escort fighters that were capable of engaging in a dogfight on anything approaching even terms with the Hellcats. Thus, in the first stage of the battle, the Americans held a formidable fourteen-to-one advantage in fighter-to-fighter confrontations. While this discrepancy appeared to be a suicidal equation on the surface, in reality the American interceptions were scattered over a huge aerial battlefield and relatively few planes could engage the enemy at any one moment. The result was an almost choreographed series of confrontations that would flare into extreme violence for seconds, or minutes at most, as Nipponese aviators engaged successive groups of aerial challengers and broke free to penetrate to the next level of conflict or fall from the duel wreathed in smoke and flames.

World War II air battles were in many respects multidimensional chess matches in which several fierce duels could be taking place in the same prism of air space but at a variety of altitudes. Escort fighters fought furious battles to keep the interceptors occupied, and, they hoped, destroy most of them, while buying precious time for the more vulnerable bombers and torpedo planes to get close enough to the enemy fleet to have a reasonable chance of inflicting serious or fatal damage on their chosen target. On the other hand, the interceptors were intent on ensuring that the intruders never had the opportunity to launch their bombs or torpedoes. Thus, in one sense, attack formations wanted fighters to engage in dog fights because they distracted the interceptors, but defending aircraft were interested only in engaging the escort fighters to the extent that these aircraft blocked their access to the real threat to the fleet below.

Obayashi's formation met its first challenge 55 miles from the fleet when Commander Charles Brewer of *Essex* spotted two formations of sixteen fighter bombers each at 20,000 and 18,000 feet. Brewer's contingent of eight fighters was outnumbered four-to-one, but the enemy planes were weighed down with bombs that hindered their maneuverability. Hellcats and Zeros swirled in a series of aerial corkscrews as altimeters unwound rapidly toward 400 or 500 feet. Brewer himself picked off four Zekes in succession, dodging exploding debris while Lieutenant J. P. Carr worked the opposite end of the enemy formation. As Carr rolled down toward sea level, he engaged in five separate dogfights that left five Zeroes spiraling into the sea, and by the time he started to climb higher, he counted seventeen oil slicks dotting the blue sea.[4]

This opening round resulted in a devastating loss of attack planes as *Essex* pilots scored twenty victories at no loss to themselves. The Japanese formation had just entered what would soon be seen as an endless gauntlet of fire.

As *Essex* planes ripped the Japanese formation from one direction, eight of *Hornet*'s fighters caught the survivors as they grimly flew eastward. The pilots of the VF22 were initially surprised to find that so many Zekes were carrying bomb loads; these made them easy targets even if they represented more of a threat to the fleet than conventional fighters. Escort Zeroes were ignored whenever possible as the *Hornet* contingent slashed through the formation, sending an additional dozen Imperial planes smoking toward a watery grave.

As the battle swirled high above, American radar sets displayed surviving enemy planes moving within 20 miles of the fleet when a company of eight cowpen planes entered the fray. The escort Zeroes lashed out at their tormentors in a brutal dogfight that destroyed a pair of Hellcats in return for four Zekes wiped from the order of battle; but this part of the attack formation paid an even higher price for this modest victory when five members of the slim line of torpedo bombers took a final plunge.

The first Japanese strike force had finally managed to get close enough to see their targets below; but to maneuver into some sort of attack position had sacrificed forty-one planes at negligible losses to the American fighter screen. There were now almost ten American planes in the air for each enemy Imperial aircraft, and the only thing that prevented almost immediate annihilation was that the American interceptors were far less concentrated than the Japanese attackers. Even the process of setting up for bombing on torpedoes would cost another half dozen planes to dozens of American fighters nipping around the edges of the formation. By the time the Niponnese plan had arrived directly over Lee's Task Group, barely twenty planes were still in the battle. Perhaps a dozen of these survivors settled on *Indiana* and *South Dakota* for their attention, and both ships jinked and weaved as the shower of lethal cargoes dropped from the sky. *Indiana* emerged with no bombs closer than 200 yards away, but *South Dakota* was not so fortunate; a single bomber broke through a wall of antiaircraft fire and caused a major explosion on the battleship. There were more than fifty casualties, twenty-seven of them fatal.[5]

One ship in the American fleet had felt the full fury and terror of being at the receiving end of an enemy carrier assault, and a moderately large number of these Americans would not survive the experience. But even the normal functioning of *South Dakota* was unaffected by this disaster, and it would prove the only tangible accomplishment of Obayashi's now disintegrating formation.

Then, as a pillar of smoke rose from *South Dakota,* surviving Japanese planes in groups of two or three turned westward and headed for the relative safety of their carriers. Eight escort fighters and nineteen attack planes were still in the air, although many limped homeward with bullet holes and coughing, dying engines. The attack on the battleship had added two more interceptors to the two Hellcats already shot down, but in essence the first phase of the battle had resulted in a ten-to-one loss rate that would continue for much of the remainder of the day. A second and larger attack formation, the one actually ordered by Ozawa himself, was already making its way toward Task Force 58; but this part of the battle would be, if possible, even more devastating to Japanese hopes than Obayashi's ill-timed gesture.

As Ozawa supervised the launch of what would be the second Japanese attack of the day, the first under his direct orders, another officer was taking an avid interest in the activities aboard *Taiho.* This superb carrier was the Japanese answer to the *Essex,* the exception being that the *Essex* would have twelve new duplicate consorts with eleven more in various stages of construction; Taiho was a "super carrier" and had no immediate prospects for comparisons. The ship was a perfect vessel to be the communications center of the Mobile Fleet and boasted a larger air group, more watertight compartments, and more speed than any other carrier in the Imperial Navy. Now, as she launched her first strike of the battle, her every move was being carefully noted by Commander J. W. Blanchard of the submarine *Albacore*. As Imperial planes climbed skyward from the *Albacore*'s flight deck, Blanchard brushed aside the problems caused by the failure of the boat's Torpedo Data Computer and, hoping that at least one would hit, fired six torpedoes. Four streaked harmlessly by the flagship; the fifth was rendered useless when an observant dive-bomber pilot, Ensign Sakio Komatsu, saw the weapon closing with the carrier and performed a suicide dive into the torpedo that temporarily saved the *Taiho*. However, one torpedo continued on its deadly approach and hit *Taiho* far forward while *Albacore* made a desperate dive to escape now fully alerted escort vessels.[6]

Like the initial reaction to the *Titanic*'s collision with an iceberg, everyone from Ozawa down to sailors in the damage-control parties breathed a huge sigh of relief when it was apparent that no vital point had been hit and that the watertight compartments had localized the flooding. However, without their knowledge, the pride of the Imperial Navy had been turned into a floating powder keg just waiting for someone to light the match.

The rest of Ozawa's strike force, minus the gallant ensign, droned over the waters of the Philippine Sea as Lieutenant Commander Tarwi led them over the outer limits of friendly ships, the wayward C Force. Suddenly, inexplicably, the very antiaircraft batteries that Ozawa depended upon to decimate Mitscher's plans as they flew westward toward the Mobile Fleet hurried into action against planes flying eastward toward the enemy. Kurita's batteries proved their accuracy when Tarwi's force was literally decimated as two planes tumbled into the sea and eight other aircraft staggered back to the main fleet to land as floating wrecks. Ten nearly irreplaceable planes had been lost before the attack force had even cleared friendly waters, and the formation's luck would only get worse.

At 11:00 a.m., Tarwi began the same cumbersome deployment and orientation activities that his predecessor had employed earlier. Lieutenant Sims carefully monitored radios and passed every shred of information to the coordinator of Combat Air Patrol operations.

This time, Commander David MacCampbell of *Essex* was the tip of the American defense spear as he led nine *Essex* Hellcats into ten times as many Japanese raiders, who were now 45 miles from the task force. Leaving four planes to provide top cover, the remaining six interceptors flew up and down the long train of enemy planes particularly intent on flaming the Yokosuka D4Y dive-bombers that fortified much of the offensive threat in this second Japanese thrust. While other wingmen tangled with the defending Zeroes, MacCampbell emerged as an almost instant ace after knocking down five of the bomb-laden Judys. His comrades were hardly underemployed: Among them, they flamed another fifteen planes, mostly Zeroes, in perhaps five minutes of multiple dogfights.[7]

Despite the tremendous losses, Tarwi's force was actually having more luck in closing on the fleet than its predecessor. The formation commander was able to deploy his surviving planes in an echelon of descending altitudes, thus forcing the defenders to scatter their own forces to meet each successive threat. Now the battle of the Philippine Sea was turning into a twentieth-century version of a series of Old West gunfights, but on levels from 24,000 feet down to wave height. *Bataan*'s VF50 engaged in a running gunfight just above the ocean as five Zeroes and one Hellcat crashed into the sea only seconds after they were hit. Pilots from *Bunker Hill* produced the same kill-loss ratio in a higher-altitude duel.

This multidimensional dogfight was ending with far more Zekes than Hellcats taking a final plunge toward the sea; but the sacrifices of the Zeroes had allowed perhaps twenty dive-bombers and torpedo planes to penetrate the airspace directly above the American fleet, the interceptors initially being too scattered to offer massive immediate interference. Lieutenant William Lamb of *Princeton* found himself alone with five operable guns confronting twelve Jill torpedo planes preparing to make their attack run. After radioing for help, he waded in and shot down three with his last bullets while two newly arrived *Enterprise* planes bagged two more.[8]

At least some survivors were able to target the huge ships of Lee's fast battleship group. *Alabama, Indiana,* and *Iowa* all received the unwanted attention that produced near hits by torpedoes and bombs, the spectacular geysers being uncomfortably close to the American spectators. Then the battle swung eastward to the carrier groups with *Enterprise* and *Princeton* the first recipients of unwanted attention. *Enterprise* veered from a bomber 750 yards to starboard and then narrowly avoided a torpedo that exploded in the ship's wake. *Princeton* barely dodged a plane exploding into the water 300 yards away.

As sailors from these ships breathed a collective sigh of relief, it was the turn of *Wasp* and *Bunker Hill* to undergo trial by fire, and for the latter luck finally ran out. A single bomber that was in the process of being shredded by antiaircraft batteries smashed into the sea just off the vessel's port elevator; a massive concussion wave was produced that severed fuel lines and initiated fires in ready rooms. Two men died and seventy-two were injured in this nautical inferno.

As the crew of *Bunker Hill* treated the dozens of injured shipmates and fought the deadly fires, hundreds of sailors on other ships suddenly noticed the eerie quiet when the second Japanese attack dissipated like the end of a ferocious thunderstorm. American planes, now almost all short on fuel, sought out their home carriers and began the laborious process of landing and securing from action. Some planes were landed by wounded pilots; other pilots who ditched into the sea calmly awaited rescue, and a few airmen never returned at all. The Philippine Sea had claimed nearly another one hundred Japanese planes as aircraft emblazoned with the distinctive red sun either burned fiercely or slowly plummeted to the sea floor. Sixteen fighters, eleven dive-bombers, and four torpedo planes, all that was left of Ozawa's second wave, sputtered westward, many with damage so severe that they would be dumped over the side as soon as the pilots were safely out of their cockpits. Ninety-seven planes failed to return, and their commander chose for the moment to insist that many of them had landed at Guam or Tinian after decimating the American carrier fleet.

But although Ozawa effectively veered from reality, he was about to be rudely awakened by a new disaster developing literally under his feet. Damage control parties were furiously attempting to counter the impact of *Albacore*'s torpedo attack as the pungent odor of aviation fuel sloshing around the hangar deck reminded at least some crew members that their ship was still potentially a floating firebomb. Then one damage-control officer hit upon the bright expedient of ordering all the ventilation ducts on the ship to be opened to dissipate the fumes seeping throughout the flight area. The fumes were spread more evenly through the vessel, but the process simply expanded the tinderbox from a relatively contained area to the entire ship. The huge vessel was now a floating powder keg that was about to explode, but not before Jisaburo Ozawa endured another crisis in a seemingly unending series of crises on this first day of A-GO.

Ozawa's interlude at the former American naval base at Tawi Tawi had been a disaster for Imperial destroyer squadrons because nearly one fourth of the vessels were sunk or put out of action near the port. Now the gaps in the Nipponese destroyer screen were reaching alarming proportions. While damage-control parties on *Taiho* struggled to cope with the vessels' encounter with *Albacore,* the submarine *Cavalla* slipped through another gap in the Japanese screen to track other prey. *Cavalla*'s skipper, Commander James Kossler, surfaced to periscope depth to discover carrier *Shokaku* peeping the launch combat air patrols while the destroyer *Usakazr* circled in a lonely antisubmarine vigil. *Cavalla* easily penetrated the porous barrier and launched six torpedoes toward the unsuspecting carrier. At 12:20 p.m., four warriors slammed into the vessel and fires broke out the length and breadth of this survivor of the glory days of Pearl Harbor. Damage-control parties were quickly overwhelmed by far more destruction than they could contain, and as the ship's bow settled lower in the water, a fire in a magazine ripped out the insides of the ship.

While captains of seriously or moderately damaged American carriers concentrated on saving as many crew members as possible, Japanese masters were notoriously cavalier about abandon ship procedures. The *Shokaku* was soon enduring a final agony amazingly similar in some respects to the sinking of the RMS *Titanic.* In an ironic comparison, the Japanese carrier initiated a final plunge into the Pacific two hours and forty minutes after the torpedoes struck, exactly the same time span remaining to the British liner after it struck the iceberg. Similarly, almost an identical percentage of those aboard were rescued as the 737 survivors of a complement of 2,100 closely matched the 705 souls rescued from the 2,200 persons on the great disaster forty-two years earlier.

But Ozawa scarcely had time to digest the loss of one of the two remaining survivors of Pearl Harbor when disaster struck much closer to home. At 3:30 p.m., thirty minutes after *Shokaku* sank beneath the waves, a violent explosive tore through the flagship; huge sections of the hull were reduced to punctured, twisted pieces of metal that were rapidly corroded by foaming seawater. While dazed survivors veered between jumping overboard and dying for the emperor, Ozawa made plans to go down with *Taiho*. However, in the almost perverse choreography of Japanese ritual suicide, Ozawa found himself trapped in a strange dilemma. It was always assumed that Nipponese captains would go down with their ships, and *Taiho*'s master was thus assured a reserved position in this ritual of honor. But Ozawa was not a ship's captain; he was commander of most of the Imperial fleet and might very well need the emperor's express permission to kill himself. Thus, the admiral's staff said emotional farewells to *Taiho*'s captain and helped Ozawa carry the emperor's portrait to a ladder to implement transfer to another vessel. Ozawa and his key subordinates took up temporary residence in the Imperial cruiser *Haguro*, but 1,650 of his crew would go down with *Taiho*; a mere five hundred seamen were plucked from the ocean.

By late afternoon on June 19, Ozawa had lost two of his premier carriers along with more than 3,000 men and about two dozen planes that joined them below the sea. The Japanese admiral believed that his pilots had already sunk three or four enemy carriers, and he still felt the exhilaration of a leader who somehow still seemed to be winning the battle. Admiral Joshima's Carrier Division 2 was still largely intact with *Junyo*, *Hiyo*, and *Ryuho*'s naval air group capable of launching nearly fifty planes for a third assault on the enemy. Another series of orders flashed through the ozone and twenty-five fighter bombers, seven torpedoes, and fifteen fighter escorts clawed their way into the air and headed eastward toward the "badly damaged" American fleet. But although most of the planes in the first two attacks were at least able to make contact with the American fleet, Joshima's squadrons failed to remain together as a concentrated threat and twenty-seven of the forty-seven planes became hopelessly separated and were forced to turn back for lack of fuel.

The twenty aircraft that actually located Task Force 58 found a daunting gauntlet of hostile planes between them and their primary targets. As the score of planes intruded on the periphery of American airspace, twelve Hellcats from *Hornet* and four more from *Yorktown* pounced like two voracious birds of prey; six Zeroes plummeted toward the sea in perhaps five minutes of battle.[9]

The surviving planes were fortunate enough to encounter a series of heavy cloud formations that temporarily hid them from more interceptors and allowed a breathing space to organize an attack strategy. However, most of the Imperial planes were either escort fighters or aircraft that had jettisoned their bombs in the dogfights so that the entire offensive power of *Joshima*'s raiders consisted of a single Zero that still carried a bomb. While other aircraft flew interference, the lone Nipponese pilot targeted *Essex* steaming below, instituted a power dive, dropped a bomb 600 yards from the vessel, and promptly disintegrated under the fire of an angry swarm of interceptors. The rest of the air armada, now divested of any remaining ship-killing capacity, promptly ducked back into the clouds and veered westward toward a friendly deck. Forty of the original forty-seven planes would actually return to the Japanese fleet, but their total impact on the battle of the Philippine Sea was exactly one large waterspout nearly half a mile from the nearest American vessel.

Now Ozawa was down to only one remaining card to play in this rapidly unraveling game called A-GO. The commander of the mobile fleet ordered all planes that weren't already assigned to Combat Air Patrol to form up for one final mighty thrust that would surely ensure an Imperial victory by nightfall.

Like Robert E. Lee before ordering George Pickett to launch his gallant but futile charge at Gettysburg, Ozawa was convinced that the enemy was near the breaking point and needed just one more push towards disaster. This aerial shove would be determined by twenty-seven Val dive-bombers, nine Judy dive-bombers, six Jill torpedo planes, ten Zeke fighter bombers, and thirty fighters for escort. These eighty-two planes represented essentially the last substantial carrier air power that Japan could utilize in World War II.

The pilots launched to the cheers of hundreds of Japanese sailors; indeed, they seemed to have a collective hunch that this was the attack that would turn the tide of war for the empire. But as these planes displaying the Imperial red sun approached the coordinates given for the American fleet, they were shocked to discover nothing more than an endless expanse of undulating blue sea. In a breakdown of command discipline that would plague the Japanese in the Marianas campaign, the air group split into three formations, forty-nine planes heading to Guam to somehow launch an attack from that island. Eight planes promptly turned and headed back to the carriers, and the remaining twenty-five aircraft decided to continue eastward in an attempt to locate the enemy.[10]

The plucky band of pilots who chose to tempt the fates by flying perilously close to the limit of their fuel tanks were rewarded in a perverse way by edging close enough to the American fleet to be intercepted by planes from *Monterey, Wasp,* and *Cabot.* Planes began their inevitable flaming descent into the Pacific, but nine dive-bombers slipped through the aerial cordon and scored near hits on *Wasp* and *Bunker Hill.*

The planes heading for Guam fared little better. As the formation made a final approach for that island, the pilots were shocked to discover more than fifty Hellcats circling above Orote Airfield, eagerly awaiting another group of victims. As the Hellcats slashed through the stunned Imperial pilots, several gull-winged Corsairs that had been providing air cover for pilot rescue activities joined the melee. A Japanese soldier peered into the sky to view the one-sided confrontation and admitted, "I was unable to watch dry-eyed as plane after plane crashed and burned as the tragedy of war never seemed so real."[11]

Guam would receive considerably more attention from American airmen in the coming weeks, but for now the pilots withdrew as fuel and ammunition ran out and the rising victory total provided ever more exuberant discussions for the carrier ready rooms. Daylight was fading rapidly and the first day of the battle of the Philippine Sea was finally over. Now it remained for Spruance and Ozawa to tally their losses and make vital decisions on the future course of the engagement. Perhaps somewhat mercifully, Ozawa's communication system on *Haguro* was erratic and primitive, and he did not yet know the awful truth: Of 374 carrier planes that the admiral had sent into battle on this late spring day, 244 would never return to their ships. The air battle over Orote Airfield had destroyed another fifty Japanese aircraft and an additional twenty-two had gone down with *Taiho* and *Shokaku*. Thus, in the worst day in the history of Japanese carrier aviation, 316 planes were destroyed and two dozen more were written off as total wrecks. This loss of 340 planes was the equivalent of the loss of the entire air fleet sent to attack Pearl Harbor thirty months earlier. In addition, Ozawa had lost two of the three most powerful carriers remaining in the Imperial navy without a single American aircraft even approaching the Nipponese fleet. With the exception of *Zuikaku,* now the soul survivor of the Pearl Harbor attack, the Imperial carrier force was centered upon a combination of retrofitted converted cruisers, light carriers, and other jury-rigged vessels that simply did not have the offensive capability of the six fleet carriers that had sailed towards Hawaii on that fateful December morning two years earlier. For better or worse, however, Ozawa knew only part of this dreary litany of disaster in the twilight of this Monday evening, and for a short time he would be permitted to continue the dream of a spectacular victory built on many American carriers burning furiously in the tropical night sky.

Several hundred miles to the east, Raymond Spruance had more specific facts, and most of these were spectacularly positive.[12]

A battle had been fought and young Americans had died. This would not be a bloodless victory. However, given the enormity of the confrontation, the American casualty list was amazingly short. Twenty-two American planes had been shot down by Japanese fighters and Imperial antiaircraft batteries on Guam, the most deadly spot of the battle being the airspace over Orote Airfield. Six aircraft were total write-offs when they landed, twenty-seven aircrews and thirty-one ships' personnel had died in action. But no American ship was in danger of sinking and most damaged ships were operating normally. The calculus of the first day of the battle of the Philippine Sea had been remarkably stark and simple. All day long, American pilots had been shooting down Japanese pilots at a ten-to-one rate, an equation that would eliminate Japanese carrier airpower in a remarkably short time if the battle continued much longer. Air combat had now come full circle since Pearl Harbor. On that Sunday morning, roughly ten American planes had been destroyed for every Imperial aircraft lost. However, the Japanese pilots had attained that stupendous ratio largely by shooting at parked planes bunched wingtip to wingtip. This reversed ratio had been achieved in full-scale air-to-air combat when the enemy was fully prepared for battle and flying in large formations.

Raymond Spruance had chosen to open the battle of the Philippine Sea by fighting a defensive action and had achieved a spectacular defensive victory. Now that the Americans had achieved favorable results in defending their own fleet, the key question facing the American commander was how quickly and how completely should he swing over to the offensive and attack the enemy fleet on its "side" of the Philippine Sea. His opponent had frittered away much of the remaining carrier air power of the Japanese fleet in a battle that so far was as futile as Fredericksburg or Cold Harbor had been to the Union cause eight decades earlier. It was now theoretically possible for Spruance to accomplish a victory of annihilation that would in most respects end the naval war in the Pacific in any traditional sense of a confrontation between two rival fleets.

13

TWILIGHT RAID ON MOBILE FLEET

B Y NIGHTFALL of this day of titanic aerial confrontation, Raymond Spruance and his subordinates were attempting to digest the enormity of the damage they had inflicted on the Imperial naval air service. The commander of the Fifth Fleet had just directed a defensive masterpiece not unlike General George Meade's orchestration of the Union repulse of Pickett's Charge eighty-one years earlier. But unlike that of his Civil War predecessor, Spruance's command was still at nearly 100 percent fighting effectiveness. However, like George Meade, Spruance had to confront the very real challenge of transforming a largely defensive victory into a follow-up annihilation of the mauled enemy forces. Meade's decision concerning an immediate counterattack, which led to the decimation of many of the best regiments in Robert E. Lee's army, had revolved around the wisdom of assaulting an enemy position on Seminary Ridge that was nearly as formidable as the Federal position on Cemetery Ridge. Spruance's major challenge was more mundane and more complex because he had to find his battered enemy in a vast sea using patrol planes that had less range than their enemy counterparts. Spruance was now convinced that he could deal the Imperial Navy a blow from which it would never

173

recover if only he could locate and attack that fleet before it had time to escape.

Throughout this balmy tropical night, Spruance paced in and out of the *Indianapolis*'s flagplot as restless staff officers reluctantly deferred to their commander's strong objections to smoking by quickly extinguishing cigarettes each time he entered the cabin and then quickly relighting seconds after he had left.[1]

Several hundred miles to the west, Misaburo Ozawa's staff was not encumbered with intermittent stoppage of their smoking activities because their commander chain-smoked as intently as his subordinates, but in every other way their stress was even higher than that of their American counterparts. At midnight on June 19–20, Imperial aviation rosters counted only slightly more than a hundred planes currently capable of a dawn takeoff, which averaged out to a meager fourteen planes for each of the seven surviving carriers. But Ozawa and Admiral Toyoda, who had been closely following details of the battle in Tokyo, estimated that Japanese airmen had sunk four American carriers, damaged six others, and destroyed more than five hundred enemy planes. This wildly optimistic estimate implied that the opposing forces were still relatively evenly matched, especially when the availability of Imperial land-based air power was considered.[2]

Toyoda and Ozawa hoped to turn what they considered a drawn battle into an Imperial victory by enticing Spruance far into the western edge of the Philippine Sea so that the Americans could be savaged by great pincers formed by the surviving aircraft of the Mobile Fleet on one side and the formidable land-based air units in the Philippines on the other. Thus, Toyoda ordered Ozawa to spend the next two days refueling the fleet, dispatching severely damaged vessels to safe anchorages, and coordinating attack plans with Admiral Kakuta for the "final" attack on the enemy now scheduled for June 22. After this expected major victory, the Mobile Fleet would be engaged in "mopping up" operations around Saipan as the retreating Americans were hounded eastward. In the curious parallel universe that was Japanese battle assessment, the worst day in naval aviation history had simply not occurred and the "real battle" of the Philippine Sea would be memorialized in Japan on June 22, 1944.[3]

On a continuum of war commanders' impressions of the relative strength of their opponents compared to their own forces, if General George McClellan occupied one end, Toyoda and Ozawa surely could claim a spot on the opposite pole. Although the first commander of the Army of the Potomac generally ascribed superhuman fighting capabilities to his rebel opponents, the senior Japanese admirals minimized American power and maximized alleged losses to Fifth Fleet to a fantastic level. Perhaps a society entertained by surrealistic Kabuki and Nó theatre and energized by belief in an emperor directly descended from a sun god blurred distinctions between reality and fantasy to a greater extent than most Western societies of the time; and surely believing that more than half the enemy carrier fleet was either severely damaged or at the bottom of the ocean was a far more congenial thought than the far starker reality offered. Yet this attitude as played out in the early hours of June 20, 1944, was putting the entire Imperial Navy in real jeopardy of annihilation if only Raymond Spruance had the good luck to discover his adversary while there was still time to inflict fatal damage. The American commander would get his wish but only in the partial sense that would leave the battle of the Philippine Sea as one of the least satisfying major victories in American military history.

The American fleet that was steaming towards the Imperial survivors was very real, almost totally intact, but, fortunately for Ozawa, still not absolutely sure of the enemy's location. All morning and early afternoon on this last day before summer, American search planes droned over the sea in extended search patterns looking in vain for a tell-tale ship's wake. Then, just when it appeared that the enemy had made a clean escape, scout planes equipped with extra belly tanks probed a little further west, broke through a dense cloud cover, and saw the Pagoda masts of their quarry. The great climax of the battle of the Philippine Sea would not occur on the Japanese timetable of June 22, but neither would it be fought on a schedule particularly favorable to American preferences.

Static-laden messages squawked on the radios of American communication centers and maps were consulted; garbled and often contradictory information arrived at the solitary chair occupied by Admiral Marc Mitscher, who began to realize that he would have to make one of the most wrenching decisions of any American commander in World War II. The commander of Task Force 58 had plenty of attack planes available, and these aircraft were flown by superbly trained pilots and aircrew. However, no level of superior numbers or training could counter the harsh reality that the elusive enemy fleet had been detected at the absolute outer limit of the range of American planes and had been discovered so late in the day that most of the return flight would be flown in the appallingly absolute darkness that only night over a vast and unforgiving ocean could present. American planes might very well arrive at their targets, and they might even strike a major blow at the enemy; but even at this time of year this close to the equator darkness would set in far before the pilots could find a safe haven.

At 4:24 p.m. on this Wednesday afternoon, a starkly simple message flashed in ready rooms: "Get the carriers."[4] Normally ebullient pilots spoke in hushed tones as they calculated the probable distances to the enemy carriers they were ordered to destroy. Two hundred and forty war planes waggled their wings and headed towards a sun that was already low on the horizon, but as engines sputtered and misfired and gauges reported operational problems, fourteen pilots broke away from the massive formation and aborted their missions. Now the outcome of the battle was in the hands of pilots and aircrew from ninety-five Hellcats, fifty-four Avengers, fifty-one Helldivers, and twenty-six Dauntlesses. The latter dive-bombers represented the only remaining combat plane that had participated in every carrier engagement of the last two years, and now these veterans of Midway were flying their last mission from American ships. The "hottest" plane of 1942 was now reduced to "venerable" status bordering on obsolescence in a telling microcosm of the ability of the United States to deploy one upgraded model after another in a remarkably brief time.

As the planes began melding into flying formation, the pilots received the sobering information that latest plot reports placed the enemy 60 miles farther west than originally believed, an alarming reality for an attack force that was already flying with no safety margin. Sixty miles may have represented only a few minutes flying time for these fast planes, but ditching a plane 60 miles away from the American fleet in a dark and pitching ocean would almost appear to be the distance from the Earth to the moon for a solitary airman whose world was suddenly reduced to the confines of a tiny rubber life raft.

As the raiding force droned across the water between Task Force 58 and the Mobile Fleet, the refueling Japanese vessels were increasingly drifting into two distinct formations. Admiral Kurita's powerful antiaircraft vessels circled comfortably nearby the carriers *Chitose, Zuiho,* and *Chiyoda* like friendly and determined guard dogs around a sheep's pen threatened by wolves. But although these three light carriers were under the formidable antiaircraft screen provided by two super battleships, two conventional battleships, and several cruisers, this force had drifted so far from the rest of Ozawa's fleet that *Junyo, Hiyo,* and *Ryuho* had only one battleship and a lone cruiser to provide a meager level of direct antiaircraft support.

At 6:25 p.m., a Japanese scout plane reported four groups of raiders approaching the Mobile Fleet. By time the sparse force of Imperial fighters flew towards interception points, the sun was beginning to slip below the horizon. When the first dogfight erupted over the fleet, perhaps twenty minutes of daylight remained on this potentially climactic day of the Pacific naval war. In a supreme effort of repair and refueling, Japanese carrier crew launched sixty-eight fighters into a growing melee while hundreds of antiaircraft guns unleashed a lethal multicolored barrage against the intruders.

Now that the Zeros were thrust into the same role as the Hellcats had assumed the day before, each pilot had to attempt to destroy as many intruders as possible before the Americans could launch coordinated assaults against the irreplaceable carriers. This was the last time in the Pacific War that Japanese carrier pilots could significantly influence the outcome of a battle, and in their grand finale they were at least moderately successful.

The American attackers had virtually no margin of error for fuel consumption and they sacrificed much of their coordination activities simply to attack the first significant target they could find. They hoped to emerge from the gauntlet of enemy fighters and antiaircraft guns still capable of dropping a bomb or a torpedo.

Much of this unwanted attention was directed at *Zuikaku,* the senior carrier in the Imperial fleet. This last survivor of the glory days of Pearl Harbor was successively pounded by helldivers from *Hornet* and *York-town* and then exposed to *Bataan* Hellcats dropping 500-pound bombs. Enough torpedoes and bombs struck home that the order to abandon ship was issued and it appeared that the last member of the Pearl Harbor strike force would join its sister ships on the bottom of the Pacific. However, almost if to offer compensation for the strange loss of *Taiho* the day before, the fates of war seemed to intervene as furiously energetic damage-control parties brought the carrier back from the brink of destruction and gained enough mastery over the spreading fires that the ship was granted an extra four months of existence.[5]

While *Zuikaku* was enduring its near-fatal agony, much of the remainder of the American attack force was concentrating on *Ryuho,* *Hiyo,* and *Junyo.* Initially, a force of Dauntlesses from *Lexington* spotted *Junyo* far below and a stream of planes dove seaward as their tailgunners kept up a steady volley against the formidable group of Zeros probing to find an easy target. The Dauntlesses scored two hits and six near misses before turning a now-burning ship over to the next group of attackers. Meanwhile, Air Group 10, led by Lieutenant W. R. (Killer) Kane, noticed that *Ryuho* had drawn away from the other carriers and straddled the ship with a series of near hits.[6]

Some distance away, *Chiyoda* began drawing unwanted attention as it steamed between *Kongo* and *Haruna.* Bombs from *Monterey*'s avengers ripped through the flight deck while *Haruna* took an equal pounding. Then *Bunker Hill*'s torpedo planes fired a spread of five potentially deadly fish that either missed their target or failed to explode.[7]

By nightfall, virtually every bomb or torpedo that could be hurled at the Imperial fleet had been expended by the Americans. The Task Force 58 pilots now faced two uncertainties: How much damage had they inflicted on the enemy fleet? Did they have enough fuel to return to their carriers? The answer to the first question was far from clear. As the planes veered eastward, *Hiyo* was burning furiously and was only moments from her final plunge. But although fires were blazing on four of the six remaining Imperial carriers, they would all return to port for extensive repairs and be joined in the dry docks by the battleship *Haruna* and two cruisers. Considering the size of the American strike force, the number of Japanese ships sunk was rather small: Just two valuable but hardly irreplaceable oilers joined *Hiyo* in the depths of the Pacific. The Mobile Fleet had been mauled, but it was still a force in being even if stripped of most of its air power. At the end of the battle, six Japanese carriers still stood between the U.S. Navy and the Japanese homeland, even if most were damaged and could launch only meager airgroups. As the Americans turned homeward in the darkness, they could see multiple fires burning on the sea, but this was not the funeral pyre for the Imperial Navy. Admirals Toyoda and Ozawa had just enough ships remaining to launch a final offensive at the western edge of the Philippine Sea, and the Americans would have to endure one more massive naval threat to their series of Pacific invasions.

The answer to the second question, individual survival, would become clear within the next few hours and produce more than a little terror and chaos for the young aviators of the American navy. Each revolution of droning engines sucked a little more fuel out of dangerously low tanks for an American attack force that believed it had gained an enormous victory; but the pilots prayed they would live long enough to celebrate their triumph on their carriers.

Unlike a lost motorist driving down a strange dark road with a fuel needle edging towards empty, these young airmen knew almost precisely where safety loomed. However, when a car runs out of fuel, it merely glides to a stop and creates more of an annoyance than a physical danger to the frustrated motorist. On the other hand, an airplane fuel needle on empty meant an inevitable spiral from the sky into the sea. And this sea was potentially more unforgiving than the most barren desert in the United States.

Even if all went well in the process of ditching a plane—and often little or nothing went well—the pilot and other air crew would be adrift in the world's largest ocean, their main tenuous link to survival a tiny rubber craft not much larger than a bathtub. The warm water in the region did produce a small mercy in that pilots and crew would not die of the brutal exposure inflicted by more frigid seas, but if rescue vessels or aircraft did not spot these tiny specks on the sea, the Pacific would eventually claim them through thirst, heat, and other more gradual forms of death by exposure.

Now, as the adrenaline of battle gradually wore off and the vastness of the ink-black Pacific gradually became a reality, more than two hundred individual survival dramas were played out in the tropical darkness. Meanwhile, dozens of miles to the east, the commander of this imperiled group of young Americans was taking the first steps to rescue as many of these men as possible.

First, Admiral Mitscher ordered every carrier to make maximum speed westward at least to partially close the gap between the returning planes and the fleet. Then he ordered the illumination of all Task Force beacons to counteract the moonless darkness. Next, brightly colored 1-foot-square lights used to identify each carrier were illuminated so that pilots with sufficient fuel could find the proper landing deck. Finally, at 8:30 p.m., the admiral took a far more significant and dangerous step. A simple order was given to every vessel's captain: "Turn on your lights."[8]

The effect was startling, and if it had been peacetime, mesmerizing, as a colorful combination of red and green running lights and other multicolored deck lights gave a Christmas-like glow; the effect was enhanced as each flagship pointed a search light into the air while cruisers and destroyers fired starshells at regular intervals. The fleet could now be seen from miles away. The display provided new hope for anxious pilots, but it could have provided a spectacular opportunity for Japanese submarines that might have been roaming these waters.

Admiral Ernest J. King, opinionated, self-assured commander of the vast American navy, was the driving force behind the controversial plan to invade the Marianas. *(U.S. Navy)*

Admiral Chester W. Nimitz, commander-in-chief of the U.S. Pacific Fleet, had mixed feelings about the benefits of Operation Forager but eventually became a staunch proponent of the invasion. *(U.S. Navy)*

Premier Hideki Tojo found that his earlier promises that the United States would not have the fortitude for a long war were badly flawed. Tojo would become the most prominent Japanese victim of The Marianas campaign as he was forced from office in the summer of 1944. *(Associated Press)*

General Holland M. Smith was commander of the ground forces during the bloody battle for Saipan. He would emerge from the battle with a promotion that effectively removed him from direct combat leadership. *(U.S.M.C.)*

Major General Harry Schmidt was commanding general of 4th Marine Division on Saipan. *(U.S.M.C.)*

Major General Roy Geiger was commanding general of Third Amphibious Corps during the invasion of Guam. *(U.S.M.C.)*

As commanding officer of Fifth Fleet, Admiral Raymond A. Spruance directed the Battle of the Philippine Sea and scored a major, if somewhat criticized, victory over the Imperial Japanese Navy. *(U.S. Navy)*

Vice Admiral Marc A. Mitscher was commander of Fast Carrier Task Force in the Battle of the Philippine Sea. *(U.S. Navy)*

Top: Despite their official designation as soldiers of support units, African-American marines were under heavy enemy fire in Saipan, but their performance under fire made a positive impression on senior officers. *(National Archives) Middle:* Marine units approaching the outskirts of Garapan were forced to make a rapid adjustment from jungle to street fighting. *(U.S.M.C.) Bottom:* Marine gunners employed captured Japanese artillery to maximize firepower in the battle for Garapan. *(National Archives)*

The grisly effects of Japanese fanaticism were particularly apparent after the Gyokusai attack. Thousands of Japanese soldiers were buried in mass graves the day after the attack. *(National Archives)*

Many Japanese civilians on Saipan were shocked to discover that the foreign invaders were not the bloodthirsty barbarians they had been warned to expect. *(National Archives)*

Top: The marines landing on Tinian approached the most constricted beachfront of the Marianas campaign. *(National Archives) Bottom:* The landing on Guam brought the Stars and Stripes back to American soil. *(National Archives)*

Top: These Zeroes were no longer the masters of the Pacific skies that they once were in the months following their attack on Pearl Harbor. *(National Archives)*
Bottom: The tactic of American island hopping left many large Japanese garrisons out of the fighting. Almost 3,000 Japanese troops on Rota never fired a shot against the invaders of Operation Forager and surrendered in large numbers. *(U.S.M.C.)*

Top: Japanese carriers, such as the *Zuikaku* (shown here under attack during the Battle of the Philippine Sea), found themselves caught between powerful American air and submarine attacks. *(National Archives) Middle:* These Essex and Independence class carriers became the most feared element of Admiral Spruance's massive Fifth Fleet. *(U.S. Navy) Bottom:* American Hellcat fighters enjoyed a 10-to-1 victory-to-loss ratio in the dogfights over the Philippine Sea. *(U.S. Navy)*

While official kamikaze units were not yet operational during the Battle of the Philippine Sea, individual pilots sometimes attempted to crash their planes into American warships. *(U.S. Navy)*

Right: American anti-aircraft batteries and fighters defeated the majority of Japanese attack planes. *(U.S. Navy) Bottom left:* Avenger Torpedo planes were far more lethal weapons than the nearly obsolete models that were almost annihilated in the skies over Midway. *(U.S. Navy) Bottom Right:* Japanese bomber crews were brave and determined but they were poorly trained and their planes had minimal protective armor. *(U.S. Navy)*

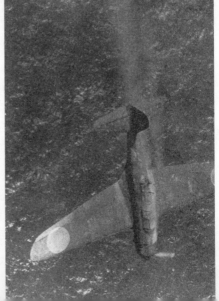

But no hostile vessels were nearby, and Mitscher's luck held. Now, from the darkness, sputtering and coughing planes, obviously sucking their last reserves of fuel, came into view individually and in pairs. Just as most passengers on a sinking ship would be less than particular about the specific life boat they boarded when leaving their stricken vessel, these increasingly desperate pilots were more interested in finding an open flight deck than in observing the protocol of landing on their home carriers.

More than one pilot ignored wave-offs and simply came hurtling down on the closest deck, sometimes crashing through barriers, tearing up flight decks and even killing their would-be rescuers. Meanwhile, as propellers whirred to a stop and engines made a coughing death rattle on their last few ounces of gasoline, other pilots prepared themselves for a landing in the sea at varying distances from the fleet. As the water loomed ever closer, flyers made a mental checklist of the seemingly mundane objects that might determine life or death. Fully-functioning life preservers, life rafts, dye markers, waterproof flashlights, and whistles were their main allies in this duel with the sea and the malfunction of any of these objects could be a death sentence. Even in the relatively confined waters of the English Channel, ditched pilots disappeared forever, and the Philippine Sea was far vaster than the waters of Britain. As moments passed, the sea between the Mobile Fleet and Task Force 58 became increasingly littered with a trail of downed American planes that stretched from the edges of Ozawa's fleet to only a few hundred yards from the decks of friendly ships.

Ditching near the enemy fleet was the most terrifying outcome of the night; the Japanese had a predilection for torturing "rescued" pilots until they had extracted all useful information and then dropping their prisoners back into the sea with attached weights; indeed, the practice was like some macabre update of seventeenth-century pirates who forced their captives to walk the plank. The second most potentially lethal outcome would involve ditching a plane in the vast no-man's-land between the two fleets. These were usually aircraft stricken with fuel leaks or engine damage from antiaircraft hits and would not be able to make it home. Although pilots who landed in this ill-defined zone between adversaries were in no particular danger of capture, rescue planes would have difficulty locating them because of the vastness of potential search patterns.

The final and most common ditching experience on this evening occurred when pilots realized that they didn't have enough fuel to cope with multiple wave-offs on deck and simply splashed down near one or more friendly vessels. For example, Lieutenant J. J. Cummings from Air Group 10 described his experience as mildly thrilling but not necessarily life-threatening:

> Our exit from the plane was speedy enough and the water pleasant. Old 52 gave her final salute by sweeping her tail around and nearly taking Lindsay and me with her. It was a sad parting. Jerry paddled around like a duck and even after Lindsay and I were squared away in the raft, he played around outside. I signaled the Baltimore with my water-filled flashlight and the hands aboard saw the dull red glow. It hurried our rescue. In about fifteen minutes from the time we hit the water, the big dark form of the heavy cruiser was sliding alongside to pick us up. Rescued! Treated like kings, and returned to the Big E two days later by destroyer *Bradford*.[9]

Fortunately for the airmen of Task Force 58, Lieutenant Cummings's experience was more common than that of pilots who simply drifted towards doom in waterlogged rafts that were never spotted by rescue planes or ships.

As the sun rose on this first day of summer of 1944, Admirals Mitscher and Spruance began to tally the known results of the American attack. Of the 226 aircraft that actually reached the enemy fleet, six fighters, six torpedo planes, and five dive-bombers were apparently shot down by enemy planes or guns. This toll of seventeen planes was not astoundingly high given the relatively large number of fighters the Imperial fleet had put aloft and the formidable antiaircraft batteries deployed by Admiral Kurita's powerful capital ships. However, Mitscher's gamble to launch an attack that was at best on the edge of

American combat range did subject the attack force to relatively high losses on the return trip. Eighty-two planes—seventeen fighters, forty-two dive-bombers, and twenty-three torpedo planes—either ditched in the ocean or were demolished in deck crashes, losses that inflated the entire operational loss to a significant ninety-nine planes, or just under half the aircraft that had embarked on the mission. But although the loss of nearly a hundred planes was a considerable blow, American aircraft production was so vast by 1944 that the planes themselves could easily be replaced. Air crews were far more valuable than aircraft, and in this respect the American losses were far less grievous. Sixteen pilots and thirty-three air crew failed to return from the twilight attack, but eighty-eight pilots and seventy-six crewmen were rescued from the water. Thus, the airmen who were forced to ditch had a better than 75 percent chance of survival, a relatively high percentage given the vastness of the sea over which they had fought. Including the deck crews killed in ill-advised emergency landings, a total of fifty-five Americans died on the second day of the battle of the Philippine Sea, a modest loss compared to the daily death toll in the battle currently raging in Normandy. The loss of ninety-nine planes and fifty-five men was balanced by the destruction of one enemy carrier and the temporary elimination of three other Imperial flattops, which, for the immediate future, left Japan with only three fully operational carriers to defend their still vast territory in the Pacific. A third day of battle in the Philippine Sea, especially if it had included American air strikes earlier in the day, might very well have eliminated the naval air power of Japan by sundown. However, as the sun rose on this Tuesday, Admiral Ozawa was determined that the confrontation would never enter a third phase.[10]

Between dawn and midnight on June 20, Ozawa underwent a roller coaster of emotion as his initial plan for "finishing off" a defeated enemy changed into an obsessive desire to steam his fleet at all possible speed to the relative safety of an Okinawan anchorage so that he could put into play the still considerable land-based air units of the home islands. Even inflated estimates of the number of intruders shot down over the Mobile Fleet could not disguise the fact that by dawn on June

21 only twenty Imperial fighters were in condition to intercept an enemy strike force. A resumption of battle would place the fate of the Imperial navy almost entirely in the hands of antiaircraft gunners; but although they might still exact a considerable toll of enemy aircraft, they would surely be overwhelmed as each successive wave of raiders droned over the tropical sea. On the other hand, if Ozawa determined to launch another attack on the presumably decimated enemy fleet, he would be hard-pressed to mobilize the two dozen dive-bombers and torpedo planes that would constitute the final roll of the dice for Imperial victory. Spruance had orchestrated a battle that rivaled *Trenton*, *New Orleans,* and *Buena Vista* for the one-sided nature of damage to the enemy in relation to American losses. However, the one-sided American victory in the Philippine Sea never quite achieved decisive status in the American mindset.

The battle of the Philippine Sea was acknowledged as an impressive American victory as its nickname, "The Great Marianas Turkey Shoot," strongly indicates. It was the largest carrier battle in history and involved a combined American-Japanese force of carriers and carrier planes that would never again be matched. Spruance had achieved a one-sided victory while simultaneously accomplishing his primary mission of preventing an enemy attack on the vulnerable vessels supporting the invasion of Saipan. Mitscher's Task Force 58 had destroyed more Japanese planes than the American victory at Midway and sunk almost as many carriers if the accomplishments of American submarines are also included. However, there remains the nagging hint that what everyone from the naval high command to the general public expected was the absolute annihilation of the Imperial fleet. Spruance thought primarily of screening the invasion fleet, but much of American opinion was far more focused on the destruction of the enemy carriers. In the absolute calculus of battle, Spruance had succeeded magnificently.[11]

In a two-day battle of epic proportions, only thirty-nine American planes were shot down in combat and only seventy-six Americans died out of nearly 100,000 men involved in the battle. No American ship was so badly damaged as to require extensive time out of action, and the support of the ground war largely continued unabated. On the other hand, Ozawa's Mobile Fleet had been badly mauled. At dawn on June 19, Ozawa could launch 430 carrier aircraft and forty-three float planes from his fleet. Forty-eight hours later, only thirty-seven combat planes and twelve scout planes were still airworthy. When Imperial land-based units were counted, Japanese losses for the battle rose to an astoundingly high 476 aircraft and 450 pilots, a loss that was simply irreplaceable at this point in the war. Of the nine available carriers at the opening of the battle, three were sunk and three more were so badly damaged as to be useless for the remainder of the summer. For the immediate future, Japanese carrier power was reduced to three operational carriers, each capable of launching perhaps a dozen planes.

Because of the battle of the Philippine Sea, the still-formidable army of 65,000 Imperial soldiers in the Marianas would fight the rest of the ground campaign with virtually no naval support and only minimal air support. The invaders had now achieved total control of the sea around and the sky above the battlefield, a generally decisive advantage in any World War II campaign. Spruance's victory did not end naval confrontation in the Pacific. The Japanese would have one more card to play at Leyte Gulf during the upcoming autumn, but the Japanese garrison in the Marianas, an army nearly as large as the Confederate force at Gettysburg, was now essentially alone in an American-dominated Philippine Sea. The bullets, rations, bandages, and tanks they now possessed would not be replaced when any of these items ran out. They would sell each foot of the Marianas dearly, and they were still capable of inflicting painful surprises on their tormentors. But Operation Forager, only a few days old, had now turned into a gigantic siege from which there could be only one outcome.

14

BATTLE BEYOND
THE BEACH

WHILE RAYMOND SPRUANCE and Marc Mitscher were conducting the nautical chess match that would sweep the Philippine Sea of Imperial naval units, a crusty, pugnacious sixty-two-year-old Marine was attempting to orchestrate the land battle that would make the Marinas Turkey Shoot worth the effort. Lieutenant General Holland McTyeire Smith was born seventeen years after the Civil War ended in Russell County, Alabama, to the son of the president of the Alabama Railway Commission. After the younger Holland Smith had finished an undistinguished career at a one-room schoolhouse and his father's alma mater of Auburn University, the family's political ties brought an offer of appointment to the United States Naval Academy. But both his parents strenuously objected to his attendance at a Yankee-dominated institution, so a naval career was sacrificed for a law career. When Smith tired of laboring in his father's shadow, he transferred to Washington to seek an army commission. He was told by his congressman that although no posts were available in that service, he could secure a lieutenancy in the Marine Corps.[1]

The lawyer-turned-combat officer came under fire in Nicaragua, Santo Domingo, and the Western Front of France; but in the years immediately before World War II, he became one of a small core of officers who had expertise in the complex and dangerous procedure of making amphibious landings on hostile beaches. Smith was passed over for the command of the newly formed 1st Marine Division, which made the corps legendary as a fighting force at Guadalcanal, but exercised significant influence in the training in all new Marine divisions as well as the U.S. Army's 7th, 77th, 81st, and 96th Infantry Divisions and in the 7th Division's battle for Attu in 1943. Finally, after fearing that he would be passed over for a command in the upcoming American thrust into the heart of the Japanese Empire, Smith was shocked to discover that he had been appointed to lead V Amphibious Corps in the invasion of Saipan.

This was a dream assignment for the general with the less than complimentary nickname of "Howling Mad Smith." The corps commander, like his ultimate superior, Ernest King, passionately believed that Saipan as the key to the Pacific War. As Smith insisted, Saipan was Japan's administrative Pearl Harbor, the naval and military heart and brain of Japanese Defense Strategy. If the Japanese, after sinking our fleet at Pearl Harbor, had landed and taken Oahu, destroyed the garrison, and caused the death of Admiral Nimitz and top army and Marine commanders, the loss would have been somewhat parallel.[2]

That the Japanese would have heartily agreed with Holland Smith's analysis was quite evident on June 16, 1944, the morning after D-Day on Saipan. An observer in a plane flying over the island on this humid Friday morning would have seen a chaotic panorama that matched the absolute violence portrayed in the climax of a Hollywood war movie. Surrounded by a series of inland ridges, Sherman tanks deployed over the rocky earth like huge mechanical dinosaurs with gears grinding and huge engines roaring, yet they were still drowned out by machine-gun fire and earth-jarring explosions. Following closely behind the olive-drab mechanical predators, hundreds of Marines charged up the sandy slopes, firing as they ran, hoping to knock out the enemy tormentors before they were themselves eliminated. Streaking overhead were deep-blue Hellcats firing down at the Japanese positions, their bullets tearing up the earth, sand, and Nipponese soldiers.

Yet this carnival of death was decidedly a two-way street. Machine-gun, mortar, and cannon fire poured from fortified trenches, cut into the looming ridges, and showered down at the men in green denim, chewing up flesh and creating expanding blossoms of blood on the tan-and-gray inclines. The Marines kept coming, their ranks thinned but not halted as each man prayed that the Hellcats and the Shermans could knock out the hellish fire before he became the next victim.

Time correspondent Robert Sherrod insisted that the Marines were now fighting in a deadly amphitheater where they were the doomed gladiators: "The Japs' from their mountainside dugouts were looking down our throats. Not only our front lines were still being pounded. Our beaches still crowded with shore parties unloading supplies. In a 1,500 yard walk down the land Captain Thomason and I hit the sand four times!"[3]

If the hurricane of Japanese steel was ever going to abate, the enemy would have to be pushed back from their first tier of defense and deprived of at least some of the formidable army that was turning much of the American line into a live-action shooting gallery. This would entail expelling the enemy from the southern end of the island and then turning this newly won ground into a springboard for the grueling drive north toward the heights of Mount Topotchau looming over every beach and field on Saipan.

All day on Friday, June 16, the Japanese shelling turned the still perilously narrow American beachhead into a tropical version of the Western Front of 1917. The shells cut a swath of death across ranks, units, and races. The 2nd Marine Division ended the day with half its company and battalion officers dead or wounded; and five companies of African Americans, the first black Marines deployed in combat in the Pacific War, watched their ranks thin as they furiously unloaded supplies and transported them a short distance to the front lines. Saito's gunners claimed the life of the Lieutenant Colonel Maynard Schultz, commander of the 1st Battalion of the 24th Marines when deadly fragments rained down on his command post. A supporting force of twelve

105 mm howitzers was reduced to one pair of operating guns by the firestorm.

General Saito's gunners were merely softening the invaders for the island commander's most audacious gambit, the largest Japanese tank attack of the Pacific War.

The Japanese counterattack on the night of the American invasion had been marked by a combination of poor coordination and the fact that Yoshitsugo Saito had not been fully convinced that he was facing the entire American landing force. Now Saito spent the hours of daylight sending runners to key units and organizing a night assault that was designed to bleed the 2nd Marine Division white and leave the enemy too battered to advance from the beaches. According to the plan, Saito's 136th Infantry Regiment and forty-four tanks of Colonel Takashi Goto's 9th Tank Regiment would smash into the 6th Marines deployed in a wide arc around the island's radio station while Admiral Nagumo's 1st Special Naval Landing Force would march southeast from Garapan and attack the northern tip of the enemy lines in the woody underbrush of the road between Charan Kanoa and the island's capital city.

No previous Japanese garrison commander had enjoyed access to a significant armored formation, and the tanks on Saipan even included a large number of Chi Ha machines which, by Japanese standards, were massively upgraded vehicles compared to earlier models. Compared to the Panthers and Tigers that Erwin Rommel was throwing at the Allied invasion force in Normandy, the 47 mm gun on the Chi Ha seemed relatively puny. However, in an energetically conducted night assault where visibility might be less than optimal for the Marines, formations of invading Imperial tanks might well inflict serious damage.

At 3:00 a.m. on the morning of June 17, Colonel Takashi Goto climbed into the turret of his command tank and ordered the forty-three remaining vehicles to advance from the foothills of Mount Fina Susa toward the immense towers that fronted the now enemy-held Saipan radio station. Goto probably briefly speculated about how formidable his formation might have been if all one hundred of his tanks had arrived safely on Saipan, and he might possibly have allowed himself a glimmer of envy for the commander of a Panzer regiment of the German allies in which the Panthers and Tigers would clearly out-gun the same Shermans that seemed so formidable in the Pacific War. Yet Goto shared one peril in common with his Wermacht counterparts: Axis tank actions always seemed to be impeded by American air supe-riority.

To spearhead Saito's planned offensive, Goto's tank companies had to drive from scattered bases to the rally point just outside Charan Kanoa. Unfortunately for the colonel, American aerial observers had spotted some of his tanks moving toward the jump-off position in the fading daylight of evening and the entire 2nd Marine Division had been alerted to the probability of an armored night attack. Bazooka teams, antitank gun crews, and tank commanders were now all waiting expec-tantly for the sound of clanking enemy armor rolling out of the foothills, but they knew that the Japanese would enjoy the initial advan-tage of choosing one small portion of the American line to strike. At 3:30 a.m., the roar of Japanese Type 97 tank engines could be heard moving down the slopes toward the beachhead. Colonel Mitsuo Ogara's infantry were now clambering aboard the iron monsters and taking up every centimeter of deck space as they rode toward the enemy lines. Suddenly, the men of the 1st Battalion, 6th Marines, realized that the clanking treads heard in the not very far distance seemed to be heading directly for their lines; their commander, Lieutenant Colonel William Jones, suddenly remembered the sobering conclusion of division intelli-gence offices that the Japanese might have deployed as many as two hundred tanks on Saipan. What if this entire formation was now ap-proaching the battalion in the dash? The enemy threat was not quite as bad as Jones's worst-case scenario, but the next few hours would pro-vide one of the most dramatic engagements of the Pacific War. Goto's tanks initiated the battle by rolling right over two of Company B's mor-tar pits as surviving Marines huddled in foxholes and watched in awe as the mechanical version of prehistoric beasts rampaged over their lairs and dripped leaking oil on green uniforms as a reminder of their threat to the unseen prey. Company commander Captain James Rollen jumped up from his foxhole and fired a grenade launcher at a passing intruder, but the tank merely ignored the minor threat in favor of bigger game and sent the officer staggering from the field with a burst ear drum caused by the concussion. Moments later, Captain Norman Thomas arrived to take command but, unlike his predecessor, he did not survive the tank attack long enough to make it to an aid station.

Major James Donovan, the 1st Battalion's executive officer, insisted that the battle evolved into "a madhouse of noise, tracers and flashing lights." This may have been a night battle, yet lights were everywhere "as tanks were hit and set afire, they silhouetted other tanks coming out of the flickering shadows."[4]

Yet the friendly weapons fire that destroyed the tanks also blinded American gun crews to the approach of newly arriving Imperial vehicles. The result was a series of ferocious, point-blank encounters that surprised even Marines and Japanese at the sustained violence. Now small groups of American tank hunters embarked on a deadly game of hide-and-seek.

Private Herbert Hodges had been a mechanic in a tank company before his transfer to an infantry unit. He insisted to his officer: "I'm from tanks. I'm not scared of tanks. I know what they can do and what they can't do. If you'll give me a bazooka now, I'll take care of them." Hodges was better than his word. Accompanied by Private Charles Meritt, the intrepid duo moved out for an extended hunt that would chalk off seven Chi Ha tanks and earn the tandem the Navy Cross. Privates John Kounk and Horace Norverson set out with four bazooka rockets and returned with three kills. Corporal John Watson stalked a tank and threw incendiary grenades at the looming menace that killed the crew as they scrambled out. The nature of the Japanese assault stunned the defenders. As one startled Marine insisted: "The Japs would halt, then jump out of their tanks. Then they would sing songs and wave swords. Finally one of them would blow a trumpet, but jump back into the tanks if they hadn't been hit already. Then we would let them have it with a bazooka."[5]

Then, in the almost predictable pattern of Pacific War battlers, the sun rose along the horizon and the surviving attackers switched directions and began streaming back toward the relative safety of Mount Tipo Pale. In a dramatic illustration of American firepower, the last tank in the receding war of armor was bracketed by a supporting destroyer that pumped more than twenty shells into the doomed vehicles and started a blazing fire that smoldered in no-man's-land for the rest of the day.

The largest Japanese tank offensive of the war had achieved some temporary penetration of the American lines and had added a new and somewhat terrifying element to Nipponese night assaults. Yet Saito had paid a terrible price for this experience. Nigumo's naval troops had been mowed down as they streamed down the coast road toward the far flank of the American lines and were thrown back in disarray. The men of the 165th Regiment had ridden to battle on tanks, but either staggered back on foot or remained behind permanently. Most important, Saito's carefully hoarded armored formation had lost thirty-one irreplaceable tanks; this made it unlikely that a repeat performance of a fully coordinated tank-infantry attack of this magnitude would be staged. The bodies of seven hundred Japanese sailors and soldiers littered the battlefield, joined in death by perhaps a tenth as many Marines. Now, as stretcher bearers carried the wounded to aid stations, burial crews interred the dead defenders and men crowded on top of inert Chi Has to inspect their new nemesis. General Holland Smith came ashore and began planning the drive that would make the Americans masters of southern Saipan.

The commander of V Amphibious Corps now planned to shift the axis of the invasion from east-west to north-south by using General Thomas Watson's 2nd Marine Division as an enormous pivot point upon which to wheel General Harry Schmidt's 4th Marine Division into a position where it could push across the lush farmlands of southern Saipan to the east coast at Magicienne and then wheel northward toward the far more difficult terrain of the central highlands, which was the gateway to the rest of the island. This huge pivot, if successful, would give the invaders control of Aslito Airfield and enable them to push enemy artillery units back far enough to eliminate at least some of the intense fire that was still raining down on the beaches. Once the southern farmlands were secured, the invasion force could be organized for the daunting task of storming Mount Topatchau and pushing the Japanese defenders all the way back to the cliffs of Marpi Point.

Holland Smith's first task ashore was to set up a headquarters and see for himself the island he was assigned to capture. The Marine general located a small house in Choran Kanoa that had suffered only minor damage in the shelling, the major drawback being the unwanted presence of a large dead carabao occupying most of the backyard. After a bulldozer had dragged away the now pungent guest, the corps commander surveyed his new command area. Normally Saipan is a pleasant island with calming patches of bright green vegetation contrasting with the brilliant crimson of fire trees, but under the tramping of thousands of feet and hundreds of heavy-tracked vehicles, the dirt roads had disintegrated into fine, penetrating dust. A passing jeep could put up a smoke screen dense enough to blot out the sun, yet when it rained, jeeps became amphibians caught in quagmires that had been roads only minutes before.

Smith may have been an opinionated, controversial general, but he admitted to enjoying the tropical beauty of the island and felt equally relaxed when he played the role of crusty but caring grandfather to troops who were often more than forty years younger. Admiral Spruance provided regular gifts of five-gallon drums of ice cream; this prompted the corps commander to shout out from the front window of his office to any Marine within earshot to hurry over and join in the icy treat. As dusty, tired men lined up with canteen cups, cracked teacups, Japanese rice bowls, or any other container that was more or less whole, the three-star general would personally dole out large scoops of the treasured dessert to bemused and slightly surprised men. Then, when the last spoonful was distributed, Smith would return to his desk, call out through the thin partition for his chief of staff to join him, and return to the business of capturing Saipan from the enemy.[6]

The first response to Saito's night armored attack was an operation in which the 2nd Marine Division would dramatically extend the northern flank of the American beachhead while simultaneously becoming a pivot point for the 4th Marine Division to advance across the island to Magicienne with the newly landed 165th Regiment of the 27th Infantry Division lunging toward Aslito Airfield near the southern tip of the island.

As seven regiments of Marines and soldiers pushed out from the beachhead perimeter, they encountered an environment that was much closer to their grandparents' experiences in the Civil War or their brothers' or cousins' experiences in Normandy than earlier battles in the Pacific War. Much of the southern third of Saipan was dominated by well-tended farms that grew sugarcane, corn, peas, cantaloupe, and potatoes. One-story farmhouses and barns were interspersed with small hamlets and villages that were now being vacated by women with babies strapped to their backs, older men and women, young children, and even Japanese males of military age who were civilian employees of the South Seas Development Corporation and who seemed to have less desire to die in combat than their military counterparts.

The farmhouses and village homes often contained cases of Japanese beer and soft drinks, a Godsend in the heat and humidity; they also contained possessions that included an array of pictures and photographs varying from Hitler to Christ; phonograph records, including Japanese music that was ignored and Western tunes that were played over and over; and an assortment of albums of schoolchildren, baseball teams, and graduations that almost for the first time in the war put a human face on an otherwise despised enemy. Most of the civilian population of Guam consisted of Chammorros, but Saipan seemed to be more of a mixture of natives and Nipponese colonists, and the advancing Americans often tried to discover which homes were occupied by the respective cultural groups based on the artifacts inside. In this strange twilight war, American medical personnel were setting up hospital facilities to treat injured and sick Japanese civilians; their own Nipponese protectors had encouraged these people to kill themselves rather than be subjected to the torture, rape, and plunder that was described as the normal behavior of the "American devils."

Now with the inferno of D-Day behind them and the hell of storming the central highlands still in the future, the American invaders were caught in a twilight war in which the terror of enemy bombardments, ambushes, and snipers was interspersed with other periods of relative quiet and in which one unit could be engaged in a fierce shootout while a mile away their counterparts were discovering a cache of saki in a deserted farmhouse. In an experience not unlike that of Vietnam a generation later, some civilians were happy to see the Americans, some were merely apathetic, and some were hiding hand grenades or pistols to take "foreign devils" with them to paradise. The orchard down the road could be a place for relaxation or it could be filled with enemy snipers. The case of beer in a farmhouse might be the treat of the day or a deadly booby trap.

The conflicting emotions of the advance through southern Saipan affected different men in somewhat different ways. Private Guy Gabaldon, a tenth-grade dropout from the barrio of East Los Angeles used his family's Spanish and his neighborhood Nisei friends' Japanese to secure a position as a scout in the Intelligence Unit of the 2nd Marines. On one day, one of his major responsibilities was to serve as an interpreter for two Spanish priests and a Russian civilian who were brought to the unit's command post. The Spaniards, Father Jose Tardio and Brother Gregorio Oroquieta, were the leaders of the Catholic community on Saipan and were interested in securing the safety of seven nuns who had been teachers in the Catholic school but were now attempting to stay alive in the hills. The Russian was in exile from Stalin and a stint in Siberia and welcomed the arrival of the Americans as liberators. Gabaldon spoke to the priests in Spanish and the Russian in Japanese, and assisted in the rescue of all but one of the nuns.

Yet, the next day, the war turned far uglier when the Marine scout discovered a cave filled with Japanese who might become valuable intelligence assets if they could be convinced to surrender. Standing just outside the cave entrance, Gabaldon yelled, "You are surrounded and have no choice but to surrender. I assure you that you will be well treated. We do not want to kill you." When he yelled his demands in Japanese, he was standing behind a 3-foot-high boulder; when two soldiers ran out with fixed bayonets, he emptied a carbine clip into them, shocked by their bravado, stupidity, and lack of imagination. "They believed that their sabres and a Banzai yell would assure victory. I can't complain, their stupidity made me the owner of many sabres."[7]

Knowing that additional defenders were still inside the cave, the scout tossed in four grenades followed by a satchel charge of TNT and got behind the boulder, insisting that the explosion "blew the living hell out of the cave." As the dust settled, Gabaldon ran into the cave and emptied two clips into the seven remaining occupants. The result was somewhat startling, but not totally unusual on Saipan: "Five soldiers and two women in the cave. . . . The women each had rifles in their hands and grenades alongside." The spectrum of emotions, from assisting in the eventual rescue of one group of women to killing another pair of women in combat was now becoming the rule of the day as the invaders surged from their beachheads to the opposite coast.[8]

After the failure of his armored counterattack, General Saito reluctantly came to the conclusion that southern Saipan could not be held even until the Imperial Navy smashed through the Fifth Fleet and relieved the garrison. However, the general was determined to fight a stubborn delaying action in that region while the main body of the Imperial force concentrated on and deployed in positions in the much more defender-friendly central highlands. As Saito began developing plans to orchestrate his fallback, he received a personal radio message from Prime Minister Hideki Tojo, who clearly explained the importance of Saipan to the welfare of the nation: "Because the fate of the Japanese Empire depends on the result of your operation, inspire the spirit of your operation, inspire the spirit of the officers and men and to the very end continue to destroy the enemy very gallantly and persistently; thus alleviate the anxiety of our Emperor." The general's reply was in the spirit of Bushido: "I have received your honorable Imperial words. By becoming the bulwark of the Pacific with 10,000 Pacific deaths, we hope to requite the imperial favor."[9]

However, any hope of reuniting the emperor's anxiety would have to be played out farther north. By the time Tojo's message was transmitted, southern Saipan was rapidly falling into American hands.

By the morning of June 19, the 24th and 25th Marines were rapidly bypassing a series of fortified cliffs and enemy-held caves to sweep eastward toward Magicienne Bay on the east coast of Saipan. A short distance to the south, the 165th Infantry Regiment was advancing toward the biggest prize at the end of the island, Aslito Airfield, and despite heavy fire from enemy dual-purpose guns, concealed in the woods of Nafutan Point the advance was about to be under new management. The defenders were simply unable to concentrate enough men and enough guns to turn the American advance on Aslito into a bloodbath, and the surviving Imperial units either streamed northbound toward the highlands or southbound toward Nafutan, which was now developing into a last-ditch stronghold not unlike the American position on Bataan in the Philippines two years earlier.

At the end of four days of sporadic but sometimes intense fighting, Holland Smith's Northern Troops and Landing Force held most of southern Saipan except for a small salient between Mount Tipo Pale the swamps of Lake Susupe outside Charan Kanoa and the wooded peninsula jutting out into the sea at Nafutan Point. In the typical overconfident spin that Japanese commanders loved to use when things were going badly, Saito sent Tokyo this message: "The Army is consolidating its battle lines and has decided to prepare for a showdown fight. It is concentrating the 43rd Division in the area east of Tapotchau. The remaining units (including naval forces) are concentrating in the area east of Garapan." What the message failed to inform the high command was that in only four days the Japanese garrison had lost the port facilities at Charan Kanoa, the main airfield at Aslito, the main radio station near Lake Susupe, and perhaps one-third of the defenders and two-thirds of their armor. Yet, on the positive side, the defenders had inflicted heavy casualties on the Americans, 2,000 on

D-Day alone, and they still held the capital city of Garapan, the harbor at Tanapag, and a small airfield on the tip of the island at Marpi Point. They also still held the best ground for defense on the island. The new line was a formidable one extending from a point just south of Garapan, past the cliffs guarding the approach to Mount Tapotchau, and on over to the northern shore of Magicienne Bay. As the Nipponese troops dug into the alternating rocky ridges and sandy plateau that would soon assume gruesome new identities in American newspapers as Death Valley, Hell's Gate, and Purple Heart Ridge, the emperor's personal spokesman transmitted an important message from the palace. Hirohito exhorted everyone on Saipan to know that he believed "the front-line officers and troops [were] fighting splendidly." Yet the message also included a stark warning: "If Saipan is lost, air raids on Tokyo will take place often; therefore you will hold Saipan." Now Holland Smith and Saito were committed to accomplish the victory that only one command could achieve. Smith insisted in his memoirs, "I was determined to take Saipan and take it quickly. Upon the outcome of the operation rested the first proof of the ability of the Marine Corps to do a big job well."

Saito was perfectly willing to lose all 32,000 defenders on the island to ensure that, after this battle, the Marine Corps would never have the opportunity to do another "big job."[10]

15

DEATH VALLEY TO PURPLE HEART RIDGE

WHEN RALPH CORBETT SMITH received a general's star in the dark days immediately after Pearl Harbor, it seemed ludicrous to anyone around him that he would either command a combat unit in the Pacific or become the focal point for one of the most bitter interservice feuds of World War II. In one respect, Ralph Smith's background was as much Northern as his future antagonist, Holland Smith's, upbringing was Southern. He was descended from a family that had come to America on the *Mayflower* and produced descendents who held important professional positions in Massachusetts before following many other New Englanders to the open lands of the Midwest. Ralph Smith spent his childhood in Omaha, Nebraska, accompanied his family to Fort Collins, Colorado, and taught in a country school after attending Colorado State College. Like Holland Smith, Ralph Smith's path to general's status was not through the military academy but through the Colorado National Guard, which, in turn, formed part of the American First Division, the first unit shipped to France after the United States entered World War I. After being severely wounded on the Western Front, the newly promoted major learned to speak French fluently enough to attend the

Sorbonne. He returned to France in the 1930s to attend l'Ecole de Guerre, one of twenty specially selected foreign officers. Thus, when the United States entered the World War II, Major Smith was viewed by the Army High Command as potentially well-suited for a significant position commanding a unit assigned to the European theatre. Yet this calm, self-assured officer found himself promoted to major general and placed in charge of the 27th Division, which was scheduled to join the still relatively small number of army divisions fighting the Japanese in the Pacific.[1]

All things being equal, Ernest King, Chester Nimitz, and Holland Smith would probably have been perfectly happy fighting the Central Pacific offensive if they had used only Marine divisions in the amphibious assaults and relegated army units to guard duty after the islands were secure. However, the Marines still did not field enough combat units to achieve sufficient manpower superiority over the Nipponese garrisons, and both Galvanic and Flintlock had been joint army and Marine operations.

Elements of the 27th Division had invaded Makin in the Gilberts campaign, and the less than diplomatic Holland Smith had made it clear that the army had far less ability in capturing enemy-held islands than his beloved Marines. Actually, comparing the fighting techniques of the two services was a classic "apples and oranges" comparison: The Marines stressed initially high-cost frontal assaults that, if all went well, tended to bring the battle to a resolution fairly quickly; the army stressed nuanced maneuver tactics that reduced day-to-day casualties but sometimes prolonged the engagement.

"Howling Mad" Smith was not exactly the epitome of nuance or subtlety in battle, or any other enterprise, and when it became brutally apparent that his two Marine divisions simply did not have the manpower to capture Saipan alone, Ralph Smith's division was called in from a sort of nautical bullpen to join the battle. Although portions of the division would quickly become involved in the fighting for Aslito Airfield at Nafutan Point, this rise or fall of the 27th's reputation would soon become inexorably linked to the looming prominence of Mount Tapotchau and its fanatically well-defended approaches.

When Holland Smith visited the summit of Tapotchau after its capture, he admitted that he was stunned by the vista it provided. "Tapotchau had fascinated me ever since I first set eyes on the mountain which rose above the smoke of our D-Day bombardment. Looking down on the island from the former vantage point of the Japanese, it was easy to see why enemy fire had been so accurate. From the summit of the 1,554-foot mountain, the observer had a Pisgah sight of Saipan. Practically, the entire island stretched visibly before him, like a huge aerial photograph."2

With the aid of a map and a powerful Japanese telescope he found there, he could reduce the 72 square miles of terrain to the proportions of a football field and study the progress of the battle in detail. But for the Marines and soldiers who had to scale these heights, it was most certainly a football field from hell.

Holland Smith's original plan to capture the central highlands envisioned General Watson's 2nd Marine Division pushing up the western edge of the high ground while General Schmidt's 4th Marine Division took responsibility for the eastern sector fronting Magicienne Bay. Yet both of these units had suffered heavy casualties in the landing and the battle for the south: Watson's unit lost 2,514 men; Schmidt's division lost 3,628. Thus, the new offensive, which would approach the most formidable terrain on the island, began with assault units short of more than 6,000 men. At the least, throwing the army division into the fray would help push the combat strength of the invaders back toward its D-Day levels. The problem with the reinforcements was uncertainty about the kind of units the Marines were going to get to carry the load in the crucial center point of the American advance up the hills. Holland Smith hinted that the unit joining his Marines seemed to be some sort of glorified social club that happened to wear uniforms and carry rifles: "The 27th Division is a New York silk stocking outfit with an impeccable reputation for annual balls, banquets and shipshape summer camps which contains the entangled roots of home town loyalties, ambition and intrigue and should be broken up and replaced with anyone on earth but former members of the New York National Guard."[3]

According to Ralph Smith and most senior army officials, the Marines were getting the services of a unit that enjoyed a proud history dating back to the Revolutionary War; included in its membership were the descendants of the famed 69th New York Regiment, which had gained enormous glory in the Civil War and World War I. Most of the New York natives were not members of New York City society but "Appleknockers" from the Mohawk Valley and central New York's farms, villages, and small cities. Whatever the background of these American soldiers, their actions over the next few days would initiate a controversy from military and naval headquarters buildings to the offices of America's most prominent newspapers and magazines.

At 6:00 a.m. on June 22, 1944, the American drive into Saipan's central highlands began. As eighteen artillery battalions opened a thundering barrage, two Marine divisions lunged northward. Companies of the 6th and 8th Marines clambered up and down through a succession of tangled, bushy ridges and deep, wooded gullies. The first few ridgelines were conceded to the attackers, but when the Marines began advancing up the slope of Mount Tipo Pale, they suddenly discovered a honeycomb of caves and tunnels that provided a wicked crossfire and pushed the men back to safer ground.

On the right flank, General Harry Schmidt carefully studied what he considered to be Holland Smith's mostly overoptimistic objective lines and hedged his bets by penciling in an intermediate line for "reorganization" 2,000 yards short of the official destination. The units of the 25th Marines, operating toward the center of the American line, faced a series of four ridges that all seemed equally formidable. When the 3rd Battalion began to clamber up the first incline in its sector, the enemy pounced from caves and killed or wounded three company commanders and several other Marines at a cost of one hundred of their own men. Meanwhile, as the 24th Marines advanced along the shore of Magicienne Bay, they confronted a seemingly endless series of gullies interspersed with rock outcroppings from adjacent cliffs. As the men maneuvered to face each new ambush from the high ground, the senior officers began to realize that they were rapidly losing contact with the 25th Marines to their left.[4]

As darkness settled on the battlefield on the first day of the American offensive, Marine commanders could look with satisfaction at an advance of 2,500 yards in some places. However, it was obvious that there were simply not enough men currently available to maintain an unbroken advance line over such formidable terrain. Now Holland Smith determined to throw the 27th Division into the battle in an attempt to produce a continuous front from east to west sea coasts. But while Smith was ordering the army into the battle, his Japanese counterpart was pouring every available unit into the highlands; by dawn on June 23, 15,000 Japanese soldiers and sailors would be deployed in one of the most powerful concentrations of Imperial forces in a small area during the Pacific War. This line was now like a magnet drawing almost every man on Saipan capable of fighting into a shoot-out in the hills.

At 4:00 p.m. on June 22, General Ralph Smith visited the V Amphibious Corps chief of staff, Brigadier General Graves Erskine, at corps headquarters. The army general was informed that Holland Smith had decided to pass two regiments of the 27th Division through the left flank of the 4th Marine Division so that the army unit would become the center of the American line and thus responsible for capturing the eastern side of Mount Tapotchau and all ancillary terrain around that hill. The rest of the mountain would be in the zone of action of the 2nd Marine Division, but Ralph Smith's men would have the more difficult approach because the eastern face was a sheer cliff falling away approximately 600 feet to a plateau of open farmland three quarters of a mile wide and almost bare of any cover between the American line and the Japanese defenders. The plateau in turn bordered on the eastern side with a range of interconnected hills that essentially formed a 150-foot ridgeline that extended north for a mile. The right flank of the battlefield, the responsibility of the 4th Marine Division, was dominated by the heights of Mount Kagman, which loomed over the Kagman Peninsula, and the sea on the east and the crossroads village of Chacha to the west.

Seven of the nine American infantry regiments on Saipan would be involved in the renewed offensive, the 2nd, 6th, 8th, 23rd, and 24th Marines, the 106th and 165th Infantry Regiments with the 25th Marines, and the 105th Infantry either in reserve or employed besieging Nafutan Point to the south. The Marine units would have somewhat easier terrain for their advance but were also moving on a wider front than the army regiments. No matter which service the men belonged to, what they saw in front of them was a huge mountain looming over them flanked by a seemingly endless succession of ridges honeycombed with caves filled with Japanese defenders.

The most significant gains on June 23 were achieved by the westernmost units of the 2nd Marine Division and the easternmost units of the 4th Marine Division. These men were moving at least partially along coast roads where the defenders did not have quite the terrain advantage they enjoyed in the center. By sunset, advance forces were within 1,000 yards of the city limits of Garapan on the western flank and had captured the town of Laulau on the northern shore of Magicienne Bay on the eastern flank. Yet, on maps in corps headquarters, it appeared that the line was already beginning to sag in the center.

The first day of action for the army division could properly be called the battle of the Caves. The infantrymen backed up by the tanks of the 762nd Tank Battalion spent a bloody and frustrating afternoon moving along the plateau between Tapotcha and the opposite ridgeline in a natural shooting gallery that was now being called Death Valley. The tanks were pounded so severely from both elevations that only eighteen of seventy-two vehicles were still functioning at sunset. The 3rd Battalion of the 106th Regiment found itself dodging a hail of mortar shells that dropped thirty-one men in less than a minute. From corps headquarters, it appeared that two reasonably fresh regiments deployed over a relatively narrow front had been stopped cold, and in Holland Smith's opinion, the division commander was responsible.[5]

Smith called in Major General Sanderford Jarman, the army officer designated to command the Saipan garrison when the island was secured. Although neither Smith nor his chief of staff had visited the front lines, the Marine general thought the army division appeared listless and flat in its progress and asked Jarman to visit Ralph Smith and convey the corps commander's dissatisfaction. Then he emphasized, "If it was not an Army division and there would be a great cry sent up more or less of a political nature, he would immediately remove Ralph Smith."[6]

Meanwhile, *Time* magazine correspondent Robert Sherrod was told by a member of corps staff, "We cannot attack Mt. Tapotchau until the 27th Division moves up and we've got to have the high ground so we can look down the Japs' throats instead of letting them look down ours. If we don't keep pressing them, they'll reorganize and dig in deeper, and casualties will shoot up higher. We can't sit back and expect artillery and naval gunfire to blast them out of the caves."[7]

General Jarman, who should have stayed out of this dispute, agreed to visit his army colleague. The subsequent meeting ultimately fueled the controversy even more. According to Jarman, Ralph Smith admitted that "the division was not carrying its full share," and the commander "was in no way satisfied with what his regimental commanders had done during the day." Then Jarman insisted that the 27th Division commander had made this damning statement: "If the division does not go forward tomorrow, I should be relieved." Ralph Smith, who lived well into his nineties and refused to break his silence about the affair until forty years after the battle, later explained that he was badly misquoted by Jarman and had merely related now much more tenacious Japanese resistance was than expected rather than express displeasure about his own commanders. He admitted saying, "If there is not a significant improvement in the situation tomorrow, they will think I should be relieved."[8]

Holland Smith reluctantly gave his army subordinate one more day to make significant progress, but the prospects for an advance anywhere near the corps commander's expectations were extremely slim.

General Saito's formidable line was essentially threatened at three places: around the approach to Mount Tipo Pale in the west, at the entrance to Death Valley in the center, and at the base of the Tagman Peninsula in the east. Although none of these points would be easy for the Americans to overrun, the center offered the defenders the most dramatic topographical advantages. Thus, when the V Amphibious Corps lurched into motion on Saturday, June 24, progress was anything but even. On the right, the 8th Marines used satchel charges, bazookas, and flamethrowers as they crawled across jagged coral hills to seal or burn the caves fronting the approaches to Mount Tapotchau.

Many of the men were confronted with a first-hand preview of the dangers the approach to the mountain's summit would bring. Corporal Bernard Riggs, a high school valedictorian and former engineer, was a member of the Combat Intelligence section of the Headquarters Company of the 2nd Battalion of the regiment when his unit found themselves in the rocky no-man's-land between the beach and the cliffs. He discovered that the caves in this part of the battlefield left much to be desired:

> I had learned that a good foxhole could be a lifesaver, so I took my little Government Issue shovel, but I couldn't make much headway as I found that in this higher mountain area there was rock hidden under the six inches of soil covering it. I was able to borrow a pick and that helped, but I kept chopping and chipping until my hands were bleeding and then I kept going until it was deep enough to afford me a little extra room to squirm.[9]

Riggs went on to describe what happened when these dirty, hungry, tired Marines dug in for the night in preparation for an expected push toward the summit next morning: "The Japanese who had control of the high ground were not going to let us have it, so during the evening they started a barrage of mortar and artillery over the mountain top in our direction." Then fiery death rained on the troops from three directions. An artillery observer was asked to call in fire from the batteries far below the mountain and to the rear, but, as Riggs recalled,

When the advance man sent range and elevation data back, something went wrong because we were getting "friendly fire" dropping on us. We were catching Hell from both sides, and our men were cursing our artillery crew. Then enemy bombers were overhead, and they were dropping their "eggs" on and all around us. It wasn't very comforting to know that your own artillery was trying to help the enemy, but finally the artillery did get the right elevation and distance . . . but we were still cursing our artillery throughout the night as medics helped to evacuate our wounded.[10]

The men of the 2nd Marine Division were suffering heavy casualties, but like their 4th Marine Division counterparts fighting their way toward the village of Chacha near Magicienne Bay, at least there was a sense of progress. As Corporal Riggs insisted, "We gained ground each day. It was not easy, and we paid a high price, but at least we were now very close to reaching the highest point of land on this island." The men of the 27th Division had no such compensation for their trial by fire.

Unknown to Holland Smith, General Saito had deployed his largest and best force to cover Death Valley, which in turn fronted Thirty-first Army headquarters, a position the commander wanted to hold indefinitely. Almost all the 9th Tank Regiment's remaining vehicles, the most intact infantry regiment, the 135th, and a large number of headquarters units pushed this defense force to more than 4,000 men. Almost every major cave on the eastern side of Mount Tapotchau and the western side of Purple Heart Ridge was equipped with a machine gun, mortar, or 75 mm gun to support the riflemen firing at the approaching Americans below.

On the morning of June 24, Ralph Smith moved calmly among his frontline units as he directed a multipronged advance in the middle of enemy artillery fire that killed several of his staff and very nearly killed him. The more literary-inclined men of the division began to discuss a morbid comparison of their plight to the agony of the British Light Brigade at Balaclava nine decades earlier. The idea of "cannon to the right of them, cannon to the left of them" was not particularly farfetched in this instance because Death Valley was now becoming a life-sized shooting gallery, the Americans being the ducks. Casualties were soaring in a battle that would eventually cost the 165th Regiment twenty-two of twenty-nine company commanders, half the battalion commanders, and three executive officers. The incessant fire held the 106th Regiment to a mere 50-yard advance in the first two hours of the battle; in that time, eight of ten supporting tanks were knocked out by enemy fire, although they did succeed in knocking out six of nine Imperial tanks launching a desperate counterattack to push the Americans completely off the deadly plateau. As the sun passed its zenith, maps of the American lines showed an increasingly pronounced U-shape, and the 27th Division was at the bottom.

By mid-afternoon, as Ralph Smith was desperately seeking an alternative attack direction for the next day, a Jeep pulled up to his temporary command post on Chacha Road. One of Holland Smith's aides handed him an envelope containing his relief orders and a stipulation that he must leave Saipan by dawn the next morning. At 5:17 on Sunday morning, June 25, Major General Ralph Smith and a solitary aide boarded a navy PBM patrol plane for the ten-hour flight to Eniwetok, and a subsequent journey back to army headquarters in Hawaii. Two hours later, the battle for the central highlands of Saipan would commence again, but now the conflict would not only be between nations but between services.

At his Charan Kanoa headquarters, Holland Smith already sensed that he had unleashed a major controversy. As he told correspondent Robert Sherrod:

> Ralph Smith's my friend, but good God, I've got a duty to my country. I've lost seven thousand Marines. Can I afford to lose back what they have gained? To let my Marines die in vain? I know I'm sticking my neck out—the National Guard will try to chop it off—but my conscience is clear. I did my duty. When Ralph Smith issued an order to hold after I told him to attack, I had no other choice than to relieve him.[11]

Actually, the "order to hold" flap had developed in the muddled action still going on in the south at Nafutan Point and revolved around a still unresolved concept of who actually commanded certain army units deployed in that region. Whatever the outcome of the fighting in the south, however, Holland Smith was furious that the main body of the 27th Division seemed to be stuck near Mount Topatchau while the flanking Marines were moving forward. Now Sanderford Jarman would receive his chance to get things moving or very likely find himself relieved of command.

General Jarman reluctantly agreed to implement a new attack plan that had been cobbled together the previous afternoon by Ralph Smith just before his relief. The 106th Regiment, led by Colonel Russell Ayres, swung eastward toward Chacha village and then swerved northward to flank enemy positions on Purple Heart Ridge, but suddenly found itself battling toe-to-toe with the defenders of Saito's Thirty-first Army headquarters, which was ringed with howitzers and tanks. Meanwhile, the 65th Regiment, which was supposed to keep the main enemy force distracted while its sister regiment sidled around the flanks, found itself pinned down at the entrance to Death Valley, caught in a murderous crossfire.

Elsewhere on the American lines, June 25 proved to be much more profitable. On the western flank, Colonel Rath Tompkins' 1st Battalion of the 29th Marines dueled the defenders in front of Mount Tapotchau in a ferocious firefight, and Major William Chamberlain's 2nd Battalion of the 8th Marines pushed up the eastern slope. A single platoon scrambled up the daunting cliffs while a battle ranged in the woods below, and the small advance force was shocked to discover that the enemy had concentrated so many men in meeting the frontal assault that the summit was nearly empty of troops.

More good news filtered in from the eastern flank of the battle. General Schmidt's 4th Marine Division utilized an expertly coordinated infantry tank offensive to surge from one end of Kagman Peninsula to the other as numerous lines of defenders vanished, occasionally counterattacked, and then fled northward.[12]

Saito was attempting to hold too many vital positions with too few troops. And even if his center still held, its flanks were unraveling rapidly.

By Monday, June 26, General Saito admitted to Tokyo that he was in serious trouble. He had barely managed to beat back American assaults toward Thirty-first Army headquarters and the ridge and valley that fronted it, but in the process had lost 3,000 of his 4,000 men in that area. Supplying the forward troops was becoming very difficult, and water supplies were almost entirely exhausted. The 27th Division may have been stalled, but they were bleeding Saito's defenders; at the same time, the Japanese flanks were disintegrating. Now still another commander took charge of the center of the American line. General George Griner, commander of the 98th Division, was appointed by Lieutenant General Robert Richardson to replace the relieved Ralph Smith. When Griner arrived on Saipan, he reported to Holland Smith and was shocked to discover that the corps commander was now holding five of the division's nine battalions under his personal control until the performance of the 27th merited its being allowed to fight as an entire unit. Griner should have refused this rump command and jumped aboard the next plane for Hawaii; but instead, he rather tamely accepted command of the mere four battalions expected to smash the strongest point in the Japanese line.

Luckily for Griner, the Marine flanking units were now rolling up both coasts, and the "U" that looked so dangerous in Holland Smith's headquarters actually appeared as a death sentence to Saito's plan to hold the center of the island. Isolated units still fought ferociously, and three tanks and four remaining cannons provided a meager support force for the last holdouts. Far to the south, five hundred desperate Imperial troops attempted to break out of besieged Nafutan Point and briefly broke through the single battalion of the 105th Regiment to destroy a handful of American planes on nearby Aslito Airfield until slamming into the rear security forces of the 25th Marines. This failed attack became the signal for the 2nd Battalion of the 105th to pour into Nafutan in full force, and another 550 Nipponese troops were killed in a battle that raged all the way back to the southernmost cliffs of Saipan.

As June approached its final hours, General Saito finally determined that his last stand would be made in the north in the area between Tanapag Harbor and Marpi Point. On the night of June 28, Saito authorized the evacuation of Saipan's capital city, and a street battle erupted between the Imperial rearguard and Marine scouts. Guy Gabaldon was one of the first Americans to see the city of Garapan. As the scout insisted,

> The town had been thoroughly bombed and strafed, but our observation posts had reported seeing Japs milling in and around the buildings. We approached a well-built concrete building in South Garapan and started crawling. I went toward the west end and Johnny right toward the east end of the building. Suddenly, two Japanese soldiers came out of the building and stood at the door. It was my first encounter with Imperial Marines. I yelled at the Japs to surrender but could see that they were not members of the Visitors' Bureau. Very unfriendly chaps, I'd say. I fired off fifteen rounds, point blank. They were so close that it wasn't necessary to aim. I emptied the clip right from the hip. They both fell, one down the steps onto the grass, the other on the concrete deck.

This was the first round in a heavily contested firefight, Gabaldon insisted: "The push through Garapan proved to be very costly in Marine lives. The town was loaded with Japs. They were hiding in almost all the buildings. House to house fighting was intense. Japs everywhere, in the buildings, under the buildings, in the cisterns."[13]

On the final day of June, American soldiers and Marines slept in Garapan on Mount Topatchau and on Purple Heart Ridge. Many of them would be sleeping there permanently. The 4th Marine Division had lost 1,506 killed, wounded, and missing in the battle for the central highlands. The 2nd Marine Division lost 1,106 men, and the 27th Division tabulated 1,465 casualties. General Griner, who was aware of Holland Smith's opinion of the 27th Division, ordered an intensive count of enemy dead in that unit's area of responsibility and reported a total of 4,311 Japanese bodies. As Robert Sherrod reported in *Time:* "The whole area seemed to be a mass of stinking bodies, spilled guts and brains. They are thicker here than at Tarawa."[14]

The third phase of the battle of Saipan was over, and fifteen days after the initial landing, General Saito's forces were scrambling into their final defense lines. Yet the Imperial forces were still capable of great acts of brute courage and violence, and the last act in the drama would produce two final shocks to the invaders, one perpetrated against them, the other against the people the Japanese defenders were allegedly sworn to protect.

16

NORTH TO MARPI POINT

NDEPENDENCE DAY OF 1944 found the Saipan campaign
entering its final phase. General Saito had succeeded in deploying
his surviving forces on a final defensive line extending from just
south of the west coast port of Tanapag through the central village of
Tarahono and over to the eastern coast and the town of Hashigoru.
The Japanese were rapidly running out of maneuvering room as the island became increasingly narrow and edged them toward the cliffs of
Marpi Point. On the other hand, Saito's dwindling garrison would be
responsible for a more compact piece of terrain that was still hilly and
rocky enough to give the defenders a decided advantage.

As the battlefront narrowed after the capture of Saipan, Holland
Smith decided to rest the 2nd Marine Division for the upcoming invasion of Tinian. Meanwhile, the 27th Division would move up the west
coast along Tarapa Harbor and the 4th Marine Division would push
along the western edge of the island toward its ultimate goal of Marpi
Point. At noon on July 5, the final American offensive on Saipan rolled
into high gear as, from west to east, the 105th Regiment, the 165th
Regiment, the 24th Marines, and the 25th Marines moved in a syn-
chronized drive along a gradually narrowing front.

As the soldiers and Marines advanced, the Americans alternated between rooting out stubborn pockets of resistance and processing hun-

dreds of civilians who had now chosen to accept whatever fate the "foreign devils" had in store for them. Much of the civilian population of Saipan had already been captured and interned or had died in the fighting, but perhaps 5,000 survivors were now caught in a shrinking perimeter between two colliding armies. On the afternoon of July 6th alone, more than seven hundred civilians, including Japanese, Korean, and Chamorro residents surrendered to American units for the largest single catch of the campaign so far while a few hundred yards away one of the last major tank actions of the campaign took center stage.

Meanwhile, General Saito had set up his final command post in a cave just outside the coastal town of Makunsha on a parcel of high ground that fronted a large depression that would eventually be nicknamed Paradise Valley and a nearby ditch that would earn the name of Harakiri Gulch. While waves of surviving defenders threw themselves into suicidal charges to push the American soldiers back from the entrance to these two valleys, General Saito and Admiral Nagumo were preparing what was to eventually become the largest Japanese "banzai" attack of the Pacific War.

As the American advance rapidly gained momentum on this Wednesday afternoon, General Saito sent his aide Major Takashi Hirakushi on an inspection trip of the front lines, which now pressed dangerously close to the command post. Hirakushi was shocked when he saw streams of Imperial soldiers retreating on their own before the enemy drive. When he reported his findings to Saito, the commanding officer was stunned and incredulous, and assertions that "it is time to end this battle" filled the cave.

As the sun set on this day of disaster, General Saito, Admiral Nagumo, and Brigadier General Keiji Igeta, chief of staff of Thirty-first Army, sat with their aides and dined on squid, rice, and the last cans of crab meat that were available. As seems typical in the Marianas campaign, no matter how desperate the defenders' plight, they never ran short of alcoholic beverages and the saki flowed freely. Only two cigarettes remained among the men, and they were passed back and forth until they were too small to hold.[1]

Saito and Nagumo had earlier contacted Tokyo and had received permission and even encouragement to stage the ultimate mass suicide charge, a "Gyokusai." Translated into English, this word means "breaking the jewel" and was considered the ultimate human doomsday weapon that could be inflicted by the Nipponese on an enemy. In the medieval and feudal drama that was still an intricate part of Japanese life in the 1940s, the three primary virtues of the Nipponese culture were represented by a jewel, a mirror, and a sword. The sword stood for the true wisdom of decisions made decisively; the mirror represented the ability to see things as they are, good or bad, to determine true justice; and the jewel was a symbol of Japanese belief in themselves as a gentle, pious people. Launching a Gyokusai essentially meant that this final virtue had been dispensed with for the duration of the national emergency and that now even poets, artists, and scholars must trade their implements for the sword. Now, every Japanese man, woman, and child would adopt a ferocity that would ultimately make the empire invincible, even against greater numbers and better technology. According to Saito and Nagumo, the immediate goal of this "super-banzai" was to kill seven Americans for every Japanese death and "Seven lines to repay our country" would become the password.

When Major Hirakushi asked Saito what would happen to the thousands of civilians who now shared caves and other strongpoints with the Imperial soldiers and sailors, the general replied, "There is no longer any distinction between civilians and troops. It would be better for them to join in the attack with bamboo spears than be captured."[2]

Now the last operational mimeograph machine churned out three hundred copies of Saito's final orders to the garrison:

> For more than twenty days since the American devils attacked, the officers, men and civilian employees of the Imperial Army and Navy on this island have demonstrated the honor and glory of the Imperial Forces. I expected that every man would do his duty.
>
> Heaven has not given us an opportunity. We have not been able to utilize fully the terrain. We have fought in unison up to the present time, but now we have no materials with which to fight and our

artillery for attack has been completely destroyed. Our comrades have fallen one after another. Despite the bitterness of defeat we pledge "seven lives to repay our country."

The barbarous attack of the enemy is being continued. Even though the enemy has occupied only a corner of Saipan we are dying without avail under the violent shelling and bombing. Whether we attack or whether we stay where we are, there is only death. However, in death there is life. We must utilize this opportunity to exalt true Japanese manhood. I will advance with those who remain to deliver still another blow to the American Devils, and leave my bones on Saipan as a bulwark of the Pacific.

As it says in the Battle Ethics, "I will never suffer the disgrace of being taken alive" and "I will offer up to courage my soul and calmly rejoice in living the eternal principle. Here I pray with you for the eternal life of the Emperor and the welfare of the country and I advance to seek out the enemy.

"Follow me."[3]

The spirit of Yoshitsugu Saito's final orders was genuine even though important elements of the text were stretching the truth. First, the Americans did not hold only a "corner" of Saipan: It was the defenders who were now backed into a small pocket. Second, although a part of Saito really wanted to wave a sword and lead the final charge from the front line, he was old enough, tired enough, and senior enough to choose the quieter, more dignified exit of Seppuku. Admiral Nagumo and General Igeta quickly joined a triple suicide pact scheduled for the next morning and a more junior officer would be tapped to lead the suicide charge.

Dawn broke on Thursday, July 6, with illusion and reality vying for supremacy in both armies. On the American side, there was a growing sense of euphoria among many units based on their belief that the visible disintegration of Japanese lines the day before indicated that the garrison had nearly been annihilated and that only mop-up operations remained. Even staff officers at places such as the 105th Regiment headquarters believed that enemy resistance would be minimal. As

Sergeant Ronald Johnson pointed out: "The intelligence was that the Japanese had been reduced to a small force incapable of withstanding an attack. We were led to believe it was only a matter of two or three days of mopping up. I think at that point our guard was down, so to speak, because we believed that the force we were facing was not very formidable."[4]

If the Americans held the illusion that the enemy was a spent force, the Japanese who had read Saito's mimeographed orders had the illusion that they really were going to kill several "foreign devils" for each of their own deaths and thus so shock American sentiment at home that the enemy would call off the drive toward Tokyo and accept a negotiated settlement. As far as many Nipponese were concerned, they possessed the ultimate advantage over the enemy, they were anxious to die for their cause, and the Americans wanted to live so that they could go home to their cars and backyards.

Although many Americans congratulated themselves on apparently surviving the Saipan campaign, General Saito politely apologized to his aide, Major Hirakushi, for preceding him to heaven by committing Sippuku instead of leading the charge. The three senior officers then proceeded to a small, more private cave near headquarters and knelt in a circle. A senior officer holding a pistol stood behind each man. Admiral Nagumo maintained a certain level of naval autonomy by requesting that a naval officer "assist" him, but otherwise the ritual suicides were almost identical. Each commander sat cross legged near the mouth of the cave attired in dress uniform. The three men bared their chests and initiated the process of using their swords to rip open their stomachs. An instant later, their "assistants" shot them in the head and then summoned help to burn the bodies and the regimental flags. Now it fell upon the shoulders of Colonel Eisuke Suzuki, commander of the 135th Regiment, to carry out Saito's orders and lead the Gyokasai during the coming night.[5]

All Thursday morning and afternoon, soldiers and Marines kept pushing northward as Japanese rear guard units fought desperate but short-lived last stands. Units from the 27th Division had now captured

Tanapag, the last significant town on Saipan, and were advancing north on Tanapag plain toward the village of Mankunsha and Marpi Point beyond. As the day's action sputtered into ever smaller firefights, the three battalions of the westernmost part of the American line started making camp for the night. Colonel Leonard Bishop, commanding officer of the 105th Regiment had received reports from prisoner interrogations of the possibility that some form of final enemy suicide attack would occur and there were hints that the action might take place in the next twenty-four hours. But although alerts were issued, the reality was that his regiment was now deployed on an open plain with little natural protection against a determined enemy assault.

The 1st and 2nd Battalions of the 105th deployed in an elongated semicircle that ran from the coastal sand dunes through Tanapag Road over the railroad line and on into the adjacent fields; the 3rd Battalion camped further inland and several hundred yards south in their own crescent formed in the vicinity of Harakiri Gulch. Meanwhile, largely unknown to the men of the 105th Regiment, the artillerymen of the 3rd Battalion of the 10th Marines had been ordered to move from their current position near Garapan up to just north of Tarapag so that their guns could bring Marpi Point under fire. The destinies of these four battalions of soldiers and Marines were about to be changed forever by several thousand Japanese soldiers, sailors, construction workers, and even civilians: Each one was determined to kill seven Americans in exchange for a ticket to heaven.

A mile north of where 1st Battalion commander Lieutenant Colonel William O'Brien was carefully deploying his antitank guns to fill in yawning gaps in the American line, Colonel Takuji Suzuki was experiencing his own frustrating early evening. Drawing units together from all over northern Saipan was difficult in ideal conditions, and now Suzuki had to deal with the human obstacle of incessant American artillery fire and the natural obstacle of a ferocious tropical thunderstorm as he sorted out the men, and some women, who would form what he hoped would be an irresistible human wave assault. Something like 3,000 soldiers and sailors were concentrated around Tanapag Road in Makasuna and perhaps another 1,000 armed construction workers and other assorted civilian volunteers had agreed to join them even if their weapons sometimes were only bayonets tied to bamboo sticks. If nothing else, the liquor supply, as usual, seemed to be almost inexhaustible as case after case of saki and beer was unloaded to generate additional enthusiasm. Suzuki's strike force would have more than a two-to-one superiority over the less than 1,500 soldiers of the two army battalions camped just down the road and peering intently northward in search of any glimmer of information about the possible banzai attack.

At 4:00 a.m. on July 7, Suzuki felt he could wait no longer for what, after all, was planned as a night attack, and with upraised sword he ordered his motley assault force to double time down Tanapag Road. These were desperate, totally dedicated men who were united by their assurance that they had a place in Japanese Valhalla if only they could die killing one, or preferably more, foreign devils. Thousands of jogging feet could now be heard at the American end of the road, and GIs checked their weapons, took a final deep breath, and waited for Armageddon. What they saw in the next few hours was a surrealistic nightmare that would be difficult to repeat even in the carnival of death that was the World War II.

Lieutenant George O'Donnell of G Company, 2nd Battalion wrote this to his parents:

> At about 0430 all hell broke loose! It was their big Banzai attack: out from the draw, below us, came the two remaining Jap tanks, followed by about four hundred Japs heading for the flats below us. It had just finished pouring, and we were all soaked, with our teeth chattering. But no sooner had we dropped our eyes on that mob, than we forgot all our discomforts! And then, from our right and below us, there came thousands of Japs! For two hours they passed by, and came right at us. It was like a mob after a big football game, all trying to get out at once! We had a hard struggle keeping them from overrunning us, and we had a field day, firing, firing, until our ammunition started to run low. The closest any of them came was

ten yards; and we were hitting them at four and five hundred yards also.[6]

O'Donnell emphasized the sports fan analogy, but 2nd Battalion commander Major Edward McCarthy, one of the few senior officers to survive the attack, likened the action to a movie: "It was like the movie stampede staged in the old Wild West movies. We were the cameramen. The Japs just kept coming and coming and didn't stop. It didn't make any difference that you shot one; five more would take his place. We would be in foxholes looking up, just like those cameramen used to be. The Japs ran right over us."[7]

This was a scale of organized self-destruction that dwarfed anything experienced at Guadalcanal, the Aleutians, or Tarawa. But it was far more than personal destruction. The attackers were taking Americans with them at an ever escalating rate. Colonel O'Brien faced the human wave like a latter day George Armstrong Custer as he emptied the contents of two pistols into the attackers and then took over a machine gun and piled up more bodies before several bullets ended his life but brought him a posthumous Medal of Honor. Sergeant Thomas Baker played the crusty cavalry trooper making a last stand in which he trades his life for several adversaries. Gravely wounded, Baker refused medical attention, propped himself against a tree, and aimed a rifle that had eight bullets left. His body was found with eight enemy soldiers sprawled around him, a higher price for death than even General Saito encouraged for his own men, and Baker also received the Medal of Honor.[8]

The American soldiers were dropping hundreds of attackers, but they were being overwhelmed by sheer numbers on a battlefield that offered few advantages for the outnumbered defenders. Like Leonidas's three hundred Spartans falling back before Persian hordes the men in olive drabs were pushed southward into the streets of newly captured Tanapag. Now surviving officers set up defensive perimeters and fought an escalating street battle as the fighting went from house to house.

As the Japanese wave surged around the now nearly besieged men of 1st and 2nd Battalons, they began pressing on the next American unit down Tanapag Road, the artillerymen of 10th Marines. Now two loosely coordinated Imperial formations were charging down the coast road and the railroad that ran parallel to it and H Battery of the 3rd Battalion happened to be deployed near a creek bed between the two avenues of approach. When the attackers got to within 600 yards of the guns, the Marines were still not entirely sure whether friendly or enemy forces were approaching. As Lieutenant Arnold Hostetter, executive officer of the battery, recalled:

> It was 5:15, just getting light, when a group of men were seen advancing on the battery position from the right front at about 600 yards. It was thought that Army troops were somewhere to the front, so fire on this group was held until they were definitely identified as Japanese at about 400 yards. We knew that our men manning listening posts were somewhere to our front so the firing battery was ordered to open fire with time and ricochet fire on the group to the right. Firing was also heard from the machine guns on the left.[9]

Now the Japanese host surged forward and according to Robert Sherrod's report in *Time*, "The artillerymen fired point blank into the Japs with fuses set at four tenths of a second. They bounced their high explosive shells fifty yards in front of the guns and into the maniacal ranks." As the guns came nearer to being overwhelmed, a number of enterprising artillerymen spotted a Japanese aircraft parts depot in a field nearby and retreated there for a final stand. The depot was filled with crates, boxes, and parts of wings and fuselages, and the Marines quickly assembled the assorted materials to create an instant fort from which they could defend themselves. The men were not equipped as infantrymen, so they used pistols and grenades to kill the first enemy soldiers who pushed toward them. Then, in a momentary lull in the action, the defenders sprinted outside the box-fort and collected the rifles and swords of their slain adversaries. At one point, the Marines' position was nearly overwhelmed and the crisis produced one of the most visually dramatic confrontations of the Pacific War: Americans and Japanese dueling with one another armed with samurai swords!

Corps and division headquarters only gradually began to appreciate the enormity of the crisis. Naval vessels sent north to lend supporting fire to the 105th Regiment discovered a furious firefight on Tanapag Beach in which overwhelming numbers of attackers were forcing the outnumbered soldiers back through the sand dunes and toward the water. As surviving Americans blasted their guns beachward and waded into the water, many were picked up by rescue boats. Army tankers only a few hundred yards from the battle over H Battery refused initially to understand the threat to the surviving artillerymen and only belatedly entered the battle for the box crates.

The 1st and 2nd Battalions of the 27th Infantry lost 401 killed and 512 wounded, which essentially temporarily ended their combat effectiveness as units. More than half the enlisted men and three-fourths of the officers of these battalions were now dead or wounded. The 3rd Battalion, 10th Marines, especially Battery H, had taken heavy casualties: Forty-five killed and 82 wounded among men who had never expected to be in a swirling gunfight that would match many Old West shootouts.

Yet, when help finally did arrive and American soldiers and Marines surveyed the battlefield they saw a slaughter reminiscent of Shiloh or Antirtim.

Lieutenant Colonel Oakley Bidwell of 27th Division headquarters staff supervised the burial details: "I don't think I can draw a picture more horrible than my memory of Tanapag Plain. It appeared to be virtually solid dead soldiers. A creek ran through a shallow ravine, emptying into a beautiful turquoise-blue lagoon. The creek and its banks seemed filled with bodies. And while I watched a huge crimson flower grew out of the mouth of the creek." When Holland Smith's chief of staff, General Graves Erskine, arrived on the scene, Bidwell noted his reaction: "He took two steps, a long breath, and promptly and efficiently lost his breakfast before immediately returning to his car and driving rapidly off."[10]

Corporal Bernard Riggs experienced a much closer acquaintance with an area already becoming known as the Field of the Dead: "At daybreak we passed through the Army lines and entered a canefield of American and Japanese corpses. Bodies were everywhere, sometimes lying over another. They were in ditches, ravines, and in the flat cane fields. There were hundreds upon hundreds lying in different positions inter-mixed with American Army and Marine bodies." Riggs had orders to search for items that might be of use to Intelligence staffs, but he was leery of booby traps and enemy soldiers who might be feigning death to get one final opportunity to kill an American: "There were truck loads of souvenirs lying about such as Samurai Swords, rifles, pistols and flags, however, at this moment we had no desire to take anymore than what had been requested of us. We watched as troops moved in the area to identify the American dead and remove their previous bodies to a proper burial ground."[11]

There were hundreds of American bodies to bury, but by the time intelligence units had tallied the number of enemy dead, the staggering total had reached 4,311 Nipponese corpses remaining on the battlefield. This loss was higher than that suffered by either the Union or the Confederate army at Antietam or Shiloh, yet was inflicted on a far smaller force. Although a significant proportion of these bodies were those of construction workers or civilians who had entered into the spirit of Gyokusai with a vengeance, somewhere around 3,000 Imperial troops died in the attack, the irony being that seven Japanese soldiers were killed for every American fatality, exactly the opposite ratio of what General Saito had ordained.

By sunset on July 7, perhaps 4,000 desperate, hungry civilians and possibly 1,000 soldiers and sailors were crammed in the northern tip of Saipan with a leviathan called the American invasion force approaching from the front and the stark coral cliffs of Marpi Point in their rear. There was simply no remaining command structure beyond the platoon level and, with only a few exceptions, lieutenants and sergeants were the ranking officers of the remnants of the Imperial garrison of Saipan. Far to the south, 10,000 Japanese civilians, including 5,000 children, were discovering that the "foreign devils" weren't quite the monsters the military had portrayed them to be, and 3,000 Chamorros were making little secret of their happiness to be rid of their Nipponese overlords. All over the island, whether buried by the Americans or rotting in caves, were the bodies of more than 30,000 Imperial troops and perhaps 5,000 civilians caught in the crossfire of war. Now the 5,000 military and civilian survivors who were still "free" in what had become a coral-reefed prison were making decisions regarding their final destiny, or having the decisions made for them. A green tide of American Marines was surging inexorably towards them and a stunningly azure sea lapped behind them. What loomed in the middle was the final agony of Saipan in the tragedy of Marpi Point.

On the morning of July 9, the 4th Marine Division occupied the last ridge that overlooked Marpi Point and the cliff wall that fronted the sea. Admiral Kelly Turner believed that organized enemy resistance was over and at 4:15 p.m. declared Saipan secured. The next morning brought an official flag-raising ceremony at Holland Smith's Charan Kanoa headquarters and the American colors now waved over what would eventually become the Commonwealth of the Northern Marianas. Yet, even as bands played triumphant martial music and congratulations were passed around, a far grimmer drama was being played out several miles to the north.

Like the terrified passengers on the *Titanic* slowly backpedaling towards the upturning stern of the ship as the bow slid beneath the freezing Atlantic waters, 5,000 men, women, and children retreated toward the cliffs of Marpi Point simply because there was nowhere else to go. As the zone of safety shrank at an accelerating pace, the Japanese civilians and soldiers of Saipan had become participants in the equivalent of a sinking ocean liner. Some people were simply lapped up by the surging green wave of Marines and, while expecting horrible deaths, actually gained survival. Some quietly committed suicide in caves or between rock formations in the pathetically small parcel of land that was still Japanese occupied Saipan.

Yet many others became swept up in the deadly choreography of the mass suicide that seemed so much a part of Nipponese culture in times of defeat and disgrace. Now American servicemen who thought they had experienced every version of violence in the cruel war gasped in horror from the nearby ridgeline and in naval vessels patrolling below as a final orgy of death began. Mothers and fathers linked arms with their children and jumped into the sea far below as a family unit. Women calmly combed and braided their hair and equally calmly walked out from the beach below Marpi Point into the ever deeper ocean as if they somehow intended to walk home to Japan. Children in miniature Imperial Navy uniforms shouted high-pitched "banzais" and jumped into the rocks below the cliff.

At home, the Japanese press reveled in this traditional exit from a disastrous situation and reveled even more in the blatant shock it created among the "foreign devils." Newspapers triumphed the mass suicides as the moral equivalent of victory on Saipan because it would make the Americans think twice about invading Japan proper. Headlines screamed the triumph of the Imperial Navy: "The Heroic Last Moments of Our Fellow Countrymen on Saipan"; "Patriotic Essence Astounds the World"; "Women Changed into Their Best Apparel, Prayed to the Imperial Palace, Sublimely Commit Suicide in Front of the American Devils"; "Women Sacrifice Themselves for the National Exigency Together with the Brave Men."

However, behind the self-congratulatory headlines there developed a much more complex reality. First, American Marines and sailors began to notice that many of the "voluntary" suicides were becoming anything but self-inflicted. Mothers carrying babies to the edge of the cliff suddenly changed their minds and, as they turned around, were shot by Japanese soldiers; teenagers engulfed by rising water decided to swim back to shore and were picked off by snipers. Groups of civilians who tried to bolt from a suicide circle were brought down by Imperial grenades. In one of the ironies of the battle, as the Japanese soldiers, the sworn protectors of Nipponese civilians, turned into murderers, the "foreign devils" interceded and saved the victims by shooting down the self-appointed executioners.

More than a thousand civilians did die, either by suicide or murder, but for every one who died perhaps three others survived. Some people simply fled into caves and emerged only days and even weeks later as it became clear the battle was over. Others, including even some soldiers and sailors, took the shocking option of surrender.

As Scout Guy Gabaldon carefully edged his way along the caves and cliffs of Marpi Point, he was shocked to come face-to-face with a dozen Imperial soldiers who seemed torn between resistance and surrender. The Marine used his excellent knowledge of the Japanese language and culture to tell the men that he was delivering a personal message from Holland Smith, Shogun in charge of the Marianas operation:

> General Smith admires your valor and has ordered our troops to of-fer a safe haven to all the survivors of your intrepid Gyokusai attack. Such a glorious and courageous military action will go down in his-tory. The General assures you that you will be taken to Hawaii where you will be kept together in comfortable quarters until the end of the war. The General's word is honorable. It is his desire that there be no more useless bloodshed.

Gabaldon believed, correctly, that many hidden Japanese eyes were concentrating on him, but he thought that if he emphasized that the offer of generous surrender terms came from a Shogun, he could possi-bly preserve Nipponese honor and make capitulation more palatable. Suddenly, he saw smiles cross their faces, probably because of his poor pronunciation: "They know that I am not Japanese. I look like a typical Chicano." A short time later, the sergeant commanding the small force left temporarily and returned with an additional fifty men, who all sat down: "They do not look like defeated men. They are proud and seri-ous—as if they haven't really made up their minds." Then, at a signal that all is well: "They start coming up. The lines up the trail seem end-less. They all look for someone in authority."

Finally, the lone Marine waved for help to a squad of comrades on a nearby hill and a march was organized to the nearest stockard. The line of new prisoners exceeded eight hundred soldiers and civilians, more prisoners than had been taken in all the previous battles in the Pacific combined.

As the last Japanese civilians and soldiers surrendered or died and Marpi Point was occupied by American Marines, the first land battle in the Marianas campaign came to an official end. A garrison of more than 30,000 men, including most of two infantry divisions, a tank regiment, and several battalions of naval ground troops was now wiped from the Imperial table of organization. Almost a thousand Japanese troops had chosen surrender over death, one hundred times as many men as taken alive at Tarawa. Yet the American invaders had hardly escaped unscathed. More than 70,000 American soldiers and Marines had been involved in ground combat on Saipan and of these 3,225 were killed, 13,061 wounded, and 326 missing, a 25 percent casualty rate that matched the deadly losses in many battles of the Civil War. Yet even as everyone—from generals to privates—celebrated a significant, though bloody, triumph, all eyes began shifting three miles across the channel to the next American objective, the night air center that was Tinian Island.

'17

INVASION ON JIG DAY

AS THE STARS AND STRIPES were unfurled at key points in newly secured Saipan, American attention almost immediately began to focus on the Japanese emblems still waving defiantly across the bay in neighboring Tinian Island. If the capture of Saipan revolved around Ernest King's insistence on cutting the enemy line of communication between its southern empire and the Japanese war machine that utilized those resources, the seizure of Tinian had its genesis in Henry Arnold's determination to use that island's extensive airfields as the springboard for the projected mass assault by the new B-29 Superfortresses on the heart of the Imperial homeland. Tinian had been useless to the Americans when a Japanese garrison of 30,000 men was camped only three miles away on Saipan; but now that force was either dead or captured and a new offensive was imminent.

One of the advantages of conducting a campaign almost contiguous to the next scheduled objective was that by the time Saipan was captured the commanders of Fifth Fleet and its ground assault forces had an excellent idea of what awaited them on Tinian. Airplanes took photographs of the island from aerial viewpoints; frogmen snapped pictures of the target from the coastline, and intelligence personnel pieced together an excellent composite model of every aspect of the new target.

In a strict geographical sense, Saipan and Tinian were twin islands, seen from the sea as a single entity but actually separated by a channel 3 miles wide. The two islands jointly were the center of the Japanese sugarcane industry, each island also featuring a moderate stretch of cornfields. At 10 miles long and 6 miles across at its widest point, Tinian was about two-thirds as large as its northern counterpart, but it contained more farmland because nearly the entire island was arable. Although Saipan contained extensive rugged, mountainous regions, most of Tinian was lush, park-like farmland interspersed with orchards. Only the immediate coastline and an extensive plateau on the southern tip of the island provided the combination of undergrowth, scrub plants and trees, coral crevasses, and rocky caves that could be turned into natural strongpoints for defenders.

Like neighboring Saipan, and very much unlike Guam to the south, Tinian's population was overwhelmingly Japanese in culture and tradition. By 1944, native islanders had mostly been driven off Tinian and replaced with nearly 20,000 Imperial subjects from the home islands and Okinawa. Local farmhouses, villages, and the capital city of Tinian Town all reflected Japanese architectural designs. The capital contained Shinto and Buddhist temples along with more Westernized record stores, movie theaters, and beauty parlors. At this time, Tinian, like Saipan, was no conquered province populated with restive natives but an integral part of Greater Japan, and it reflected most aspects of the homeland's culture and world view. These residents were also terrified of the prospect of an American invasion and had been warned to expect the worst if the enemy ever came ashore.

The person who was nominally charged with preventing the nightmare of an American invasion was Admiral Kakuji Kakuta, commander of all land-based naval air units in the region. Kakuta had his headquarters on Tinian, which contained four major airfields dominated by the airstrip at Ushi Point at the northern tip of the island. However, in many respects Kakuta was an admiral without a command as most of his aircraft had been destroyed during the battle of Philippine Sea. Operational command of the ground forces on the island devolved to

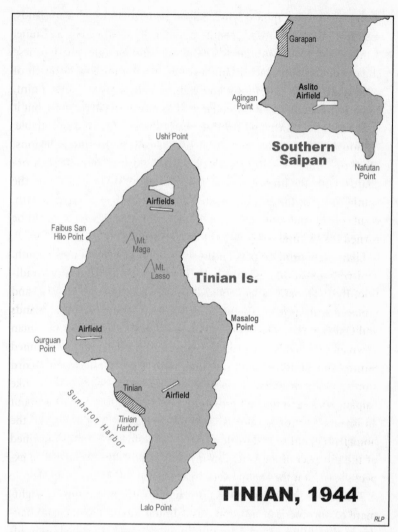

Tinian, July 1944

Kakuta's subordinate, Captain Goichi Oya, and the senior army officer present, Colonel Kiyochi Ogata.

Captain Oya was responsible for coastal and air-defense artillery on Tinian; this array centered around ten 140 mm coast defense guns, seven 12 mm dual-purpose guns, eight 75 mm howitzers, three 75 mm dual-purpose guns, and three British Whitworth naval 6-inch guns. Oya's post also gave him command of security for Tinian's four air-fields, and in that capacity the captain had hurriedly issued rifles to almost 2,000 seamen who were now designated as naval infantry. Altogether, Oya could count just fewer than 4,500 officers and men on his naval rolls.

Colonel Ogata commanded approximately the same number of soldiers, but most of his men belonged to combat units. Earlier in the spring, Ogata's own regiment, the 50th Infantry Regiment of the 29th Division had been involved in the mass transfer of units from Manchuria to the Pacific front. Then, on a stroke of good fortune for Ogata, but not for the defenders on Saipan, a battalion of the 135th Infantry Regiment had been involved in amphibious exercises on Tinian when the Fifth Fleet arrived in June and, with no available transportation back across the channel, had been incorporated into Tinian's garrison. Ogata's four available infantry battalions were augmented by a battery of twelve 75 mm mountain guns, a battery of six light antitank guns, and a formation of twelve light tanks. These regular forces could be aided to some extent by several companies of militia recruited among the local inhabitants, but these men were only lightly armed and equipped. Thus Ogata and Oya had less than a third as many men as the garrison on neighboring Saipan and about two-thirds as much territory to defend as their counterparts. Moreover, the garrison of Saipan could make maximum use of ground particularly situated for defense, but Tinian offered few places where forces could dig in and hold indefinitely; indeed, it was a tanker's paradise in a potential battle in which the invaders were likely to have far more tanks than the defenders.[1]

Ogata and Oya, like so many Imperial commanders before them, were committed to destroying the Americans on the beach, and, if nothing else, they thought they had narrowed those invasion beaches to only two possibilities. The most likely invasion point seemed to be Sunharon Bay, which fronted the capital city of Tinian Town on the western side of the island. Tinian Town occupied about the same point on Tinian as Charan Kanoa on Saipan and was the junction for several roads and railroad lines as well as housing harbor facilities, the island radio station, and most of the shopping facilities for the inhabitants. The bay also featured the only extensive beaches on an island mostly surrounded by coral cliffs, some of which rose 100 feet from the sea.

The second most likely invasion point seemed to be on the east coast, where a modest 125-yard stretch of beach wound along Asiga Bay between Asiga Point and Masalog Point. This spot seemed much less likely as an invasion point because the bay offered no port facilities and was a distance from the capital. Nonetheless, this location still received constant attention from the garrison commanders.

Finally, Ogata and Oya largely discounted the only other point on the island that contained beaches. The northwest coast of Tinian almost opposite Ushi Point Airfield featured two tiny beaches of 60 yards and 160 yards separated by 1,000 yards of jagged coral cliffs. These two points seemed the least attractive enemy invasion point because the beaches were heavily broken up by coral formations stabbing onto the sand and the heavy undergrowth at the edge of the beaches would make it far more difficult to penetrate inland that Sunharon or Asiga Bays. This position was not totally ignored, but only a small detachment of beach-defense personnel were permanently assigned to this craggy strand.

Not only were the Japanese outnumbered and outgunned but they were plagued by the same creaky command structure that cursed the Nipponese throughout the war. Army-navy relations were, as usual, frosty at best. Army personnel were furious that the Imperial fleet had seemingly abandoned the Marianas and left the soldiers to die with no hope of victory. Even the equally doomed sailors on Tinian seemed able to enjoy their remaining days in greater comfort than the army forces. As one soldier wrote in his diary, "The navy stays in barracks buildings and has liberty every night with liquor to drink, while we huddle in the rain and never get out on pass." Another entry noted the incompetence of navy antiaircraft protection on the island as "navy guns spread black smoke where the enemy planes weren't. Not one hit out of a thousand shots." The sailors seemed competent in only one activity—stealing: "The naval aviation people are robbers, when they ran off to the mountains they stole army provisions."[2]

In many respects, the American troops who invaded Tinian would be fighting two separate battles against parallel forces of army and navy personnel. Colonel Ogata and Captain Oya had a murky relationship in that each commander seemed to accept tacit responsibility for specific points on the island while merely hoping that the other service would somehow cooperate in the enterprise. Ogata deployed the 2nd Battalion of his own regiment, a platoon of engineers and a battery of four 75 mm guns to guard against an attempted landing on the Asiga Bay beach. The 3rd Battalion, supported by another engineer platoon and artillery battery, would defend the beaches along Tinian's capital. The hooked protrusion of Faibus-San Hilo Point halfway up the coast between Tinian Town and Ushi Point had no landing beaches but still rated the presence of an infantry company and an antitank battery.

These beach area deployments still allowed Ogata to retain a modest reserve force that would be rushed into action once the pattern of American attack had been deciphered. A general reserve of two infantry companies was stationed at the foot of Mount Lasso in the north-center region of Tinian. Slightly to the south of this promontory was a junction of several roads at a radio communication center, and this point was chosen as the location of Ogata's Mobile Counterattack Force, which included the orphaned battalion of the 135th Infantry, his tank formation, and a motley army of trucks. Finally, the colonel established his own headquarters at the top of Mount Lasso and this command post featured a signal company, supply company, and engineer and medical detachments.

Colonel Ogata knew that this force was spread far too thinly but assumed the tacit cooperation of Captain Oya once the American invasion began. Oya deployed most of his coastal defense guns to cover Sunharon Harbor and the capital and then deployed 1,400 hastily organized naval infantry to guard the guns. Then he issued arms to the roughly 1,000 seamen who formed the base personnel for Ushi Point Airfield and tacitly agreed with Ogata that this force would be unleashed in a counterattack against American landings in the northern third of the island.

Ogata and Oya had also reached an understanding that if the enemy had landed an overwhelming force on Tinian, all surviving units would conduct an extended retrograde movement that would terminate in a last stand on the southern tip of the island. The southern coast of Tinian could be approached only by scaling a formidable cliff line that extended from the east coast to the west coast 2 miles north of Lalo Point. This seemed to be an ideal rallying point for the sort of dramatic final gesture that was so much a part of the choreography of a doomed Japanese force. Most, or preferably all, of the Imperial forces would die, but they would die with the satisfaction of having killed large numbers of invaders.

While Ogata and Oya made their defensive dispositions, on the other side of the narrow channel their American counterparts were debating the best way to ensure that the Japanese had few Americans joining them in the afterlife. The next stage of the Marianas campaign would now entail somewhat overlapping invasions of Tinian and Guam and would force Kelly Turner and Holland Smith to orchestrate two operations more than 60 miles apart. Thus, onsite naval and ground commanders would be needed for what was now the northern axis of a dual invasion. Rear Admiral Harry Hill, who had served as second-in-command of both the Joint Expeditionary Force and the Northern Attack Force at Saipan, appeared to be the logical choice to command the naval aspects of the new invasion. Meanwhile, Major General Harry Schmidt, who had proved more than capable in his position of commander of 4th Marine Division on Saipan, now became a de facto corps commander, and Major General Clifton Cates was assigned to take over Schmidt's old unit.

Turner, Smith, Hill, Schmidt, and their staffs now focused on one overriding challenge: how to land an amphibious force on an island that had practically no beaches. Tinian was a beautiful island filled with park-like grounds and surrounded by warm azure seas, but it was missing the one ingredient that dominated promotional literature for tropical paradise vacations. The island was almost completely surrounded by jagged coral cliffs that rose as high as 100 feet above the waves. Just as wise vacationers would always attempt to ensure the availability of convenient beachfronts, the men who planned amphibious invasions were essentially searching for the same item, and Tinian was hardly an ideal choice.

Sunharon Harbor was the obvious choice for a landing, but it was so obvious that the Americans knew that this was where the Japanese commanders would deploy most of their men and guns. The American commanders were far too imaginative, humane, and sensible to do just what the enemy expected, so all eyes began to focus on alternatives. Asiga Bay's one 125-yard stretch of beach appeared to have possibilities until reconnaissance units of frogmen came back with the dismal news that this site, now designated as Yellow Beach, featured water approaches that were heavily potholed, filled with jagged underwater obstructions, and laced with large numbers of enemy mines. The beach beyond was heavily entrenched with pillboxes and gun positions that could roll up a large tally of Marine invaders.

Only one other spot on this island offered access to the sea, but no one had ever given that location a name. Located on the west coast half way between Ushi Point and San Hilo Point was an area now designated as White Beach 1 by the Americans. White Beach 1 was a 60-yard stretch of sand huddled between 3-to-10-foot coral cliffs. The beach was so narrow that only eight amtracs could land at one time, and four of them would still have to nudge against the lower parts of the cliff wall. Then, beyond another 1,000-yard stretch of insurmountable heights, was another 160-yard beach now designated as White Beach 2. This beach was wider, but not continuous as it was interspersed with coral rocks and swaths of undergrowth jutting seaward from the ground immediately beyond the coast. Planners calculated that White 2 could accommodate sixteen alligators at a time; but, here again, half would have to ram up against steep cliffs to disembark their passengers.

When Kelly Turner saw the limitations of the White Beach plan, even Sunharon Harbor suddenly looked much better. The area fronting Tinian's capital might be heavily defended, but Turner insisted that it had several redeeming features: "It does not have the extensive swamp that proved so troublesome at Saipan; once a beachhead has been gained there is a quite good small craft harbor with a narrow entrance and a shallow protective reef that would permit unloading in all but seriously heavy weather." In turn, according to Turner, "an advance down the length of Tinian from White Beaches would be too time consuming; the beaches were far too narrow to be exploited; and artillery would be difficult to land in such narrow confines."[3]

Smith, Schmidt, and Hill formed a united front against "Terrible Turner," and the crusty but intelligent admiral spent considerable time reconsidering the plan. Finally, he submitted his request to invade through White Beaches 1 and 2 to Raymond Spruance. The stage was now set for the second of three great amphibious invasions of the Marianas campaign.[4]

Each American amphibious invasion of the Pacific War had a unique and definable flavor that set it apart from its counterparts. The landings on Guadalcanal two years earlier were dominated by the feelings of a desperate shoestring operation whereby the first American offensive against the Japanese would rapidly turn back into a defensive struggle against an enemy that had more men, more planes, and more ships than the invaders. The assault on Okinawa, a year after Forager, reflected the vastness of an American war machine at its peak of productivity. Yet the invasion force soon faced the dual emotions of confronting an enemy that at first ceded the landing beaches virtually without opposition and then shattered the eerie silence with the suicidal roar of the kamikazes of the divine wind. The battle for Tinian was no different in its particular personality of place and time. The invasion would not be easy—no battle against the Japanese ever was—but now the invaders knew much about the objective they were going to attack, enjoyed a substantial numerical advantage over the defenders, and owned the sky above and the sea around their target. Unlike the situation in the European theatre, there was no hope that a cornered enemy would make the logical decision of surrender and thus save numerous lives on both sides. Even a German SS unit trapped in similar circumstances would give serious consideration to capitulation after fighting long enough to preserve their honor. The Marine invaders, who were hardly the barbarous gangsters the Japanese high command presented them to be, would have welcomed mass enemy surrenders if they came without trickery; but as experience had taught them that few adversaries would take this way out of combat, they prepared for the usual grisly scenes that this form of warfare would produce.

In this invasion, the date of attack was designated "J-day," and for this "Jig Day," the two focal units were the 2nd and 4th Marine Divisions. These units had ended the battle of Saipan with 11,000 casualties and would enter the new campaign decidedly understrength because only 2,000 replacements had arrived. More reinforcements would arrive as the battle progressed, but the initial invasion force would number perhaps 32,000 men to be put ashore by the 533 amtracs that had survived the enemy barrages on Saipan. On the positive side, the 1,000-mile trip from Eniwetok to Saipan was reduced to a 3-mile channel crossing from an already secured island that would serve as a platform for enormous support activities.

General Schmidt decided that if he was going in over narrow beaches, he would concentrate much of his power around one division while using the other division to hold the enemy defenders in place in their erroneous deployments. Thus, the initial assault force, the 4th Division, would temporarily inherit most of the armor and artillery from the 2nd Division while that unit took part in a carefully orchestrated diversion at Sunharon Bay. If the scenario proved successful, those forces would then gradually be shifted to the northern landing beaches.

The trial of the Tinian garrison began concurrently with its Saipan counterpart and lasted far longer. As soon as the Fifth Fleet arrived in

Marianas waters, several bombardment ships were assigned to shell Tinian and the process went on day and night for more than six weeks. Then, once Saipan had succumbed, even more ships were shifted across the bay to alternately wreak havoc on emplacements and convince the defenders that the invasion would take place at Sunharon Bay. Battleship *Colorado* and cruisers *Cleveland* and *Louisville* were tapped for this especially valuable task of convincing Colonel Ogata and Captain Oya that the full fury of the Americans would fall on the beaches fronting the island capital.

Although Tinian was not spared the attention of carrier air strikes, two days before the invasion the garrison was subjected to a lethal new innovation in air warfare. U.S. Army Air Force and U.S. Navy ordinance experts had recently demonstrated the awesome destructiveness of a jellied concoction of naphtha and gasoline when dropped from jettisonable fuel tanks. Most of the currently available supply of the new weapon was designated for the invasion of Tinian, and Colonel Lewis Sanders of the U.S. Army Air Force was dispatched to Aslito Airfield on Saipan with two squadrons of P-47 Thunderbolts to drop the deadly bombs. On July 22, 1944, two days before the invasion, eighteen P-47s made the short flight from Saipan to Tinian and attacked artillery emplacements scattered across the island. The next day, the planes swooped low over the invasion beaches and seared the area with flames that turned many of the pillboxes into raging infernos.

Finally, the day before "J-day," thirteen artillery battalions deployed near the southern tip of Saipan joined the deadly chorus of fire by opening one of the most devastating ground bombardments of the Pacific War. The American commanders were taking full advantage of the proximity of newly captured Saipan to the next objective and anything that moved on the northern half of Tinian was now subjected to a deluge of shells that would reach a crescendo when the first Marines clambered ashore.

Now, on Sunday afternoon, July 23, LSTs (landing ship, tank) pulled next to the pier on Tanapag Harbor, Saipan, and loaded supplies and ammunition; meanwhile, down the coast at Charan Kanoa, the assault troops boarded their own transports. Marines who had lived on canned meals for weeks were pleasantly shocked when the ships' crews served a menu of meals that seemed fit for a holiday cruise. Then engines started throbbing and one by one vessels steamed southward for the brief journey across the channel separating Tinian from Saipan. The major question on the minds of most assault troops was whether the complex diversion drama would actually keep most of the enemy soldiers occupied while the real invasion was beginning on the narrow strand to the north.

The first order of business on "J-day," July 24, 1944, was to fix the defenders in place fronting Sunharon Bay. Battleship *Colorado*, cruiser *Cleveland*, and destroyers *Remey* and *Norman Scott* steered ever closer to Tinian's capital and transports carrying the 2nd and 8th Regiments of 2nd Division lowered landing craft as troops clambered down cargo nets in plain sight of Japanese observers. Then, as transports and warships edged closer to the beaches, Captain Oya's most potent weapon, the trio of British Whitworth guns, barked destruction from a well-concealed cave mouth just beyond Tinian Town. In one of the most dramatic sea-land confrontations of the war, the defenders' 6-inch guns scored twenty-two hits on *Colorado* and nearly as many on *Norman Scott.* The duel between American sea batteries and Imperial shore batteries reached a crescendo of violence as the Whitworths were demolished, one by one, in the very process of inflicting serious damage on their tormentors.

Colorado lost a 5-inch gun, completely knocked out of action, two more were damaged, the catapult for spotter planes was destroyed, two fuel compartments were flooded, five light guns were put out of commission, and thirty-three sailors and ten Marines were killed in action. The list of wounded included an additional 166 seamen and thirty-two Marines. *Norman Scott* lost a 5-inch gunmount and a 40 mm gun; a searchlight was demolished, radar system damaged, and several hundred holes ridded the superstructure. The vessel's captain and eighteen other men were killed and forty-seven additional crew members wounded. Bombarding enemy shore positions was always a potentially hazardous enterprise, but seldom had a single defending battery inflicted such damage and so many casualties on American ships. However, the sacrifice was not in vain because Japanese attention was now firmly fixed on the blood-stained waters of Sunharon Bay and few Imperial troops were deployed at the real American landing site.[5]

At 7:47 a.m., the first wave of amphibian tractors crossed their departure line 3,000 yards from shore and began their run into White Beach 1 and 2. Cruisers *Montpelier* and *New Orleans* pummeled the shoreline while *Birmingham* and four destroyers directed their fire at enemy artillery emplacements on the slopes of Mount Lasso. At 7:30, fifteen LCI (Landing Craft Infantry) gunboats wheeled into formation and sped toward shore as they unleashed a barrage of rocket and automatic weapons fire. Then specially marked P-47 Thunderbolts flew at low altitudes from the line of departure to the shore and provided aerial shepherds for the run to the invasion beaches.

This was the fury and drama of battle in microcosm. Saipan's invasion beaches had been measured in miles, but landing sites on Tinian, where each landing craft had to be in perfect alignment with its equally densely packed neighbors, were calculated in yards. At White Beach 1, a slim force of eight alligators carried elements of Company E, 24th Marines. The four most fortunate vehicles waddled up on to a relatively open beach and an equal number of counterparts nosed up against adjoining coral barriers that required deft teamwork to put men in position to clamber over the cliff and down on to the scrubby bushes beyond this natural seawall.

Colonel Ogata may have focused his attention on Sunharon Bay, but he had taken the precaution of deploying a small detachment of troops amid the jagged coral walls and crevasses that rose up around the American landing site. For a short while, cleverly concealed defenders pierced the morning haze with rifle and automatic weapons fire that ensured, at the very least, that the invaders would not simply saunter ashore. Yet the shootout could end in only one outcome because from every four to ten minutes another wave of amtracs replaced the set of eight that had just wheeled seaward and even the best cover could not completely negate overwhelming numbers.

The immediate threat of small-arms fire now gave way to the longer-range threat of howitzers and mortars as Imperial gun positions on Mount Lasso responded to the invasion by pouring fire onto the invasion beaches. The beach defense detachment may have been annihilated, but there were still plenty of choice positions along the coast road and the Japanese bombardment provided time for riflemen to select an excellent place from which to contest further enemy advances. Captain Irving Schechter and the men of Company A quickly learned this truth as they wheeled left off the beach and trotted northward to protect the regiment's flank. Their rear was now threatened by the guns on Mount Lasso, and their front faced a long stretch of rocky outcroppings and fissures that sheltered Japanese sharpshooters who would pop up, fire, and then disappear as if they were a lethal offshoot of an arcade shooting gallery back home.[6]

A few hundred yards down the coast, a second drama was unfolding on the shores of White Beach 2. Nominally, this landing beach was nearly the size of two football fields, but the expanse was dotted with long fingers of scrub bushes and coral formations that broke up the 160 yards into compartmentalized landing sites. Somehow, sixteen amtracs could be rammed ashore like autos in a badly overcrowded parking lot; but, as on White Beach 1, half would have the dubious distinction of fronting a cliff face that required an ingenious assortment of group contortions to get each Marine over to the other side of the barrier with all his limbs intact. At the cliff line, two Marines would stand in the bow of the LVT and assist other men up the wall to a point where they could gain a grip on the coral rim and then clamber down to the landward side beyond. Just to make the process a bit more interesting, the defenders had planted mines on the invasion beach and placed a variety of booby traps on the far side of the cliffs. Three alligators were turned into twisted pieces of metal when they ran afoul of the mines. Then souvenir-hunting invaders came upon an inviting assortment of watches, swords, pistols, and cases of beer all rigged to explode as soon as they were touched. This time caution triumphed over greed: The landing troops notified demolition teams and moved inland hoping for similar items minus the explosives at some later point in the campaign.

The chief nemesis to the move inland from White Beach 1 was the rock formations and coral crevasses that nature had provided the defenders. The main barrier to exploiting the landing on White Beach 2 was primarily manmade. Two enemy blockhouses just beyond the road and railroad line had somehow escaped destruction from air attack and naval bombardment and now they were crammed with machine guns, light cannon, and more than fifty defenders. Two assault battalions from the 25th Marines now began to concentrate their fire on the Japanese fortifications as more and more men disembarked from amtracs and increasingly crowded the beaches until passage inland could be secured. As mortar shells wafted across the hazy sky and crashed onto White Beach 2, the impetus for clearing these blockhouses gained momentum as assault squads converged from every possible approach position. Once again, the defenders could slow, but not halt, the American advance, and, as the last inhabitants of the fortifications succumbed to American fire, the push inland began in earnest.

When the Tinian operation was in the planning stage, the tiny White Beaches looked like an invitation to a gigantic jam up as thousands of invasion troops picked their way over the narrow expanses of sand. Yet a rigidly enforced timetable and the inability of the defenders to pin the Americans to the beaches enabled the landing force commanders to move 15,600 troops ashore by sunset on the first day of invasion. The landings were not walkovers and the Imperial troops fought tenaciously individually and in small groups. Yet the American casualty toll of 77 killed and 470 wounded was more a result of Japanese shore batteries striking *Colorado* and *Norman Scott* than of ground troops killing disembarking Marines. The actual landing force had lost a relatively modest 15 killed and 225 wounded on the first day of battle, a tiny fraction of the extensive losses on Tarawa and Saipan. Colonel Ogata and Captain Oya had spent most of July 24 fixated on the Tinian Town beaches while allowing the enemy to enter the island by the side door. Now an American landing force of nearly twice the size of the garrison was safely ashore and supported by a rapidly expanding formation of artillery and tanks. A Japanese counterattack was desperately needed, but was it already too late to throw the invaders into the sea?

By nightfall on July 24, Kiyochi Ogata and Goichi Oya had separately come to the conclusion that the American landings on the northeast coast were a mortal threat to the Imperial garrison, whether or not the enemy planned a thrust from Sunharon Bay. Ogata peered through his binoculars from his headquarters atop Mount Lasso and watched a growing mass of enemy troops congregate between Ushi Point and San Hilo Point. Captain Oya's command post in a cave on high ground outside Tinian Town was far less panoramic, but his erratic communications system hinted strongly that the enemy was closing rapidly on the Ushi Point Airfield, which was the navy's responsibility to defend. Both senior officers were imbued with the Imperial emphasis on "pushing the enemy into the sea" as a solution to an amphibious threat, and each commander now set in motion his service's version of that prime directive.[7]

Colonel Ogata had access to four infantry battalions that could theoretically launch a counterattack, but the sobering reality was that only a portion of this force could be concentrated in time to be of any benefit. The 1st Battalion of the 50th Infantry was already deployed between the invasion beaches and Mount Lasso and could be thrown into a counterattack on relatively short notice. The 2nd Battalion was holding defensive positions along the possible landing site at Asiga Bay, but this part of the island was relatively narrow, and a 3-mile march would bring the unit into contact with the enemy. Thus, roughly 2,000 army personnel could be thrown into a night assault on fairly short notice, but any hope of success depended upon other units joining the battle before sun up, even if they were not coordinated with this first wave.

Ogata's so-called Mobile Attack Force was not really very mobile because it had few vehicles and its Marpi Point bivouac was about as far as one could get from the White Beaches and still be on Tinian. The

Japanese road system on Tinian was actually fairly well designed, but because American aircraft and ships were frequently attacking these avenues of approach, the senior officer of this force, Captain M. Izumi of the 1st Battalion, 135th Regiment, would be obliged to march his men through cane fields and orchards at night, an action that hardly suggested a speedy arrival at the battle. Ogata's tank formation could also move across the fields and at a faster speed than the infantry. The quandary was whether to throw the armor into action as soon as it arrived or wait until the infantry caught up.

Captain Oya had deployed nearly 1,000 armed seamen around the perimeter of Ushi Point Airfield, now less than 2 miles from the forward positions of the enemy invasion force. However, rather than ordering his men to push through the fields and hit the center of the American line, Oya opted to send this detachment on a somewhat roundabout march northward and then organize an attack on the enemy left flank via the Ushi Point–San Hilo Point road. Thus, with a minimum of interservice cooperation, the Japanese commanders had organized a jury-rigged three-pronged offensive that would hit the American left flank, center, and right flank from three directions sometime before dawn on July 25. In what must be considered a minor miracle, considering the circumstances, the defenders would manage to make the Marines' first night on Tinian a memorable one by launching all three attacks within ninety minutes.

Midnight of a new day began with a gradually rising crescendo of Japanese artillery fire that increased in ferocity over the next two hours. Then, around 2:00 a.m., the armies of the night began to advance, and the first all-out battle on Tinian began to develop in earnest. At this moment, the moonless darkness was pierced on the extreme left of the American lines by the screaming concentrated mass of Captain Oya's naval infantry. The seamen pushed down the main coast road waving rifles and swords and manhandling an assortment of machine guns that had been stripped from disabled planes dotting Ushi Point Airfield. The men of the 1st Battalion, 24th Marines, were not aware of the fact that their adversaries were under navy, not army, command, but this was the farthest thing from their minds as hell was unleashed upon them.

For four hours, a vicious melee surged back and forth across Ushi Point Road and its adjoining beaches and fields. Company A seemed to be in the epicenter of the Japanese offensive and, as the outnumbered defenders occasionally seemed at the verge of being overrun, engineers, radio operators, and even corpsmen grabbed rifles to shore up the firing line. At one point, only thirty men in this endangered unit were both unwounded and in possession of rifles that still had ammunition, and this small band would have to parry the enemy thrust until ammunition and reinforcements could be brought up to the front line. Then the familiar and welcome sound of clanking armor treads was heard in the distance, and as the first glint of gray light pierced the darkness, the Shermans of Company B, 4th Tank Battalion, lurched forward and added their fearsome firepower to the proceedings. The welcoming night was over for the attackers; as the sun rose, Oya's men pulled back toward the airfield, leaving behind 476 dead comrades and carrying perhaps 200 wounded on improvised stretchers fashioned from the tin roofs of military buildings.[8]

Captain Oya had dented but not pierced the American left flank and had paid for this minimal accomplishment by losing two-thirds of the defenders on the most important piece of real estate on the island. Unless Colonel Ogata rushed units from his own thinly stretched lines to aid in defense of the airfield, the advancing Americans would face far fewer than three hundred armed seamen in their path when they approached their objective.

While the forces of the Imperial navy were slashing at the American left flank, Ogata's army units were desperately searching for a weak spot on the enemy center and right. Some combination of luck and effective observation drew the assault battalions of the 50th Regiment to one of the danger points on the Marine perimeter, the seam between the 24th and 25th Regiments. Even the relatively numerous invaders did not have the manpower to fashion an airtight line around their entire perimeter, and a little after 2:30 a.m., perhaps two hundred Imperial soldiers charged against the thinly manned boundary between American units and surged toward the rear. The assault force divided into two roughly equal prongs and as the drive continued, one formation found itself in sight of 25th Regiment headquarters. Headquarters personnel and support staff quickly turned back into frontline riflemen and blazed away in a massive gunfight as a reserve platoon deployed for just such an emergency hustled to the rear and smashed the intruders in the flank. Eight or nine survivors withdrew to seek a more congenial enemy target, but more than ninety other Nipponese warriors died where they stood.

The second part of the Japanese breakthrough party discovered its first significant target in the 2nd Battalion, 14th Marines. Three batteries of gunners suddenly found that they were no longer supporting the front lines and instead were fighting for their lives. While artillerymen fired back with rifles and pistols, well-placed machine guns at the flank of each battery roared into action and, according to one officer, "literally tore the Japanese to pieces."[9]

Then infantrymen from Company C, 8th Marines, were rushed to plug gaps and wade into the breach until there were no more enemies left to fight. Two machine gunners had died manning their weapons, but they were joined in death by more than a hundred adversaries sprawled on the field in silent testimony of courage and defeat. Yet these men had been relatively successful; they had penetrated, though not broken, the American perimeter. Most of their comrades from Ogata's 50th Regiment spent the night engaged in futile charges against Marine infantry and tank units, which left three hundred attackers dead in exchange for minimal casualties among the invaders.

Now, in the last hours of darkness, the main action gradually shifted to the right flank of the American perimeter as troops of the 135th Regiment ended their odyssey from the south and linked up with Ogata's main armored unit. The men of the 2nd Battalion, 23rd Marines, heard the distinctive sound of approaching tanks very much as their counterparts on the northern end of the perimeter had, but this time the noise signaled the approach of hostile armor as six Japanese light tanks clanked up Ushi Point Road from Tinian Town and

closed to within 40 yards of the Marine positions. The American response to this threat was rapid and violent. As the tanks lumbered up
the road with infantrymen sprawled all over the exterior of the vehicle,
star shells whooshed skyward and an array of bazookas, antitank guns,
and half-track-mounted 75 mm guns erupted from positions adjoining
the road. Five tanks erupted into fireballs, infantrymen crumpled from
machine-gun fire, and the advance wavered and then halted. In the un-
fathomable calculus of Japanese victory and defeat, the attackers then
began to do the Marines' work for them. Ogata's plan was to use his armor to punch a hole in the enemy lines and then push a special force of
attackers into the rear. These men were equipped with portable mines,
which were strapped to their chests; once the line was breached, the
mines would then be used to blow up American cannon. Now, as it became obvious that hopes of penetrating were slim, the Imperial soldiers calmly triggered the weapons on their own bodies. As one incredulous Marine explained, "Jap bodies began to fly ten to fifteen feet in
the air and we knew that hand grenades did not have the power to
blow a man that high and could not figure out what was happening."

The only initial certainty was that the enemy was again dying in
large numbers and the Marine perimeter was holding firm. Sunrise
brought the situation into stark clarity. At a cost of less than one hundred Marines killed or wounded, 1,241 Imperial troops had died and
an additional 800 were dragged from the field with serious wounds.
Nearly one-fourth of Tinian's garrison was now effectively out of action, but no American unit had suffered significant losses. During the
first twenty-four hours of the invasion, roughly twenty Japanese troops
were dying for every American they killed. This ratio simply could not
continue for very long, and if the Marines were exhausted from staging
an extensive amphibious landing and then deflecting a major counterattack, they also realized that if the enemy continued to fritter away
their finite manpower at this extraordinary rate, the battle could not
continue much longer. The Americans did not realize it at the time, but
Colonel Ogata was about to shift his tactics significantly and turn the
Tinian campaign into a very different kind of battle.

'18

TINIAN HEIGHTS

THE FAILURE OF THE JAPANESE counterattack on the first night of the American invasion forced Colonel Ogata and Captain Oya into the unenviable position of either conceding most of Tinian to the enemy or ordering their men into a battle of annihilation on ground that offered few advantages to the defenders. Given the reality that the Imperial Navy seemed incapable of regaining control of the waters around the Marianas, it was clear to the senior officers on Tinian that the garrison would eventually be overwhelmed by the invaders. The only decision (for the surviving Japanese) remaining was how to inflict maximum casualties on the enemy while dying in the most glorious way possible. Thus, while abandoning most of an island that they had been charged by the emperor to defend seemed an abhorrent action, the army and navy commanders reluctantly, and rather separately, admitted that a glorious final stand on the more defensible southern tip of Tinian was the proper response under the current conditions. Thus, Ogata and Oya set in motion a complex series of retrograde movements that would turn the next week into a series of rearguard actions culminating in the final stand on the cliffs above Marpo Point.[1]

General Harry Schmidt and his division commanders had little inkling of their counterparts' intentions as they tallied the results of

251

the enemy counterattack on the morning of July 25, 1944. It was now clear that the defenders did not have the power to concentrate a force large enough to push the invaders into the sea and, in turn, the American commanders were naturally attracted to the nearest enemy-held objectives, Ushi Point Airfield, and Mount Maga and Mount Lasso looming over the American perimeter with their still-functioning artillery and mortar batteries spitting fire into the Marine positions. Although Ogata and Oya had no intention of fighting the major battle on Tinian for these positions, they deployed enough men around the obvious targets at least to delay the enemy while a slow withdrawal to the south got fully underway. Thus, as two long columns of men in green denim snaked out from the invasion beaches on this cloudy, stiflingly humid Tuesday morning, other men wearing uniforms the color of brown wrapping paper did their best to slow, if not stop, the American tide.

Colonel J. M. Batchelder's 25th Marine Regiment drew the assignment of capturing the nearest objective, the 390-foot heights of Mount Maga. Detailed air reconnaissance had revealed a sheer half-moon-shaped northern cliff face between the Marines and the summit, but the east and west approaches were more accessible but more open to enemy fire from the summit. Batchelder had no intention of throwing all his assault battalions against the steepest cliff, so while the 2nd Battalion deployed in plain sight to the north, the 1st and 3rd Battalions used the cover of powerful artillery fire and a massive strike by P-47 fighter bombers to sidle over to the alternative approaches. The defenders used excellent small-unit tactics, leapfrogging individual platoons from firing positions on the lower slopes to new deployments higher above as the Americans used riflemen, flamethrower units, and tanks to secure each successive elevation. However, the higher the assault troops clambered, the more furious the defensive fire became, and while elements of the 1st Battalion clambered up to the summit, on two occasions they were at least temporarily thrown off by a furious enemy counterattack. Yet the Japanese simply did not have enough men to parry American attacks from three different directions, and by

3:00 p.m., the last defenders were either dead or scrambling down Mount Maga's south face to retreat back to the relative safety of Mount Lasso looming just over a mile away.[2]

While the 25th Marines were slogging up the cliffs of Mount Maga, the beaches far below were the scene of a sort of organized confusion that marked the follow-up landings after the initial beachhead was secured. Up to this point, the battle of Tinian had been fought primarily by the battalions of the 4th Division, but now members of the 2nd Marine Division were pouring ashore as rapidly as the slim beach front would allow. While Japanese artillery on Mount Lasso kept up an intermittent barrage on the landing beaches and the sea immediately beyond, columns of landing craft would drop their ramps and allow the next unit of Marines to wade to the beach 100 yards across the warm, shallow water. As these men established themselves on the island and prepared for new orders, the overall perimeter was being expanded relentlessly outward to prevent congestion and push closer to key objectives.

By nightfall on July 25, Schmidt's forces were ready to storm both Mount Lasso and Ushi Point Airfield. The 25th Marines had set up lines 1,000 yards from the slopes of Mount Lasso, the 23rd and 24th Marines covering their flanks, and the 8th Marines had established forward outposts only 400 yards from Ushi Point Airfield. A general advance was now planned for the following morning to ensure that all of northern Tinian would be in American hands in the very near future. Standing on Mount Lasso's summit, which was now less than a mile from the American front lines, Colonel Kiyochi Ogata surveyed the coiled enemy snake that seemed about to strike and decided that the battle for these heights would be no more than a delaying action to buy time for the withdrawal to the final defense line in the south. He had deployed men in spider holes, caves, and rugged undergrowth all the way from the enemy lines to the approach to the mountain, but the headquarters itself would shift from Mount Lasso to the southern tip of the island.[3]

As the Marine campaign stretched into late July, American operations would become increasingly influenced by the rainy season that was beginning in this region. Troops who had contended mainly with the relentless heat of Saipan now saw long periods of sun punctuated by ever more frequent torrential downpours that could quickly turn roads and fields into quagmires. Yet, despite bursts of monsoon-like rain and wind, the third day of the Tinian campaign began with American drives toward Mount Lasso and Ushi Point Airfield. Division commanders General Thomas Watson and General Clifton Cates and their staffs huddled around a table surrounded by dripping wet trees and pored over maps and charts to determine how to turn the previous single-division drive into a dual-pronged attack. Armor and artillery units loaned to the 4th Division for the initial assault were now returned to 2nd Division control. The former unit took over responsibility for pushing straight southward, and the latter formation would swing due east to the coast and then turn south toward Marpo Point.

Mount Lasso was the first barrier to the 4th Division's journey, and at 7:55 a.m. on July 26, thirteen battalions of XXIV Corps Artillery opened a massive barrage on the approaches to the hill that soon included naval gunfire from the *Tennessee, Cleveland,* and two destroyers. Five minutes later, the lead units jogged forward through wet cane fields and sporadic Japanese machine-gun fire. Two of the battalions of the 25th Regiment that had seized Mount Maga the previous day now began to take on the role of mountain fighting specialists as they pushed toward the approaches of the larger hill to their south. However, while well-covered riflemen blasted at the assault force from trees and shrub growth, no serious fire came from Mount Lasso itself. Marines clambered up the slopes of their objective and were astonished to find that the summit was empty. Observations from their newly conquered heights revealed a formation of enemy tanks and infantry deployed along a ridge perhaps a mile south, but the Americans were not sure whether this force was preparing to counterattack or was in the process of withdrawing. A requested air strike arrived in the early evening darkness while the Marines hunkered down for the night and prepared for the always realistic possibility of an enemy assault.[4]

Meanwhile, the other major target for the American offensive was now coming within striking range. As the 2nd Marine Division swept eastward toward the rocky opposite coast, units of the 8th Marines marched across the Ushi Point flats at the northern tip of the island and began to sweep south toward Ushi Point Airfield. Captain Oya had initiated the same fighting withdrawal as his army counterpart and the American advance alternated between eerie silence and the clamor of enemy counterattacks. The Japanese invariably came out on the short end of these brief firefights and, at a cost of sixteen casualties, including two men killed, advance units probed cautiously towards the airfield and found an airstrip soaked and puddled from the now frequent rain but utterly silent except for the wind passing through the carcasses of the unflyable Imperial planes that had been left to their fate in the Nipponese retreat. Soon, the silence would be pierced by the clanging of machines as the Seabees of the 121st Naval Construction Battalion swarmed over the newly acquired prize and began the transformation into a powerful American base.

The capture of Mount Lasso and the airfield prompted General Schmidt to conserve the energy of worn-out men and equipment by ordering a systematic but relatively slow push southward with the two divisions taking turns in their respective advances. For much of the next three days, Marines and Imperial troops played a deadly game of hide-and-seek as Americans would advance a little bit further under the cover of massive artillery bombardments only to be confronted by well-concealed adversaries whenever the thundering cannon halted their fire. Lieutenant William McMillan, commander of a tank platoon screening the 2nd Division, was advancing southward when a concealed Japanese machine gun suddenly came to life: "I got on the ground, and I was on the telephone. There was a burst from a Nambu machine gun. There was an infantry kid right beside me. He got it right across the waist. They got me across the legs. I couldn't walk. . . . We got the two Japs that had the machine gun. Before I gave up, we killed them. I hopped around there, and they evacuated me."[5]

Wounded for the third time in the campaign, Lieutenant McMillan was on his way back to the United States when his companions continued their careful advance southward. Much like the bush and jungle of another war a generation later, seemingly innocuous stretches of cane fields and farmhouses could turn into places of deadly peril. Melvin Swango, a radio operator in a Marine tank battalion, noted, "Those cane fields were treacherous because you never knew what you were going to run into. A friend of mine, Herschel Fulmer, was a radioman in one of the tanks. His tank commander was killed. They were in a cane field. He had his hatch open for some reason and got shot and killed."[6]

Every ambush sprung on an American infantry or tank unit seemed to give Ogata and Oya precious extra time to prepare the high ground at the tip of Tinian for its intended purpose as a final bastion. Marines who had gained much of their combat experience in the close quarters of jungles and scrub growth were now forced to adapt to a new peril as they found themselves subjected to long-range enemy fire while standing in an open field with no cover in sight. Then, on July 30, the march southward through the grasslands gave way to a new vista, the battered streets and buildings of Tinian's capital.

General Schmidt and his division commanders suspected that the enemy might very well seriously contest an American entry into Tinian Town, and they began to feel that their hunch was correct when advance units came under massive shellfire from the northern outskirts of the town. As the Japanese artillery raked the advancing Marines, armored amphibians moved along the coast road to duel with enemy gunners concealed in caves while Satan flame tanks poured streams of fire into the interiors. Then, in mid-afternoon, the noise from natural and man-made thunder came to an abrupt halt, and at 2:20 p.m., the 24th Marines marched in and captured an almost empty Japanese capital. A single straggler formed the minute Japanese rearguard, and when this lone warrior died in a hail of gunfire, the Americans had accomplished virtually every pre-invasion objective.[7]

By sunset on July 30, General Schmidt and his division commanders began to suspect that their Japanese counterparts had pulled the bulk of surviving defenders back to the ominous-looking plateau that loomed over Tinian Town from the south. In seven days of fighting, the 2nd and 4th Marine divisions had captured 80 percent of the island, including the capital and all four airfields. American planes were now operating from Ushi Point Airfield and the other airstrips would enter service shortly. Yet the dominant topographic feature of Tinian was still in enemy hands; it would have to be seized before the island could be secured for the purpose for which it was intended, that is, as the springboard to air attacks on Japan.

The most significant high ground on Tinian was formed around a rugged plateau that extended from the road and rail line just beyond Airfield Number 4 back to Marpo Point, which overlooked the sea at the southern tip of the island. This plateau was ideal fighting ground for outnumbered defenders because it featured a succession of ravines, gulches, rocky crevices, and caves, all of which were interspersed with particularly thick underbrush. Even the process of getting up onto this uninviting battlefield would be an arduous task for the Marines because the plateau was separated from Tinian's gentle lowlands by a 100-foot limestone cliff that alternated between sheer rock face and dense jungle-covered ascent routes. A single access road peppered with hairpin curves wound a tortuous path upward from the edge of the airfield to the craggy plateau far above. This nightmarish jumble of woods, cliffs, and caves would become the stage on which the last drama of the battle for Tinian would be played out.

At precisely 6:00 a.m. on the last day of July, the gun turrets of two battleships and three cruisers swung into firing positions and began sending their lethal messages into Tinian's southern plateau. Marines hunkered in their foxholes at the base of the cliff as explosions shattered the early-morning stillness. Then, seventy-five minutes later, the shell fire came to an abrupt halt as eighty-six Thunderbolts shot out from Aslito Airfield on Saipan, roared over the American lines, and hurled rockets, bombs, and napalm on a target that would not have looked out of place in Vietnam two decades later. The P-47s were followed in turn by twenty-four torpedo bombers from escort carrier *Ki-*

tunbay and sixteen B-25 medium bombers unloaded their lethal carriers from 800 to 1,000 feet. As the drone of the aircraft receded in the distance, the sound of naval guns began to grow once again, competing with multiple batteries of artillery for dominance in this symphony of destruction.

At 8:30 a.m., 150 minutes after the sea, air, and land barrage began, lead elements of regiments of Marines scrambled from their foxholes and moved toward the heights looming above. The combination of the intensive bombardment and Colonel Ogata's shortage of manpower meant that the Americans would not be advancing into the full fury of a tightly formed defensive line blasting away from the summit. Yet this advantage for the attackers was somewhat nullified by the fact that the Japanese commander had deployed part of his force on the approaches to the cliff in an attempt to bleed the Americans before they even began scaling the heights.

The 23rd Marines found the fields between Airfield Number 4 at the cliff base sprinkled with farmhouses and small villages that offered cover for Japanese defenders as they blasted away from every available window and doorway. Tanks accompanying this regiment's 1st Battalion stumbled into a clever ambush from a well-concealed enemy 47 mm gun. One tank from C Company of the 4th Tank Battalion was hit by six antitank shells in a matter of seconds and, while other crews fired smoke grenades and called for suppressive artillery fire, a second vehicle was disabled by six more rounds. Two surviving tanks bracketed the newly located pillbox from front and rear and obliterated the strongpoint and twenty fleeing defenders, but such incidents turned the advance into an often-dangerous crawl.[8]

The first unit assigned to scale the cliff itself was the 8th Marines, and the two assault battalions of this regiment endured a gauntlet of enemy fire from the fields below and heights above as they sprinted across the open ground fronting the approach road. Nipponese suicide squads rushed out to attack supporting Shermans while the tanks were firing into underbrush on the road above. Then the tanks advanced upward in single file, covering engineers lifting the mines that dotted the narrow road. As the disposal units engaged in their deadly craft, Imperial troops rolled grenades down the slopes and into the road.

While the 1st Battalion and its support units wound their way up the seemingly endless road to the top, the men of the 3rd Battalion were clambering directly up the pocked limestone cliff. As Shermans and Satan flame tanks sprayed shells and flames at the defenders crouching in the underbrush above, the Imperial troops whittled down the attackers at an alarming rate. However, the losses in this unit were not in vain because Japanese concentration on this threat weakened their ability fully to halt the Marine advance up the road. As the sun slipped toward the horizon, a group of panting, exhausted men of the 1st Battalion staggered to the summit and established a perimeter on the plateau; at the same time, regimental commander Colonel Clarence Wallace pushed G Company from 2nd Battalion and a pair of 37 mm guns to the heights to stiffen the line against the inevitable enemy counterattack.

The American front line, if such a term could really describe the Marine deployment on this final night in July, started at the base of the cliff and meandered up through the woods and thickets dotting the cliff face up to the gnarled plateau of the summit. In several instances, one Marine's foxhole would be several feet above that of his nearest companion; the configuration made the battlefield take on the appearance of a three-dimensional chess board. This jury-rigged American line was managed from a temporary headquarters established in the field below that fronted the parallel courses of the road ascending the cliff and the rail line extending westward toward Tinian Town and the sea.

The entire American line was so meandering and pitted with gaps that it seemed to present a perfect opportunity for a Japanese night attack, a fact that Colonel Ogata was not reluctant to recognize. The colonel's first target was control of the sole access road to the plateau, and soon after midnight a hundred Imperial soldiers slipped around the flank of 1st Battalion and established a roadblock halfway down the cliff. As the Nipponese forces began the ambush, they set fire to two captured ambulances and created a fiery barrier to American traffic.

Relief units from 2nd Battalion below were sent clambering up the dark cliffside until they reached the burning vehicle and cleared the roadblock in bitter hand-to-hand fighting.

Just as this position stabilized, probing attacks against the Americans on the plateau started gaining in intensity. At just past 3:00 a.m., the 2nd Battalion reinforcements from G Company and one of the two 37 mm guns were rushed by Imperial troops while competing mortar barrages from both armies flashed through the night sky. Two hours later, E Company was hard-pressed in a furious battle by flare light. The Japanese were now coming from several directions at once and were barely held at bay by the pair of American guns that barked incessantly, even though one crew after another fell to enemy fire. Screaming attackers closed to within 5 yards of the Marine position, and the line nearly buckled; but at a cost of 80 percent of the gun crews, the American position on the plateau was still holding at daylight on the first morning of August.

Midmorning on this new day brought massive numbers of Shermans, Satans, and flamethrower teams to the plateau, and the Marines edged through scores of enemy dead toward the last ridgeline between themselves and the sea. Suicide squads as large as fifty men would pop up from cover for a final Wild West–like shoot-out, but the result was always large numbers of Japanese deaths, a few American casualties, and another surge forward to the sea. As the Marines approached the glistening water far below, the final tragedy of Tinian began to play itself out in a mirror image of the horror on Saipan. The climax on Saipan had occurred on the island's northern tip at Marpi Point. Now, at the southern point of what were in many respects twin islands, a parallel drama was unfolding. Unlike General Saito on Saipan, Colonel Ogata was never accorded the time or the luxury of ritual suicide: He died slumped over American barbed wire as he led one of the final night attacks. The bodies of Admiral Kakuta and Captain Oya were never found, and, like Admiral Nagumo on Saipan, were presumed to have joined their ancestors in the privacy of one of the innumerable caves that dotted both islands. However, while senior army and navy officers joined the list of war dead relatively voluntarily, many of Tinian's 18,000 civilians were given far less choice in the matter.

The enormous fertility of Tinian's soil had convinced Japanese officials to forcibly transfer virtually the entire native population to less-desirable islands, and by 1944, there were only twenty-six Chamorros still listed in residence. As on Saipan, the Nipponese civilians had been warned of the barbarism of the approaching Americans and were highly encouraged to commit suicide and kill their younger family members rather than suffer the indignities of enemy torture and death. Although more than 5,000 civilians had been caught up in the American drive southward and had mostly survived to be lodged in growing interment camps, 13,000 others followed their retreating soldiers to the heights and began hiding in the region's hundreds of caves. As the Japanese lines steadily contracted, Japanese-speaking Marines and sailors used loud speakers to urge the civilians to leave the caves or come down from the edge of the cliff above the sea to receive food, water, and medical attention. One of the first civilians to accept this offer was the superintendent of Tinian's largest sugar refinery and his wife, and this couple, in turn, convinced others to join them in safety. However, most of the remaining civilians wavered in a twilight world between surrender and suicide until their Imperial protectors decided to expedite their decision for death.

One by one, Japanese soldiers marched from their shrinking defense line to the edge of the cliff and, after a final salute to the emperor, jumped into the sea 200 feet below. When civilians seemed reluctant to join the parade of self-destruction, a party of Japanese soldiers imposed a bloodier exit for the terrified families when they roped fifty men, women, and children together and began pitching grenades into the group. Now these supposed guardians of Nipponese families became the barbarians and, as groups of victims were being formed, thousands of panicked civilians bolted for the American lines, dragging children and senior citizens as rapidly as they could move them. Unlike the horror at Marpi Point, the mass suicide at the southern tip of

Tinian would be predominantly a military ritual. One final terror in a seeming war without limits had been mercifully avoided.

At 6:55 p.m. on August 1, 1944, General Harry Schmidt declared Tinian secured and almost immediately the middle chapter in the Marines' trilogy would become a subject for discussion in the high commands of both countries. The battle had extended for nine days, although on most days the intensity of combat was more limited than at Tarawa or Saipan. Five thousand Japanese dead had already been counted and thousands of other corpses would be discovered in caves during the next several months. A modest contingent of 252 prisoners had been processed, but this total would drift upward as other isolated defenders surrendered in the future. A total of 3,027 Marines had died, and 1,571 men were wounded in the ground battle; 62 men had been killed and 325 wounded aboard the naval bombardment ships. Even this composite total was only a small fraction of the loss on Saipan and, in effect, twenty Imperial soldiers or sailors had been killed for the loss of each American.

At Saipan, U.S. forces had traveled 1,000 miles to meet the enemy; on Tinian, they had journeyed 3 miles in what some strategists labeled a large-scale river crossing. This was a battle in which senior American commanders made few serious errors in judgment. They chose the right beach on which to land, had excellent cooperation from naval and air units, and refused to get sucked into bloody frontal assaults when flanking attacks would get the job done. Once the by now almost ritualistic enemy night counterattack was over, the invaders could get on with the job of annexing the island a mile or two at a time while meeting constantly undermanned countermoves.

Given his limitation in manpower and equipment, Ogata did about as much as could be expected under the circumstances and prevented the Americans from simply rolling over his forces. A reasonably sane Western commander would have surrendered sometime during the battle on the plateau and would have been congratulated by the victors on his tenacious defense. However, this was not the Japanese way, and, at least Ogata and his men gained great face in a homeland where casualties inflicted on the enemy in these now traditional last stands were inflated almost beyond comprehension. According to Imperial news agencies, 9,000 Nipponese warriors would probably take 30,000 or 40,000 foreign devils to their graves with them, and the public could be justly comforted by this profitable transaction. However, when the Stars and Stripes were raised on Tinian, only one more Imperial garrison remained in the Marianas. When and if the defenders of Guam went to their final glory, no matter how many invaders they took with them, those four splendid airfields on Tinian would make excellent bases for the American air forces. Deep within the hushed chambers of the Imperial Palace, men who knew the true situation about the Great Pacific War realized that the enemy had just the right plane to fly from those bases and that they would bring a fiery death on much of the Japanese homeland. As long as Guam held out, the Americans would at least be obliged to look nervously to their southern flank when they set about the task of turning Tinian's lush fields into a springboard for bringing hell upon the homeland. However, only that one bastion remained, and the fall of Guam would surely signal the descent of the furies upon Nippon.

'19

ASSAULT ON GUAM

THE INITIAL CONCEPT of Operation Forager was based on the expectation of relatively simultaneous landing on Saipan and Guam by the separate invasion forces, V Amphibious Corps, and III Amphibious Corps. However, the intensity of the early fighting on Saipan and the growing evidence that Japanese garrison was much larger than expected necessitated using Forager's floating reserve, the U.S. Army's 27th Division, for the contest on that island and forced a postponement of the Guam landings until the 77th Division could be transported from Hawaii. The invasion of Guam, designated W-Day, was now set for July 21, five weeks after the first assault on Saipan. This would certainly provide the defenders with extra time to enhance their defenses but, in turn, would allow time for one of the most concentrated extended bombardments in history.

The new composition of III Amphibious Corps centered around the 3rd Marine Division, the 1st Provisional Marine Brigade of two reinforced regiments, two additional Marine Defense Battalions, and the 77th Infantry Division, along with a large number of attached units ranging from a single bomb disposal squad to a reinforced tank battalion. The officer who would command this diverse but powerful corps of just more than 50,000 men was Major General Roy Geiger, a Marine aviator who had first gained national fame leading the outnumbered, multiservice Cactus Air Force during the perilous days of the Guadalcanal campaign. Geiger had welded U.S. Navy, Marine, and Army Air Force pilots flying a bewildering assortment of planes into a force that had scored significant victories over Japanese air and naval units and helped turn a shoestring operation into a major American victory. Geiger had proved his ability to work in an interservice environment, but would now operate under the shadow of the still-seething controversy over the firing on Saipan of an army general by a Marine general.[1]

The officer ultimately responsible for getting the men onto the beaches and supporting them once they were there was Rear Admiral Richard Connolly, commander of the Southern Attack Force of the Joint Expeditionary Force of Operation Forager. Connolly was a colorful, versatile mariner who had begun the war in command of Admiral Halsey's destroyer screen, transferred to the Atlantic command for the Allied invasion of Sicily, and was back in the Pacific for Operation Flintlock, the invasion of the Marshalls. During the invasion of Roi, the admiral had placed so much emphasis on maneuvering battleships into extremely close-in firing range that by the summer of 1944 he was now recognized as "Close-In Connolly." Geiger and Connolly were rapidly developing a cordial relationship that went far beyond mere professional courtesy: "My aim is to get the troops ashore standing up," the admiral emphasized to the assault commander. "You tell me what you want done to accomplish it and we'll do it."

Connolly and Geiger faced challenges that were similar to those the Saipan invasion, yet also distinct. The proportion of attackers to defenders was very similar in both operations as the roughly 75,000 Americans facing 30,000 Japanese in the previous battle was almost exactly matched by the 50,000 invaders engaging 20,000 defenders in the upcoming operation. Guam, like Saipan, was the site of various villages and towns representing the possibility of street fighting virtually absent in the earlier island campaigns. But although most of Saipan's population consisted of either Japanese subjects or pro-Japanese natives, the residents of Guam were essentially American citizens who would prob-

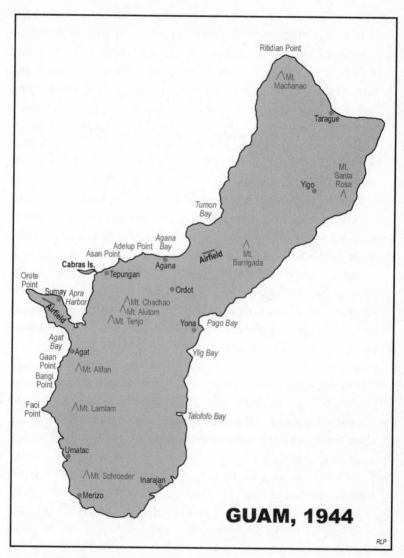

Ritidian Point

Mt. Machanao

Tarague

Mt. Santa Rosa

Yigo

Tumon Bay

Agana Bay

Adelup Point

Asan Point

Cabras Is.

Tepungan

Agana

Airfield

Mt. Barrigada

Orote Point

Sumay

Apra Harbor

Airfield

Ordot

Mt. Chachao
Mt. Alutom
Mt. Tenjo

Yona

Pago Bay

Agat Bay

Gaan Point

Agat

Mt. Alifan

Ylig Bay

Bangi Point

Faci Point

Mt. Lamlam

Talofofo Bay

Umatac

Mt. Schroeder

Inarajan

Merizo

GUAM, 1944

RLP

Guam, July 1944

ably aid the invaders but might have to be rescued from massive reprisals on the part of the defenders.

Beyond the population differences, Guam was roughly twice the size of Saipan, which provided the defenders with more maneuver room but, in turn, spread their forces more thinly. The island was 34 miles long and 5 to 9 miles wide and surrounded by coral reefs anywhere from 25 to 700 miles wide that were covered by only 2 feet of water at high tide. The entire northern half of the island featured seaside cliffs rising up to 600 feet that ruled out any possibility of a landing; the east coast was exposed to prevailing easterly winds and a heavy pounding surf that would complicate a landing from that direction. These factors essentially reduced feasible landing areas to the 17-mile stretch of beach from Tumon Bay to Facpi Point, the same sector used by the Japanese invaders just over thirty months earlier.

The topography of Guam represented three distinct regions, yet all parts of the island were affected by the location, just over 100 miles south of Saipan, a factor that made the place definitely more tropical than its northern neighbor. The northern part of Guam was dominated by a limestone plateau heavily covered with tropical forests, weeds, and underbrush interspersed with small roads and jungle trails. The dominant feature on the western side of the region was Fonte Plateau, which was the location of Japanese field headquarters. The east coast was dominated by Mount Barrigada and Mount Santa Rosa, which represented the Japanese fallback position in the final stages of the battle.

The central part of the island between Agana on the west coast and Pogo Bay on the east coast featured marshy lowlands and rice paddies draining into the Apra Harbor. Mount Alifan and Mount Tenjo served as the gateway to a combination of steep, rocky hills and lush grasslands alternating down to the southern tip. The two major objectives of the invasion were Apra Harbor, the most valuable port facility in the entire Marianas chain, and Orote Airfield, which had been constructed by Japanese engineers almost adjacent to the old Marine barracks and was now coveted as a B-29 base by the U.S. Army Air Force. Once these objectives had been secured, the invasion force would secure the capital of Agana, rescue the natives from Japanese captivity, and drive the defenders toward sea in whatever direction they retreated.

The invasion plan developed by the American high command envisioned a two-pronged assault, north and south of the two initial objectives, Apra Harbor and Orote Peninsula. The northern landing force would center on the 3rd Marine Division, which would land three regiments just below Agana in the area of Asan Bay between low jutting land masses called the "devil's horns," Asan Point, and Adelup Point. Unlike the Japanese northern landing in 1941, this force would not initially be concerned with capturing Guam's capital but would wheel south to seize Piti Navy Yard and Apra Harbor just beyond while also securing the high ground just inland from the beaches. The southern landing force would consist of the two regiments of the 1st Provisional Marine Brigade followed closely by the 77th Infantry Division. This force's task was to capture the Marine barracks and adjacent airfield on Orote Peninsula, secure the southern end of Apra Harbor, and link up with the northern landing force to push the defenders into the sea wherever the Japanese concentrated to make a stand. During this final phase of the operation, it was expected that the unified landing force would capture Agana and liberate the native population.

The Japanese officer who was most responsible for preventing this disastrous sequence of events was Lieutenant General Takeshi Takashima, the field commander of Guam's garrison. Takashima was technically subordinate to Lieutenant General Hideyoshi Obata, the commander of the Thirty-first Army and who had been more or less stranded on Guam while making an inspection tour early in the campaign. Obata would play a significant role in the last few days of the battle for Guam, but the senior general gave Takashima a free hand in developing the defense of the island.

Takashima was an experienced, aggressive officer who had spent the last three years commanding the 29th Division in Manchuria, fighting a war of maneuver in wild, open country. The general wanted to fight the same sort of battle on Guam by using combined tank-infantry columns to smash the invading Americans at points where they were most vulnerable.

However, American air and submarine attacks would at least partially unravel Takashima's strategy. When the 29th Division was ordered to Guam to form the core of Japanese defenses, American planes and torpedo attacks pounced on the transport ships and sent most of the tanks and field artillery to the bottom of the Pacific along with nearly all the men of the 18th Infantry Regiment. A second round of attacks decimated the 50th Infantry Regiment and forced the survivors to land on Tinian, where they would add nothing to the defense of Guam. Thus Takashima's powerful division was now reduced to his headquarters personnel and the 38th Infantry Regiment, which had been the only major unit to arrive on Guam intact. As somewhat of a consolation, there was an opportunity to cobble together some sort of coherent defense plan based on the units already on the island before Takashima arrived.

The major army units deployed to defend Guam included Takashima's own 38th Regiment; the 48th Independent Mixed Brigade, which fielded four battalions made up of an assortment of units that were either directed to Guam or had survived American attacks on their transports; and the 10th Independent Mixed Regiment, which fielded two infantry battalions and two engineer companies, eighty-one pieces of field artillery, eighty-six antitank guns, and a formidable array of coastal defense batteries that completed an army garrison of about 12,000 men.

However, Takashima could also field a fairly formidable naval force on Guam as Captain Yutaka Sugimoto, who had previously been island commander, deployed nearly 7,000 men ranging from naval construction battalions and naval air units to coastal defense batteries and anti-aircraft units. The safe arrival of all units assigned to defend Guam would have given Takashima a formidable force of 35,000 men and more than a hundred tanks; but, in reality, the Japanese commander would win or lose the battle of Guam with 19,000 men and about three dozen tanks. Takashima could still win the battle, but there was very little margin for error on the Japanese side.

The battle for Guam was fully joined on July 4, 1944, when first American naval planes bombed and strafed Japanese coastal batteries and then a night destroyer bombarded enemy defenses around Agana, Asan, and Agat. Four days later, Rear Admiral Turner Joy's cruisers appeared off the coast and began bombarding the beach front along Guam's west coast. On July 14, Connolly, on the bridge of his flagship *Appalachian,* personally directed a bombardment by battleship *Colorado,* three destroyers, and a destroyer escort.[2]

This was the first volley in a virtually nonstop shuttle bombardment in which American warships would pound Guam, return to Eniwetok or Saipan for reloads of fuel and ammunition, and then rotate back to the target zone for a new series of fire missions. By July 19, the waters around Guam were crowded with six battleships, six cruisers, and several flotillas of destroyers raining shells on the island while planes from up to seven escort carriers and fleet carriers swooped from the sky to add an aerial dimension to the noose that was tightening around General Takashima and his garrison. Admiral Samuel Eliot Morison rated the naval bombardment of Guam as "superior to any other operation in the Pacific prior to Korea," and insisted that "the small amount it fell short was unavoidable." Japanese defenders largely agreed with Morison's evaluation. As one soldier noted: "On the island, no matter where one goes, the shells follow." A Japanese officer noted that "after several days of successive attacks scattered outbreaks of serious loss of spirit occurred." He admitted that "some of the men could not perform their duties in a positive spirit."[3]

By nightfall on Thursday, July 20, the eve of the American landings, roughly 6,000 14-inch and 16-inch shells, 4,000 8-inch projectiles, and 16,000 5-inch shells had obliterated almost every coastal gun in the open and about half of the artillery in caves, blockhouses, and other strong points. On the other hand, most of the Japanese communication system was still intact and the pattern of bombardment allowed Takashima to focus his attention on a relatively small part of Guam's coastline.

The Japanese field commander had established his headquarters on the Fonte Plateau overlooking Asan Bay and had deployed most of his service units, tanks, and reserve artillery as well as a battalion of the 38th Regiment in that vicinity. Takashima envisioned an American assault in almost exactly the same place that Japanese naval troops had landed in 1941—the wide beaches between Tumon Bay and the capital of Agana, and his largest concentration of army units, the 319th, 320th and 321st Battalions of the 48th Brigade covered the beachfront in that region; only one battalion, the 322nd, was deployed along Asan Bay, the actual landing spot for the 3rd Marine Division.

The two infantry battalions of the understrength 18th Regiment were deployed in the vicinity of Piti Navy Yard and charged with blocking an American thrust either up or down the main road from the navy yard to the capital. Farther south, in the area dominated by the Orote Peninsula, Takashima deployed one battalion of the 38th Regiment to cover the Agat Bay beaches, and a second battalion to occupy the base of the peninsula. This force would be heavily supported by the navy's 54th Naval Ground Force, which had scattered from Agat Town to the approaches to Orote Airfield.

The Japanese commander believed that he had divined American assault plans and had enough firepower to drive them into the sea. One of Takashima's senior deputies, Major General Kiyoshi Shigematsu, echoed this sentiment in a message to his command which had responsibility for the Agana-Tumon Bay:

> It has been decided that the enemy is going to launch and attack in force at dawn in the region of the Agana sector. When he lands, the Division will be quick to seize the opportunity to attack him in the sector with a powerful force and crush him at the beaches. The Garrison Unit will await its initial opportunity and will completely destroy the enemy landing force upon the beaches.[4]

Several miles away, on board the *Appalachian,* Admiral Connolly considered the excellent weather forecast for Friday morning, the impact of the naval bombardment, and the firepower of the assault force and sent a dispatch to the task force saying that "conditions are most favorable for landing."

The predawn hours of Friday, July 21, 1944, impressed one American naval officer, Commander Hal Smith, as a "tropical sky bespangled with stars," a scene of beauty in which the upcoming battle seemed totally out of place.[5]

But even before the sun could poke above the vast Pacific, the business of war was underway as four battleships stationed off Orote Peninsula let loose with their big guns; meanwhile, inside Agat Bay, the *Pennsylvania* pounded the cliff line at the very tip of the peninsula. Just as dawn broke, twenty-six planes from the carrier *Wasp* appeared overhead and assumed their station as a roving combat air patrol, a new feature of the island invasion experience.

At 7:00 a.m., thirty-two LSTs sailing 12,000 yards off Guam's shoreline opened their doors and disgorged 360 landing craft; at the same time, sixty Sherman tanks began their journey in their special landing vessels. As the gray craft chugged toward their target in intricate patterns along the sea's surface, two hundred planes, including eighty-five fighters, sixty-two bombers, and fifty-three torpedo planes flew in a spectacular sweep along the 14 miles of beachfront from Agana to Bongi Point, bombing gun emplacements and shooting up anything that moved.

As the landing craft began their final run toward the coral reef, eighteen specially equipped gunboats took the lead as gunners manned 20 mm and 40 mm weapons and a new innovation, a battery of forty-two rocket launchers that had been retrofitted on each craft. As gunboats closed in to 200 yards from the reef, one of the most awesome sights of World War II was seen as an almost simultaneous salvo of 9,000 rockets whooshed through the blue sky and onto the invasion beaches, evoking memories in more than one of the leathernecks of the most spectacular Independence Day fireworks displays of childhood.

Just as in two other spectacular amphibious invasions of that momentous summer of 1944, at Normandy and Saipan, the initial assault on Guam began essentially as two separate engagements that would become a unified campaign only when the landing forces linked together after several days of fierce fighting. The Northern Assault Force, primarily a heavily reinforced 3rd Marine Division, stormed ashore across 2,500 yards of beachfront between Asan Point and Adelup Point, which defined the waters of Asan Bay. Colonel Carvel Hall's 3rd Regiment came ashore on Red Beach 1 and Red Beach 2, and veered slightly northward toward Adelup Point and nearby Chonito Cliff at the far left side of the invasion beach. Colonel Arthur Butler's 21st Regiment landed on Green Beach and focused on capturing the town of Asan and sprinting toward the first line of hills a few hundred yards beyond. Colonel Robert Craig's 9th Marines landed on Blue Beach adjacent to Asan Point with an initial goal of seizing the Agana-Piti Road, which was the gateway to Piti Navy Yard and Apra Harbor.

The invasion troops benefited from the many lessons that had been learned since the assault on Tarawa almost eight months earlier. As the new rocket boats launched their deadly salvos, a Marine air observer reported that, despite a few projectiles falling short, the "rockets are landing and giving them hell."[6]

As the landing vessels closed on the beach, airplanes dropped white parachute flares that signaled the big guns to raise their fire inland while attack planes hovered over the beaches. Amphibious tanks and tractors provided close-in fire support right up onto the beaches.

Each Japanese defender still believed that his actions could tip the scales of battle and that his death could become one small part of annihilating the enemy on the beaches. The diary of one beach defender revealed this mindset: "I will not lose my courage but now is the time to prepare to die! If one desires to live, hope for death! Be prepared to die! With this conviction one can never lose . . . look upon us! We have shortened our expectancy of 70 years of life to 25 in order to fight. What an honor it is to be born in this day and age!"[7]

These determined Nipponese defenders still manned machine guns and artillery batteries that the air attacks and naval bombardment left undamaged, and an alarming, if not overwhelming, number of landing craft spouted into flame to attest to the defenders' tenacity.

Captain John L'Estrange, an officer in command of thirty DUKWs (popularly called "ducks"), quickly experienced the deadly accuracy of still-concealed Japanese guns. "On Guam we weren't kept in the dark very long," he recalled. "I lost three of my DUKW's from enemy fire on the way in, with the worst yet to come. Where we were landing was really like a huge amphitheater surrounded by hills and cliffs. It was this high ground that turned the beach into an inferno." Another startling discovery added to the confusion: "No one had bothered to tell us about the coral reef. Every one of the damn rubber tires had been cut to ribbons coming in. There was no way we could move over vehicles on land."[8]

While the men of the Northern Assault Force stumbled through an amphitheater that was rapidly becoming a giant shooting gallery, their comrades to the south were facing their own perils. The Southern Assault Force was centered on a Marine initial invasion group and an army follow-up force. The leathernecks were formed around the 1st Provisional Marine Brigade commanded by Brigadier General Lemuel Shepherd. This unit was an improvised merger of the 22nd Marine Regiment. The original 4th Marines had gone down fighting at Bataan and Corregidor, but now the regiment was reconstituted by merging raider and parachute battalions into a new organization. They would form the initial assault force that would storm ashore along Agat Bay and then, reinforced by successive landings of the three regiments of the 77th Infantry Division, drive both eastward into Guam's interior and northward to seize Orote Peninsula and the southern approaches to Apra Harbor.

At 8:30 on the morning of W-Day, at almost exactly the same moment the 3rd Marine Division landed along the Asan Bay beaches, the 22nd Marines stormed ashore from Agat Bay on Beaches Yellow 1 and 2, just south of the town of Agat, and the 4th Marines seized White Beach 1 and White Beach 2 south of Gaan Point. The Marines were quickly caught in a joint Japanese army-navy crossfire as guns from the north on Orote Peninsula, from the east on Mount Alifan, and from the south at Bongi Point epitomized the ability of the defenders to use camouflage and concealment at least to partially counteract the power of American naval and air superiority. An American intelligence officer described the emplacement as a "particularly well-concealed battery of a 75 mm and 37 mm gun located in a double cave, one above another. The mouth of the cave could not be seen from the sun and trees and shrubs prevented them from showing up in aerial pictures."[9]

The smoking wreckage of nearly twenty landing vehicles attested to the fact that the Japanese were still dangerous opponents who would fight for every foot of the island.

Within an hour of the arrival of the first assault waves, it was becoming apparent to Takashima that if these landings were not clever diversions, then the chances of annihilating the Americans on the beaches were becoming very dim. The units that were deployed at the point of contact were fighting well, but most of the general's best infantry and armored units were either too far inland or too far north to enable the defenders to throw the invaders into sea. However, from his perch atop Fonte Plateau, Takashima did have the consolation of watching his outnumbered beach forces ensure that the enemy landing would be no walkover.

The first major hurdle to an American drive off the beaches was Chonito Cliff, which loomed over the Red beaches as a fearsome, inanimate sentry. The cliff was actually pocked with dozens of caves of assorted sizes bristling with Japanese weapons. As Company K of the 3rd Marines tried to cross a stream bed that would provide access to the far side of Chonito, enemy defenders rolled grenades down the cliff and peppered away with expertly concealed machine guns. A few minutes later, a company of Sherman tanks and several flamethrower units deployed along the beach road and fired directly into the caves, an action that provided enough cover for the foot soldiers to push a few hundred yards inland but did not completely eliminate the threat from the cliff.

The other immediate obstacle to a successful move inland was Bundschu Ridge, a jungle-covered piece of high ground 400 feet high and 200 yards square that loomed over the road that connected Afana with Piti Navy Yard. Shortly before the American landings, this obvious

Japanese strongpoint had been named for Captain Geary Bundschu, commander of Company A of the 3rd Marines. Now, less than an hour after the first landing, Bundschu's company was pinned down in a gully just west of the ridge by Japanese mortar and machine-gun fire. As Bundschu's men groped their way through the gully to gain the approaches to the high ground above, the defenders exacted a steady toll of men and by twilight, when the Marines were finally in a position to attack, only slightly more than half the company was still standing. The company commander led a desperate, early evening assault, but Bundschu and dozens of his men climbed up the steep slope; then, shot by the defenders, they fell backwards to the ground far below. By full darkness, Bundschu was dead, the few survivors who had reached the crest were nearly overwhelmed by the counterattack, and the left flank of the 3rd Division was far from secure.

The middle assault regiment on the northern front experienced nearly as much frustration on W-Day. In a series of actions that would become known later as the battle for Banzai Ridge, the three battalions of 21st Marines encountered a seemingly endless succession of ridges crammed with Japanese automatic weapons and mortars. One single ridge position held fourteen Japanese machine guns and six mortars and required a grueling battle to secure a series of entrenchments that also yielded the first two live prisoners in that area. One exhausted officer noted that "every ridge gained by the 21st Marines disclosed another pocket of the enemy behind it." The regiment assigned to the right flank of the assault, the 9th Marines, made the most impressive gains of W-Day when the unit faced more open ground as it wheeled south toward the Tatgua River and the Piti Navy Yard about a mile beyond. But as the lead units splashed across rice paddies toward the first water barrier, the Nidual River, the Marines were caught by heavy fire from Japanese guns concealed on the high ground of Asan Point. As the first company from the 2nd Battalion approached the bridge over the Nidual, a carefully concealed battery of machine guns and antitank guns let loose and took a high toll of leathernecks. By nightfall, the 9th Marines were only 100 yards short of the Tatgua River, but the beachhead was dearly won: Twenty officers were dead or wounded and several companies had been severely mauled.

The inland thrust of the southern attack force encountered fewer impediments such as Bundschu Ridge and Banzai Ridge had presented, but the men of the 1st Provisional Brigade still faced heavily entrenched enemy that could call on more direct artillery support from their comrades from the north. The Japanese army and navy units charged with guarding the approaches to Orote Peninsula had established an extensive network of concrete pillboxes and blockhouses and each strongpoint had to be captured in a series of miniature battles. The first major objective for the southern assault force was the town of Agat and by mid-morning the 1st Battalion of the 22nd Marines had wheeled left from Yellow Beach and sprinted toward the town. While one company advanced along the beach road and a second company plunged through the adjoining rice paddies, Japanese defenders crouched behind piles of rubble and blasted the invaders. The battle now surged through town until the Marines secured the center of Agat and pushed northward into the outskirts. As they picked their way through abandoned, badly damaged buildings, the Americans encountered a mass of hill underbrush concealing several Japanese machine guns. As one platoon leader admitted later:

> The Marines didn't know where the emplacements were and many of them died trying to find out. Then occurred one of those inexplicable things known to every Marine who had fought Japs and understood by none. Down track leading to the center of the trench marched 12 Japs. They carried the machine guns, three heavies and a light, which had held up the American advance all afternoon. The Japs were riddled by machine gun bullets.[10]

The Americans had now recaptured the first town on Guam; but as the sun disappeared below the horizon, the Marines dug in for one of the trademarks of the Pacific war, the Japanese night counterattack.

Ever since the frightening early days on Guadalcanal, nearly two years earlier, American Marines and soldiers had been forced to condition themselves to the fact that the Japanese rarely allowed the night of an invasion day go by without launching a desperate counterattack. The first day on Guam had produced modest but definite gains, and the 1,050 causalities, including just under two hundred dead, was proportionately much lower than the first day at Tarawa. But the Japanese were viewed as enormously resourceful and tough-minded night fighters, and the only question in the American beachhead was when, not if, the enemy would attack.

General Takashima fully intended to launch a massive night counterattack, but he felt that prospects for success would be much greater if he could concentrate the units covering Agana and the Fonte Plateau into one strike force and then coordinate and offensive with the naval units on Orote Peninsula. This attack would take several days to organize, however, and meanwhile the Japanese commander gave lukewarm support to Colonel Tsumetaro Suenaga's plea to launch an immediate night assault against the southern beachhead employing the three infantry battalions of the 38th Infantry Regiment and the single tank company deployed in that area. The Japanese colonel had observed the American landing force capture Agat in one operation and then thrust into the lower slopes of Mount Alifan with other forces. Suenaga was determined to push every rifleman and tank he could gather down Harmon Road, push the American away from the approaches to Alifan, and then launch a three-pronged drive for the invasion force into the sea heartened even the cautious Takashima and the plan was approved.

At just 1:00 a.m. on Saturday morning, July 22, American Marines deployed along Harmon Road and on the adjacent foothills of Mount Alifan heard the unmistakable clanking of tank treads in the darkness up the road. A series of calls was placed to the support ships offshore and suddenly the night was transformed by the eerie, strobe-like glow of illumination shells fired by the fleet. The sudden brightness revealed a column of eight Japanese tankers clattering down Harmon Road supported by dozens of riflemen hanging from the tanks or quick-marching alongside. Cannons and machine guns sprayed death through the woods while a handful of bazooka teams played a deadly game of hide-and-seek with their armored adversaries. Then, just as the American outposts were about to be overrun, five Shermans that had been parked farther down Harmon Road for just such an eventuality rumbled forward and used their heavier guns to turn four enemy vehicles into fiery infernos while a lone bazooka crew accounted for two more.[11]

The Americans had won the first armored duel on Guam, but other groups of Japanese troops were pushing down gullies and ravines and emerging on the landing beaches to spread destruction. One unit that was hard hit by the attack was the vanguard of the 305th Infantry Regiment of the 77th Division. Unlike the Marines, most of the soldiers had not been provided with amphibious landing craft and were forced to wade ashore in water from waist deep to neck deep. As the GIs staggered ashore, overloaded with equipment and drenched, they were shocked to encounter Japanese soldiers with demolition charges strapped to their backs and aiming for nearby artillery pieces scattered on the beach. In one vicious firefight, seven soldiers were killed and another ten wounded, but not before more than fifty of the attackers lay sprawled in the sand.

The enormous supply of illumination shells kept large parts of the beachfront relatively bright and eliminated the Japanese perception that they "owned" the night. As one survivor admitted: "We had been thinking that we might win through a night counterattack but when the star shells came over one after the other one could only use our men as human bullets and there were many useless causalities and no chance of success."[12]

Just before dawn, Colonel Suenaga personally led a charge downhill from his command post on Mount Alifan towards the beaches below; but the colonel went down in a hail of bullets and joined six hundred of his comrades dead or dying on the battlefield. The steady stream of wounded soldiers limping or being carried to rear-area hospitals soon pushed the Japanese casualty total higher than 1,000 in exchange for fifty American dead and a hundred injured. The 38th Regiment, the key army unit in the southern sector, was now nearly finished as a cohesive force as two battalions were cut to pieces and the third was backpedaling westward along Harmon Road to make a stand on Mount Alifan. The defense of Orote Peninsula was now largely in the hands of the Japanese navy, which even now was preparing for its own banzai in the near future.

20

RAISING A FALLEN FLAG

THE NEXT PHASE of the American operation on Guam rivals in complexity Robert E. Lee's Chancellorsville campaign and Ulysses S. Grant's Vicksburg operations as two separate American forces were in turn subdivided into smaller entities to launch attacks at almost every point on the compass. Meanwhile, General Takashima attempted to parry each successive thrust while concentrating a force that could launch a devastating counterattack four days later.

The most northerly American operation during the second phase of the battle was the attempt to secure the bloodstained crest of Bundschu Ridge. On the morning of July 22, Major Henry Aplington, commander of the 1st Battalion of the 3rd Marines, sent small groups from three companies to work their way gradually onto the high ground while the 2nd Battalion of the regiment maintained constant pressure on the Japanese defenders. However, the defenders had too many concealed mortars and machine guns and there were never enough Marines concentrated in one place to hold the crest from enemy counterattacks. General Allen Turnage, commander of the 3rd Marine Division, now planned an all-out attempt to capture Bundschu on Sunday morning because this position was the main impediment to linking the 3rd and 21st Regiments for a unified drive inland.

As the Marines spent the night preparing for their concerted push up the ridge, the Japanese defenders made Turnage's job much easier as they launched a poorly coordinated counterattack that charged American machine guns at point-blank range. By day, only fifty of five hundred attackers were still alive and, although these survivors contested every foot of Bundschu in an all-day battle, the ridge was in American hands by late Sunday night.

Although much of Turnage's command was attempting to push inland, the men of the 9th Marine Regiment were advancing down the beach road toward Piti Navy Yard. On Sunday morning, the Marines pushed across the Tatgua River and then split to capture two objectives. While one battalion embarked on landing craft to secure Cabras Island 500 yards off the coast, the remaining forces stormed into the navy yard and reclaimed the base for the United States. One of the liberators, Captain L'Estrange, marveled at the impression he received of going back in time as he walked through the complex: "I walked into one of the buildings and the first thing I saw as a desk calendar that was still open at December 10, 1941, the day the island had been captured. Not a thing had changed. I guess the Japs felt time was going to stand still for them."[1]

Time was definitely not standing still on contemporary Guam as both assault forces lunged toward their primary objectives. Although the capture of Piti had put the northern force in a position to secure one end of Apra Harbor, the southern force was launching a simultaneous attack northward in a drive to secure the gateway to Orote Peninsula.

The drive toward Orote began in earnest on the morning of July 22 as lead units of the 22nd Marines pushed northward from the outskirts of Agat. But as the leathernecks moved along the Agat-Suman Road and through adjacent rice paddies, they encountered the first in a series of mutually supporting pillboxes that had to be captured one strongpoint at a time. The Americans inched toward the base of the peninsula as they weathered a succession of localized counterattacks launched by a combined army-navy infantry force supported by small groups of tanks. The first day of the drive gains were measured in yards because the defenders were able to use the marshy terrain to maximize advantage. The halt line Sunday night was only a third of a mile outside of Agat.

As the American drive up Agat-Suman Road continued to be reduced to a crawl on July 23, General Shepherd decided to switch tactics and change the axis of his advance. A perusal of the map showed two roads leading into the peninsula, the Agat Suman Road, which passed Dadi Beach on the left side of Orote, and the Old Agat Road that led to the town of Atantano and then swung along the right-hand coastline. It might take a day or two to secure the second road; but, if all went well, the Japanese would be forced to cover two avenues of approach and it seemed likely that the Americans could find a weak spot somewhere. However, as the men of the 1st Brigade began their dual advance, General Takashima was preparing to ensure that the invaders would never get within sight either of Orote Airfield or of the Marine barracks, which was gaining more symbolic importance every day of the battle.

As early as the afternoon of July 23, General Takashima was convinced that the only remaining change for outright Japanese victory was a well-organized counterattack that either recaptured the landing beaches or inflicted such horrendous causalities on the invaders that they reembarked the assault force.[2]

The Japanese commander could not wait much longer to strike because his front-line units had been adsorbing very high casualties. The division field hospital near Fonte Plateau was now overflowing with wounded men and the nearby Fonte River was so fouled by the blood and bodies of soldiers killed in firefights that it could no longer be used as a source of drinking water. At 1:00 p.m. on that Sunday afternoon, General Takashima decided to launch a major strike in the predawn hours of Wednesday, July 26, and he admitted to his subordinates that this action would determine the fate of Guam.

The core around which the northern attack would be launched was the force of the three infantry battalions, two tank companies, and several mobile artillery batteries that had been deployed to counter an American landing at Agana. These units would stiffen the badly mauled front-line battalions as they poured down through a series of ravines to the landing beaches.

Despite the intense American bombardment and air attacks, Takashima's communications network was still more or less intact, and he secured the promise of substantial support from his naval counterpart, Captain Yutaka Sugimoto. First, Sugimoto agreed to move a substantial part of his 54th Naval Infantry Force north from the Orote area and personally lead them into battle against the 3rd Marine Division. Also, the naval officer directed his subordinate, Commander Asaichi Tamai, to utilize much of the remaining naval garrison on Orote in launching a southern prong of the counterattack at the Americans, who were advancing towards the entrance to the peninsula.

Takashima's basic plan was to use his remaining armor, about twenty-five tanks, as spearheads for a series of thrusts toward Asan Point, Piti Navy Yard, and the beaches in between; at the same time, Tamai's men would burst out of Orote, smash the Marine units near the neck of the peninsula, and then lunge toward the invasion beaches at Agat. The counterattack was designed as an all-out effort in which the wounded would hobble into battle and sailors and army service personnel without rifles would wield swords, baseball bats, or any other object that might kill or wound an American invader.

Soon after midnight on July 26, American units began reporting Japanese probing attacks along the northern front. The first unit to feel the full fury of the enemy counterattack was the Reconnaissance Company of the 9th Marines, which was deployed between the left flank of their own regiment and the right flank of the 21st Marines. Japanese scouts had discovered the gap and, just before 1:00 a.m., a wave of attackers smashed into the isolated Marines. A wild melee followed in which nine Americans were killed or wounded; the leathernecks inflicted thirty-five casualties as they backpedaled toward the relative safety of their regimental lines.[3]

A few minutes later, much of the 9th Marines' front was wreathed in flames as attackers poured down the hilly paths and roads that led from Fonte Plateau towards the ocean and engaged in a frenzy of close-quarters combat. The attackers nearly rolled up the 2nd Battalion of the 9th Marines, killing or wounding three hundred men. One American emplacement changed hands seven times in the ebb and flow of battle as the Japanese seemed to pour down from Fonte in unending waves. Sergeant Alvin Joseph, a Marine combat correspondent, provided a graphic account of the battle: "A wave of Japs appeared from nowhere and a Marine automatic rifleman blasted them with his B.A.R. From the darkness a lone, drunken Jap raced headlong at the Marine, tripped several feet away over a body and flew through the air. There was a blinding flash as he literally blew apart. He had been a human bomb, carrying a land mine and a blast charge on his waist."[4]

Takashima was now utilizing one of his primary advantages, the Japanese held the high ground, and had carefully studied the deployment of the American forces. As Colonel Robert Craig, commander of the 9th Marines, noted after the battle: "We found three huge telescopes of 20 power. Looking through these scopes one could almost make out individual features of Marines below us. Practically every part of our lines and rear areas, as well as my own CP, could be seen through these glasses from this high ground."[5] The result was several disturbingly deep penetrations through seams in the American lines.

For example, one Japanese assault force utilized a gap in the American lines to penetrate all the way to the 3rd Division hospital near the landing beaches. Doctors and corpsmen immediately began evacuating patients from the tents while other hospital personnel and walking wounded formed a defensive line. When attackers penetrated the wards, bedridden patients fired pistols in a last desperate stand. Captain L'Estrange, a member of a force ordered to relieve the hospital, described the chaotic battle this way: "What a sight it was! The wailing wounded, bandages and all, are banging away at the Japs. Some of the more seriously wounded men were firing from their beds. After it was all over they even found several dead Japs in the surgical tent. The Marines lost some men but we killed the Nips in bunches!"[6]

The Japanese troops enjoyed two initial advantages in this offensive: They were attacking from high ground and they were able to locate seams in the American lines. On the other hand, as the battle continued, Takashima's men were increasingly handicapped by three major problems. First, the attack plan was developed on the premise that tanks would provide an armored spearhead for the infantry. However, the core of Takashima's armor, two entire tank companies, became lost in the darkness and failed to engage the Americans. Second, the Japanese officers sought to enhance the fighting power of their men by distributing enormous quantities of sake, beer, and other spirits from the huge liquor supplies stashed on the island. Although these inebriated troops were more than willing to charge American lines, discipline began to unravel to the point that unit cohesiveness virtually disappeared. Finally, in the spirit of Bushido, high-ranking officers wielding ceremonial swords took the lead position in attacks and so became prominent targets for American marksmen. For example, Captain Yutaka Sugimoto, the senior Japanese naval officer on Guam, was cut down only moments after he led his sailors into action. By dawn, an incredible 90 percent of all officers involved in the attack were dead or mortally wounded.

By early morning, the attack was degenerating into a massacre as massive American firepower began to take effect. Sergeant Thomas Josephy described one moment in the climax of the battle this way:

> A last wave of Japs charged over the top of the hill. It was the wildest, most drunken group of all, bunched together, howling, stumbling and waving swords, bayonets, and long poles. Some were already wounded and swathed in bandages. The Marines yelled back at them and chopped them down in their mad rush. In a moment it was over: the last wave of the three-hour attack died to a man.[7]

Several miles to the south, the 1st Marine Brigade faced a similar attack, but from the opposite direction. The 4th Marines and 22nd

Marines were just in the process of deploying across the neck of the
Orote Peninsula when Commander Tamai, the senior officer on the
peninsula, initiated the main naval contribution to the offensive. Rifles
were in relatively short supply for the sailors, so Tamai's men were
equipped with pistols, baseball bats, pitchforks, knives, swords, and
even broken bottles. It was possible that the navy outdid the army in
the distribution of liquor before the attack commenced: Groups of
sailors sang songs, boasted about their prowess in battle, and began
group cheers and chants to the awe and mystification of the Americans
deployed only a few hundred yards away.[8]

Then a wave of white uniforms surged forward and rolled across
mangrove swamps and rice paddies towards the entrance to the peninsula and the now fully alerted Marines. The Japanese were met in close
combat with automatic rifles, bayonets, and grenades while machine
guns and mortars fired at point-blank range only 40 yards behind the
front lines. American and Japanese adversaries locked in deadly em-
braces from which only one person would emerge alive.

Within a few minutes of Tamai's attack, an awesome assortment of
army and Marine artillery wheeled into action and poured shells into a
screaming crowd of Japanese marines as they surged between the gaps
they had broken between the two American regiments. Japanese tanks
never appeared, but Shermans began lumbering onto the scene and the
tide of battle gradually ebbed back into the woods. The exhausted
Americans were content to let the enemy retreat under the encouragement of a last flurry of artillery shells. The Japanese left four hundred
dead sailors at the field and carried perhaps another six hundred dying
or seriously wounded men back toward Orote Airfield. Seventy-five
Marines awaited burial and an equal number required hospitalization.

By mid-morning, a stunned General Takashima began tabulating
the reports of the few surviving officers. Four thousand Japanese soldiers and sailors had been left on the battlefield, and another 2,000
mortally wounded Japanese would soon join them in death. In a few
hours, Takashima had lost nearly as many men killed or mortally
wounded as Robert E. Lee or George Meade had lost in the entire three

days of Gettysburg, and every regimental or brigade commander on the island had been killed. At a cost of 241 dead and 650 wounded, the American invasion force had won the climactic battle of the campaign, and now 50,000 soldiers and Marines were poised to drive perhaps 10,000 defenders into an inevitable final stand that would unfold first on the Orote Peninsula.

On Friday morning, July 28, exactly one week after W-Day and forty-eight hours after the collapse of Takashima's offensive, a massive forty-five-minute-long air strike engulfed Orote Peninsula. This attack was followed by a thirty-minute naval bombardment and a thirty-minute artillery barrage by Marine and army guns. Then, at 8:30 a.m., one week to the minute after the initial invasion, platoons of Marine and army tanks rumbled forward, followed by the men of the 4th Marines and the 22nd Marines. General Lemuel Shepherd, commander of the 1st Marine Brigade, had spent the last two days probing Japanese positions and blasting through an extensive network of Japanese pill-boxes and entrenchments. Now, for one of the few times in the Pacific War, enemy defenders broke from their entrenchments and ran in the face of American riflemen and tanks. By dusk, American advance units were only 300 yards from the old Marine rifle range and the Marines reluctantly halted to await sunrise.

Saturday, July 29, dawned clear and hot as eight cruisers and destroyers, six battalions of artillery, and the greatest concentration of air power since the invasion provided a carpet of covering fire as the Marines sprinted for two objectives: the ruins of the Marine Barracks and the adjacent Orote Airfield. As enemy troops made last stands from the old rifle range to the airfield control tower, the last defenders died and, in the quiet of the humid afternoon, a stream of dignitaries inspected the barracks grounds.

At 3:30 on this Saturday afternoon, a bugler played "To the Colors" on a captured Japanese horn and the American flag was unfurled and raised on the barracks flagpole. Among the officers and men giving the first official salute on Guam since the Japanese invasion were Admiral Spruance, General Holland Smith, General Roy Geiger, and an honor platoon of men who repossessed the barracks for the Marine Corps. Ironically, the speed of the Japanese collapse prevented the timely arrival of another important figure, Captain Charles Moore, Jr., Spruance's executive officer and the son of Lieutenant Charles Moore, USN, and the takeover of the island government by the Navy Department.

General Shepherd spoke for the thousands of Marines who had fought to retake this highly symbolic plot of land: "On this hallowed ground, you officers and men of the first Marine Brigade have avenged the loss of our comrades who were overcome by a numerically superior enemy three days after Pearl Harbor. Under our flag this island again stands to fulfill its destiny as an American fortress in the Pacific."

The first American flag surrendered in World War II had been replaced by the emblem of a powerful avenging nation that now boasted the power that Captain McMillen and his tiny garrison could only dream about two and a half years earlier. Now that same powerful force was about to liberate nearly 25,000 fellow citizens who had suffered greatly for their refusal to repudiate their loyalty to the United States. A fallen flag had been redeemed; now a hostage people would be liberated.

The death of General Takishima in the struggle for Orote left only one senior Japanese officer still alive in the Marianas. Lieutenant General Hideyoshi Obata, the commander of the Imperial Thirty-first Army, had established his headquarters in Charan Kanoa; but when Saipan had been invaded, he was on an inspection tour of defenses in the Carolines. When the Fifth Fleet appeared of the Marianas, Obata could travel no farther north than Guam before the Americans established a naval blockade. He spent most of the campaign in little more than nominal command of Tinian and Saipan. Now all of his senior field commanders were dead and Obata felt obliged to orchestrate the final defense of the Marianas.

The Thirty-first Army commander established a temporary headquarters in the central Guam town of Ordot and began concentrating a motley force of 1,000 surviving army combat forces, eight hundred naval infantry, 2,500 assorted support troops, a dozen tanks, and a similar number of cannons. The general assumed that other units had retreated northward after the final Banzai attack, but radio communications were minimal and the 4,300 men under his immediate command represented the last organized force on Guam.

Obata, determined to cobble together a temporary defense line stretching eastward from the capital city of Agana through Ordot and over to the town of Yona near the east coast in order to delay the invaders long enough to establish a more formidable position, centered on the high ground around Mount Barrigada with a final redoubt on Mount Santa Rosa at the northern tip of the island. Obata knew that each successive line was covered by increasingly dense woodlands and jungles that would not only offer excellent concealment and cover for the defenders but also make penetration by the enemy difficult.

General Geiger was equally aware of the fact that the high ground of northern Guam strongly favored the Imperial troops, but he was not sure where the enemy would seriously contest the American advance. When the 307th Regiment reached the town of Asinan, on the south beach of the Pago River, late in the afternoon of the last day of July, the forward units discovered that the enemy had abandoned both their defensive positions and a large concentration of camp holding more than 2,000 Chamorros. Now ecstatic, liberators and tearful captives met in embrace as troops passed candy, cigarettes, and food to people who were overcome with joy at once again seeing Americans. The fatigue of a long and tiresome march through hot, difficult country was quickly forgotten as for a moment. Liberation replaced combat as the major objective of the day and tired GIs watched in awe as Guamanians brought out tiny American flags that they had hidden, under threats of death if discovered, for the past thirty months.

Meanwhile, while the army was liberating a concentration camp, the Marines were returning the captured city of Guam to its legitimate government. The city of Agana had been the scene of bitter street fighting during the Japanese invasion of December, 1941, but now was more dangerous to the Americans because the Imperial defenders had planted mines and booby traps. Advance units of Colonel Thomas James's 3rd Marines pushed continuously through rubble and mined buildings until they reached the main plaza; this city square had been the scene of a desperate stand by a handful of Marines, sailors, and insular police more than two years earlier. Now, only wounded or dead enemy forces were discovered, and the capital city of Guam was finally back in American hands.

While the Marines were delighted to recapture what was the first American-owned city to be occupied by the Japanese in World War II, the next American objective was coveted more for its water supply than its symbolism. The town of Barrgada was hardly a household name among the invasion forces, but it was the site of a huge reservoir capable of pumping 20,000 gallons of water a day for seriously thirsty troops. Elements of the 305th and 307th Regiments pushed northward just as General Obata dispatched reinforcements southward to fight the "battle of the reservoir."

At just after dawn on August 2, fourteen light tanks of Company D, 7th Division, and the tank battalion were pushing towards the reservoir when the trees suddenly became alive with Japanese soldiers. Fire poured down on the lead tanks and 20 mm cannon and heavy machine guns sprayed lethal torrents at the rear of the column. Soon, reinforcements from both sides were pouring into a battle that swirled around a newly constructed Buddhist temple and a two-story greenhouse reinforced with a concrete wall. American infantrymen had no sooner overrun the temple when a Japanese tank roared down the road, plowed into the building, shifted gears, and forced its way out the other side, caving in the roof and pinning American machine gun crews under the debris. Then, as the Chi Ha tank veered off, advancing Shermans rambled towards the greenhouse, knocked out a second Imperial tank, and discovered a new assault on the greenhouse.

By the evening of August 2, the men of General Andrew Bruce's 77th Division held the outskirts of Barigada and most of the water supply, but the defenders still held the town itself. General Bruce had served in Panama during the 1930s, and, like many of his Marine counterparts, had a good sense of fighting in the jungles. Bruce secured General Geiger's permission to largely ignore unit flanks and "keep pushing to the main enemy body." The corps commander instructed, "Do not hold up for small pockets which can be mopped up later."

The first week of August was a time of slow but steady advance that forced Japanese troops defending Barrigada towns and farther north to pull back toward Mount Santa Rosa or risk being isolated by a green-tinted juggernaut. Now what seemed like relatively short distances on army and Marine maps took on new proportions for the men slugging through the hilly jungle. As one soldier recounted:

> The distance across the island is not far, as the crow flies, but un-luckily we can't fly. The nearest I came to lying was while descending the slippery side of a mountain in a sitting position. After advancing a few yards you find that the bolt handle of the machine gun on your shoulder, your pack and shovel, canteens, knife and machete all stick out at right angles and are as tenacious in the grip on the sur-rounding underbrush as a dozen grappling hooks. The flies and mosquitoes have discovered your line of march and have called up all their reinforcements who regard us as nothing but walking blood banks."[9]

These sweating, overexhausted troops may have been waging a battle with the local mosquitoes, but they were, in turn, forcing the Imperial defenders out of the Mount Barrigada line. General Obata was now obliged to pull the survivors back to the final Japanese stronghold in the mountains, the crest of Mount Santa Rosa. Obata's remaining twelve artillery pieces were shifted from one position to another in a giant shell game, but the far more numerous American batteries soon changed the competition to a cat-and-mouse game. Finally, as massed battalions of American artillery pounded Mount Santa Rosa, elements of the 77th Division stormed the heights. By the afternoon of August 8, at a cost of 145 casualties, the GIs had secured the last enemy-held high ground and counted more than five hundred dead defenders.

Now, in a final desperate tide of retreat, streaks of Imperial soldiers and sailors pulled back to the cliffs of Pati Point at the northern tip of the island. At the same time, General Obata relayed a final message to

Tokyo: "Officers and men have been lost, weapons have been destroyed and ammunition expanded. We have only our bare hands to fight with. The holding of Guam has become hopeless. Or souls will inhabit the island to the very end, we pray for the serenity of the Emperor."

On the morning of August 9, the Marine patrols worked their way down from the cliffs to the beach and engaged in a final firefight for the last Japanese-held soil on Guam. At 11:31 a.m., General Geiger read a report of the skirmish and decided that it was time to declare Guam secured. But capturing the island had not been cheap or easy: A total of 1,567 Marines and 177 soldiers died in combat, and 5,308 leathernecks and 662 GIs had been wounded in a battle that had already produced 10,971 known Japanese dead, with many hundreds more to be discovered during the coming weeks. Yet the first American territory lost to the Japanese offensive following Pearl Harbor was now back in possession of the United States and the Chamorros had traded the dubious advantages of membership in the East Asian Co-Prosperity Sphere for the more tangible benefits of citizenship in the American Republic.

The day after General Geiger declared Guam secured, a plane landed at Orote Airfield and disembarked Admiral Chester Nimitz, Lieutenant General Alexander Vandergrift, commander of the Marine Corps, and other notable members of the American high command. Meanwhile, Admiral Raymond Spruance docked his flagship *Indianapolis* in Apra Harbor. Soon, the senior officers were holding the first in a series of conferences on future operations in the Pacific that had now become feasible with the capture of the Marianas. The third other epic trilogy of land battles that was the Marianas campaign was now over, and those victories combined with the overwhelming defeat of the Imperial Japanese Navy in the battle of the Philippine Sea now provided new horizons for the Americans and new terrors for the Japanese. Yet, while the American commanders were meeting to salute their fighting men and plan future operations, the commander of the army that had opposed them was saluting in his own way the 65,000 Imperial soldiers and sailors who had died defending the islands. In other cultures and other times, General Hideyoshi Obata might have been having dinner

296 / HELL IS UPON US

296 / HELL IS UPON US

with his senior American counterpart, toasting one another's courage and their contending forces. Yet this was not the Imperial way; while the victor of Operation Forager was considering the future, the defeated commander was contemplating his past. While seated in a cave, dressed in his finest uniform, General Hideyoshi Obata said a final prayer for the prosperity of the Japanese Empire, raised a ritual dagger, and joined in death the tens of thousands of subordinates who had died in the crucial battle for a now dying empire.

21

THE COST OF VICTORY

AUGUST 1944 WAS a month of joyful relief for Americans who had endured the uncertainty and frustration of the June invasions of Normandy and Saipan. Within two weeks of one another, the first American territory captured by the Japanese after Pearl Harbor and the largest European city under German occupation were both liberated. Hitler's Atlantic Wall and Tojo's Absolute National Defense Line had both been inexorably breached and the Axis forces were gradually backpedaling toward the homelands from which they had set out to dominate the globe several years earlier.

But World War II was far from over, as bloody battles at Arnheim and Pelilieu would demonstrate in September. Yet, in the glow of the late-summer sunshine, the American president, military leaders, and the general public could all take a moment to digest the monumental accomplishments of what had been in many respects the Summer of Liberation.

In Europe, by the end of August 1944, Rome and Paris had been liberated, most of France was free of a four-year occupation, and Hitler had come very close to being assassinated. Although German troops had shown their tenacity, and German machine guns and tanks had demonstrated their superiority over Allied models, the Wehrmacht was being pushed back into the Fatherland from east and west. In the

Pacific, the Marianas campaign had ended with decisive land, naval, and air victories for the United States. At the end of the Marianas campaign, the Imperial Japanese Navy was no longer capable of functioning as a modern carrier force and was reduced to searching for opportunities to engage the Americans in a conventional ship-to-ship surface battle because the battleships and cruisers were the only significant cards the Nipponese navy still had left to play. The Japanese dream of using carrier air power to dominate the Pacific was born at Pearl Harbor and died in the battle of the Philippine Sea. Now Japan's only hope was somehow to turn the clock back to 1905 and try to replicate the battle of Tsushima Strait, Americans replacing Russians as unprepared victims. The Marianas campaign had ended the brief two-year reign of carrier versus carrier warfare as the epitome of naval conflict; the burgeoning American carrier force was now mistress of the Pacific and no comparable enemy vessels were left to fight in anything approaching equal combat. Admiral Ozawa's surviving carriers, largely denuded of planes, would receive one final opportunity to sail into harm's way at Leyte Gulf, but they would enter battle as pawns, not queens, when the Pacific war briefly reverted to a surface battle of the World War I Dreadnoughts.

On land, III Amphibious Corps and V Amphibious Corps, a force roughly the size of the Army of the Potomac under Ulysses S. Grant, did something in one summer that it took Federal forces nearly a year to accomplish: They utterly annihilated an army to the size of Robert E. Lee's Army of Northern Virginia from the chess board of war in an eight-week campaign in which the ferocity of the 1864 Overland Campaign was matched without the stalemate that would plague American forces by the end of that summer. Japanese forces had fought with courage, tenacity, and a brilliant perspective on the advantages of terrain to defenders. They had excellent artillery—and knew how to use it—as well as more armored formations than in previous battles, and their generals were intelligent, dedicated, and competent. Yet, in the end, an army of 65,000 men was either dead, surrendered, or hiding on the verge of starvation in caves, to emerge weeks or years later only to discover that the war had either passed them by or had ended.

The Marianas campaign was the first American offensive in the Pacific in which superlatives could be legitimately used to describe it. If the first offensive at Guadalcanal was nicknamed Operation Shoestring, Forager was Operation Cornucopia. The fleet of warships assigned to support the ground invasion was larger than the combined Anglo-American fleet deployed at Normandy. The combined force of American and Japanese carriers at the battle of the Philippine Sea was the largest concentration of those vessels that would ever meet in combat. The ground troops designated for use in conquering the Marianas was nearly ten times as large as the force initially committed to the invasion of Guadalcanal.

The Marianas campaign was fought in a time frame that very closely intersected the Normandy campaign in Europe, and, given the Allied priority in defeating Hitler before Japan, the scope of the battle in France was certainly wider. Ultimately, most of the American army would be involved in the march through the Continent. Yet the Marianas campaign was hardly ignored. Among the principal players in Forager, carrier pilots and Marines were among the most glamorous fighting elements in the entire American arsenal, and they were fighting enemies even more loathed in most American communities than the Nazis. At the outbreak of World War II, there was relatively little fear that the United States would be invaded by the Germans. But there was a genuine fear that snarling, buck-toothed Nipponese soldiers would somehow occupy Los Angeles or that Japanese dive-bombers would strafe helpless civilians on the beaches of Malibu. Japanese forces had penetrated as far as Alaska, and intelligent people wondered how much farther they could push. Thus, when American forces turned the tables and actually invaded real Japanese towns and cities in territory that even the enemy admitted was part of their inner empire, there was almost universal rejoicing across the United States. The farther the American warriors pushed into Japanese territory, the less likely it was that Nipponese warriors would ever threaten Seattle or San Francisco.

Yet, although all Americans could savor the heady spirits of absolute victory, the means by which this history had been achieved was open to debate from the highest circles of command down to the newspaper-reading public. Much of the prosecution of the Pacific War was interwoven with a running subplot of debate over whether the army or navy was actually better qualified to orchestrate the eventual march to Tokyo. The commander in chief made few attempts to conceal the fact that the navy was "his" service, but public opinion was far more divided. Many Americans believed, especially after the bloodbath at Tarawa, that Douglas MacArthur was far more capable of orchestrating an endgame against Japan without piling up enormous casualties than the senior members of the U.S. Navy and Marines. Other equally intelligent people believed that the senior army officer in the Pacific was an egotistical show-off and that the Pacific theatre was more water than land anyway, so the U.S. Navy by right of tradition should have preference in this theatre. Why not raise several more divisions of Marines, turn the whole Pacific over to the navy, and let the army worry about defeating Hitler?

This feud had been simmering on several levels since Pearl Harbor. Even Hollywood was not immune: Some war movie producers and screenwriters emphasized the superior capabilities of the U.S. Army and the U.S. Army Air Force, but others tilted toward the U.S. Navy and the Marine Corps. For example, in the film *Wake Island,* the Marines are shown annihilating much of the Japanese navy, air force, and army before dying to the last man behind stacks of Nipponese corpses; but in *Air Force,* the U.S. Army Air Force B-17s sink the entire Japanese navy at Midway while the American fleet dithers in confusion. If mere movies could provide ammunition for debate, what could be better than a fully-fledged and true controversy in the very real battle of Saipan?

The issue of the relief of General Ralph Smith by General Holland Smith began to escalate from command decision to national debate when the fired commander of the 27th Division reported to General Robert Richardson in Hawaii. As senior army officer in the Pacific

Ocean region, Richardson told his subordinate to take as much time as needed to develop a report on exactly what had happened on Saipan. Smith wrote a thirty-four-page document that included a number of annexes and copies of orders to and from the 27th Division by Holland Smith's headquarters. This report was forwarded to Richardson's office on July 11, and copies were also sent to Admiral Nimitz. Even before the report was finalized, Richardson had appointed a board of army officers to investigate the issue of Ralph Smith's relief. Lieutenant General Simon Bolivar Buckner, who had directed the Aleutians campaign, chaired a board of four generals that convened between July 7 and July 26 to examine documentary evidence and interview witnesses.[1]

Holland Smith had relieved his army division commanders because he felt that the 27th Division's failure to advance in the central highlands was endangering the whole offensive; but, in a form of bureaucratic overkill, the corps commander padded his official termination order with charges of insubordination based on almost incomprehensible additions and subtractions of army units between division and corps responsibility in the days leading up to the relief. A review of Holland Smith's communications to Ralph Smith displayed enormously sloppy staff work on the part of corps headquarters, and the Buckner board was hardly loathe to challenge the Marine general on that basis. Buckner's committee acknowledged that, as corps commander, Holland Smith had every right to relieve a divisional commander for whatever reasons he chose to enumerate. However, the board severely criticized the Marine officer on two fronts. First, Holland Smith's charges of insubordination on the part of his division commander were centered on operations against the besieged Japanese forces on Nafutan Peninsula; this is where the corps commander issued extremely vague orders on divisional control and then charged Ralph Smith with attempting to issue orders to battalions the corps headquarters had never specifically removed from army command. Second, the Buckner board emphasized that neither Holland Smith nor his chief of staff had ever been anywhere near the 27th Division's front lines during the opening phase of the central highlands offensive and thus possessed little first-hand knowledge of the enemy defenses that Ralph Smith's men were ordered to overrun. The board stated, "The bulk of the 27th Division was opposed by the enemy main defensive position on a difficult piece of terrain, naturally adapted to defense, artificially strengthened, well-manned, and heavily covered by fire."[2]

While the Buckner board was deliberating in Hawaii, General Richardson decided to launch his own army offensive by flying to Saipan to assess the situation for himself. The army commander was aware that Chester Nimitz as theatre commander still outranked him and thus took the precaution of securing the admiral's verbal permission to visit the front. He also paid a perfunctory courtesy call on Holland Smith. Richardson exploded and insisted, "You had no right to relieve Ralph Smith. I want you to know that you can't push the Army around the way you have been doing; you and your Corps commander aren't as well qualified to lead large bodies of troops as general officers in the Army, yet you dare to remove one of my Generals." According to Smith, Richardson closed his tirade with the charge: "You Marines are nothing but a bunch of beach runners anyway. What do you know about land warfare?"

Smith recounted that although he (barely) held his temper[3] and did not go into "Howling Mad" mode, when Richardson subsequently visited Kelly Turner's command ship, "Terrible" Turner launched a proactive strike at the army officer, vehemently questioning Richardson's right to exercise any command functions in the battle area, and when the general responded that he had permission from Nimitz, the irascible admiral demanded to see proof. After a final visit to Raymond Spruance had elicited a "What do you expect from Turner" shrug, Richardson returned to Hawaii to a request from the theatre commander to answer charges from Spruance and Turner questioning the legitimacy of his trip to Saipan.[4]

The escalating controversy within the headquarters of the Pacific command structure was now about to escalate into the nation's mass media. The powerful Hearst family staunchly advocated the appointment of Douglas MacArthur as supreme commander of the entire war against Japan and used Holland Smith's relief of Ralph Smith as an example of the mediocre leadership emanating from the Navy Department. The *San Francisco Examiner* called the relief of Ralph Smith a disagreement of tactics between the subtle, intelligent army commanders and the one-dimensional Marines: "Allegedly excessive loss of life attributed to Marine Corps impetuosity of attack has brought a break between Marine and Army commanders in the Pacific." According to the *New York Journal American*, "Americans are shocked at the casualties on Saipan following already heavy losses by Marine commanders on Tarawa and Kwajalein." The newspaper accused Holland Smith of firing his army subordinate when Ralph Smith protested "reckless and needless waste of American lives" and suggested that things would be enormously different in the Pacific if Douglas MacArthur were entrusted with supreme command.[5]

On the other hand, the Luce family, publisher of *Time* and *Life*, strongly supported Ernest King's plans to end the war by increasing the force and speed of the Central Pacific drive and viewed the Marines as far better trained for amphibious warfare than their army counterparts. *Time* reporter Robert Sherrod became very close to Holland Smith during the Marianas campaign, and although his stories concerning Marine courage and enthusiasm were essentially accurate, the correspondent spent almost no time with army units and he massively overplayed the Marines' disgust at the 27th Division for not holding up their part of the offensive. Sherrod strongly hinted that while Marines were making massive gains against tough resistance, entire army battalions would be held up for hours by a single Japanese gun position or sniper.[6]

As the Smith-versus-Smith controversy was fought out in the news media, the men in senior military command positions ardently wished the whole affair would simply go away. George Marshall, Ernest King, and Hap Arnold were more interested in orchestrating successful new offensives to terminate the war than re-fighting a dispute between Robert Richardson and Holland Smith. When Chester Nimitz, who genuinely seemed to respect and like Ralph Smith and was at best lukewarm about Holland Smith, attempted to push the relief up to the Joint Chiefs of Staff, this triumvirate quickly told him to forget the whole matter. Marshall ordered Richardson to get Ralph Smith entirely out of the Pacific theatre and Ernest King adamantly insisted that Holland Smith had done an excellent job on Saipan.

Ultimately, the controversy was managed without further damage, and, ironically, Ralph Smith probably ended up less tarnished and more professionally satisfied than his Marine namesake. At first, General Richardson essentially traded unit commands, giving Smith George Griner's 98th Division in Hawaii when that officer assumed command of the 27th. However, Marshall's determination to get the general out of the theatre without prejudice to his career resulted in the fluent linguist being assigned as military attaché to Charles de Gaulle's new provisional government of liberated France. This was a prestigious appointment for a general who should have been assigned to a position in the European theatre in the first place, and the courteous, French-speaking general was a major asset in dealing with the prickly leader of the new French republic.

In turn, Ernest King was determined to reward Holland Smith for a successful Marine campaign. The general had been arguing, correctly, that because the Marines were now effectively operating in the Pacific as the equivalent of an army, not a corps, there should be a Marine Headquarters established to administer the six divisions, twenty-eight artillery battalions, twelve Amtrac battalions, and four air wings that were now engaged in fighting the Japanese. September 1944 brought Holland Smith a promotion to the newly constituted Fleet Marine Force, Pacific, with headquarters in Hawaii. It was a mixed blessing for the fiery general: Although it carried enormous prestige, the position largely removed Smith from front-line command and placed him in a desk job amazingly similar to that of this adversary, Robert Richardson. Smith managed to get on the fringe of the Iwo Jima campaign, but certainly did not see himself as a rear-echelon commander and he fretted at the growing distance between the battle and his office. He would also receive the mixed blessing of receiving a coveted fourth star, but only at the time of his retirement two years later.

Beneath the surface civility surrounding the resolution of this crisis, a significant rethinking of the command structure of the Pacific War was accelerated by Holland Smith's actions. The Marine Corps was about to expand from five to six divisions and raise its authorized strength to almost 600,000 men, a number beyond the wildest dreams of its senior officers only five years earlier. However, projected assaults against Okinawa and the home islands of Japan would require far more divisions than even a massively expanded Marine Corps could provide. Preliminary plans for Operation Olympic, the invasion of Kyushu, called for using thirteen assault divisions, including three airborne divisions; and Operation Cornet, the invasion of the main island of Honshu, would be initiated with twenty divisions, other units to be added rapidly once a beachhead was secured. Although the Marine Corps was expected to utilize virtually its entire combat strength in these operations, the Army would still provide the bulk of invasion forces because the roles of the Central Pacific campaign were about to be reversed. As the command structures for these huge operations were being discussed and debated in Washington, the Smith-versus-Smith affair kept spreading wider ripples.

At first, the army's senior officers focused on Holland Smith's alleged shortcomings as an isolated incident. General Richardson sent a scathing report to George Marshall:

> I feel it is my duty to make of record my urgent and considered recommendation that no Army combat troops ever again be permitted to serve under the command of Marine Lieutenant General Holland Smith. So far as the employment of Army troops are concerned, he is prejudiced, petty and unstable. He has demonstrated an apparent lack of understanding of the acceptance of Army doctrines for the tactical employment of larger units.[7]

However, the particulars of Holland Smith's apparent issues gradually shifted to the generality of army units serving under Marine commanders. General Sanderford Jarman, Ralph Smith's replacement, was relatively critical of his predecessor, yet still insisted, "It is my earnest recommendation that in future operations of any kind where the Army and the Marine Corps are employed that under no circumstances should any Army divisions be incorporated into the Marine Corps. Their basic concepts of combat are far removed from that of the Army."

Army and Marine units would serve together in the future, most notably on Okinawa, but there the senior officer was Simon Bolivar Buckner, who would also become the highest-ranking American field commander to die in combat in World War II. Yet the Marianas campaign would be the last time in the war in which a mixed Army and Marine invasion force would serve under Marine command.

The second issue from the Marianas campaign that stirred widespread discussion on several levels was the general reaction to the highly publicized mass suicide on what was now called Banzai Cliff in Saipan. At the time of the invasion of Saipan, the American high command and the public in general had accepted the reality that Japanese military forces would essentially fight to the death and that few prisoners could be expected. Yet, on Saipan, the first encounter with large numbers of Japanese civilians had produced the gruesome climax at Marpi Point, which had been filmed extensively by Marine and navy cameramen. In actuality, the majority of civilians on Saipan did surrender. By mid-July, 1,500 civilians and nearly 1,000 construction workers were in American custody out of perhaps 22,000 noncombatants who were still in residence on Saipan at the time of the invasion. Most of the 6,000 fatalities had occurred in the crossfire of battle as the struggle moved northward to the landing beaches, and only about 1,000 of the deaths occurred in the last orgy of suicide at Marpi Point. However, the gruesome sight of 1,000 people committing voluntary, assisted, or involuntary suicide in the space of a few hours was a gut-wrenching, jarring experience, even for battle-hardened warriors, and films of the mass self-destruction were among the most intense live action chronicles of the entire war. An overriding question now hung over the celebration of victory in the Marianas: Had the Americans seen a preview of the Armageddon that would be unleashed when their fighting men attempted to invade the Imperial homeland?

Robert Sherrod stirred up widespread national discussion of this issue in an August 7 article titled "The Nature of the Enemy." This article was, to say the least, graphic in content and provided gruesome descriptions of schoolboys struggling to stay afloat after changing their minds about suicide and snipers shooting parents who had led their children to the edge of the cliffs and then appeared to have second thoughts. The final section, gruesomely titled "Death for 80,000,000," asked, "What did all this self-destruction mean? Did it mean that the Japanese on Saipan believed their own propaganda which told them that Americans are beasts and would murder them all? Many a Jap civilian did beg our people to put him to death immediately, rather than suffer the torture which he expected." Yet the correspondent was perceptive enough to realize that "many who chose suicide could see other civilians who had surrendered walking unmolested in the interment camps." A whole new inhuman world of warfare had now been entered, and Saipan was its portal: "Saipan is the first invaded Jap territory populated with more than a handful of civilians. Do the suicides of Saipan mean that the whole Japanese race will choose death before surrender? Perhaps that is what the Japanese and their strange propagandists would like us to believe."[8]

Robert Sherrod was more perceptive than he knew. For in the aftermath of the Marianas campaign, this image of total racial self-destruction, accompanied by huge numbers of "foreign devils," was exactly what a tottering Japanese high command wanted to recoup from the disaster in the Central Pacific. By midsummer 1944, it was obvious to the Imperial military and civilian officials that the Marianas were gone and there was virtually no chance of retaking the islands. An entire Japanese army and most of the navy's carrier air power had been annihilated. Now, the question arose, could a positive spin be placed on the otherwise unmitigated disaster? Although the leaders of wartime Japan were generally relatively stolid, unimaginative men, occasionally they could be creative, and in this instance, they had found a positive aspect of defeat.

The leaders of the Japanese military knew that the Americans had suffered substantial casualties when invading the Marianas. In fact, the real, and substantial, number of 26,000 killed, wounded, and missing was multiplied several times over in the usual wildly inaccurate Nipponese accounting system. Now, the reasoning went, if the American devils had suffered tens of thousands of casualties capturing three relatively small islands and killing 65,000 Imperial troops, what would become the calculus of destruction in defeating 4 million Japanese soldiers on the much larger home islands? If the Americans could be induced to believe that the carnage at Marpi Point would be repeated on an enormously larger scale by civilians and soldiers in the heart of Japan, the United States government and military might just acknowledge that a negotiated peace short of total victory would be better than sacrificing their own generation of youths to physically conquering Nippon. Soon, Japanese newspapers were filled with carefully edited versions of American and other foreign accounts of the mass suicide at Marpi Point; the implication was that the world was "astonished" at the courage of Japanese civilians and that this was what the enemy could expect many times over if the homeland was invaded. Yet, ironically, in the midst of this celebration of death, the person who perhaps was the most responsible for its employment was about to be deposed.

Although Emperor Hirohito was cordially despised in America, so little was known about the personality of the "living divinity" even in Japan that people in the United States needed a more tangible and accessible villain with which to identify. Along with Admiral Yamamoto, the architect of Pearl Harbor, stood the Nipponese prime minister, and when the admiral was shot down in 1943, Hideki Tojo became the personification of the brutal militarism that was Imperial Japan.

Yet although Tojo was frequently paired with Adolf Hitler in American rogue galleries, the Japanese premier never had the absolute power enjoyed by the fuhrer. The prestige and power of the emperor and the Imperial Navy allowed members of the royal family and senior admirals a nuanced but real criticism of the prime minister, and by the time of the fall of Saipan, the attacks were becoming less and less veiled. By late June, Tojo's wife was getting anonymous phone calls asking whether her husband had committed suicide yet, and members of the emperor's advisory council began edging toward running the general out of office and substituting a person who was more capable of either pursuing the war more effectively or exploring the possibilities of a negotiated peace.[9]

Finally, on July 16, Marquis Koichi Kido, Lord Keeper of the Privy Seal, inflicted the harshest criticism possible on the premier when he informed Tojo that "the Emperor himself is extremely annoyed." The prime minister was now thoroughly shocked and offered a major shake-up in his cabinet, but a cabal centered on Tojo's predecessor, Prince Fuminaro Konoye, plotted to remove the leader himself. Konoye assembled a conference of Jushin, retired senior ministers, who advised the emperor, and the group unanimously advised Hirohito to oust his premier.

On the evening of July 18, Konoye informed Tojo that the successful enemy penetration of the Marianas had alarmed the emperor to the point where a major change of leadership had been approved, and a new prime minister would be installed the next day.[10]

The choice of the Jushin was General Kunishi Koiso, the senior military official in Korea, known to be a quiet but persistent critic of Tojo's war policies. The navy demanded near parity in decisionmaking authority for the new navy minister, Admiral Mitsumara Yonai, who was expected to function as a virtual co-premier with the general.

The general and admiral were whisked into the emperor's presence on the morning of July 19 and given nuanced, oblique instructions from Hirohito to avoid antagonizing the Russians and to consider ways in which the "current difference" with the United States could be resolved before the enemy invaded the homeland. However, although there was general agreement that a succession of land barriers would discourage a ground invasion, for the immediate future the ongoing collapse in the Marianas would unleash a far more imminent disaster.

Japanese intelligence had closely followed the American development of the Superfortress, and earlier in the spring had forced down, but not destroyed, a B-29 on a training mission. Applying their usual brutal methods of interrogation, the military gained an extremely accurate idea of the new aircraft's range and capabilities. It did not take a huge leap of imagination to realize that a significant reason for the enemy invasion of the Marianas was to secure bases that were within range of the major cities of Japan.

As each successive Imperial airfield on Saipan, Tinian, and Guam fell to the American invaders, the industrial and population heart of Japan was pushed one step closer to aerial Armageddon. The dreaded enormous silver predators would not come tomorrow or even the next day, but as the Stars and Stripes replaced the Rising Sun on each island in the Marianas, enemy construction crews would repair and expand Imperial airfields; young American air crews would take up residence in former Japanese quarters and giant Superfortresses would come lumbering in from the innumerable American aircraft factories that were constructing B-29s around the clock. The fall of Saipan and the rest of the Marianas had caused the downfall of the man most responsible for initiating a war against the American colossus, and now a new set of leaders was being gently prodded by some of the emperor's most trusted advisors to produce a miracle in which peace could somehow be secured, short of the total annihilation of Nipponese culture. Yet although nuanced, oblique discussions of peace with less than victory were being held, the most bitter fruits of defeat in the Marianas were beginning to ripen. As Vice Admiral Shigryoshi Miwa, one of Hirohito's most trusted advisors, warned his emperor, the loss of the Marianas would open a portal to the destruction of the Japanese heartland by aerial demons. Soon the Flying Fortresses would take off from the gateway to the Japanese Empire, and then, according to Admiral Miwa's admonition to his sovereign, "Hell is upon us."

AFTERWORD

O N OCTOBER 17, 1944, the *Joltin' Josie,* piloted by Brigadier
General Heywood Hansell, touched down on Isley Field,
Saipan, as a long line of air crewmen on the former Aslito
Airfield sent up wave after wave of lusty cheers and took turns inspect-
ing the huge silver Superfortress. A few days later, General Emmett
O'Donnell, an aviator who had flown one of the tiny fleet of B-17s
covering Douglas MacArthur's retreat into Bataan Peninsula in 1942
arrived to open the 73rd Bombardment Wing Headquarters. On
November 24, O'Donnell's *Dauntless Dotty* roared down Isley's run-
way, left the coral lagoon of Saipan far behind, and set course for
Tokyo. Ninety-three B-29s unloaded their bombs on Nakajima aircraft
factory, just 10 miles from Emperor Hirohito's palace. More than a
hundred Zeros roared into the air to challenge the gleaming metal
predators, and one pilot crashed his plane into a Superfortress to inflict the only loss in the formation. The weather was heavily overcast
and only about fifty bombs hit the factory, but even the less-accurate
projectiles blasted a dockyard and a residential neighborhood, causing
extensive damage to both. Imperial authorities quickly realized that
cloud cover would not last forever and they had no effective defense
against the new firebombs that could turn Japan's largely wood-con-
structed cities into infernos.

Thus, even several months after the last organized fighting had
ended in the Marianas, the capture of those islands was exerting an
enormous influence on the direction of the Pacific War. This extensive
impact of one of the decisive campaigns of World War II encouraged
consideration of a number of pertinent issues regarding the battle.
Those issues included how the battle was won by the Americans and
lost by the Japanese, and the consequences of that outcome to the
long-term strategies of both nations.

Exploring the "how" of a battle that produced a clear-cut victor can encourage somewhat dangerous smugness that assumes that the winners did almost nothing wrong and the losers did almost nothing right. In some instances, such as Yorktown during the Revolutionary War and Fredericksburg and Vicksburg during the Civil War, this is a safe assumption: George Washington, Robert E. Lee, and Ulysses S. Grant orchestrated nearly perfect victories; Lord Cornwallis, Ambrose Burnside, and John Pemberton suffered abject failures. Yet the Marianas campaign is somewhat more complex. The United States won both the land and sea elements of the Marianas campaign to a large extent because they were able to combine a ready acknowledgment of errors in previous battles, introduce excellent weapons provided by the American "arsenal of democracy," implement generally sound tactics, and inspire unwavering, yet not suicidal, determination among the fighting men, all of which provided a recipe for success. Raymond Spruance and Marc Mitscher were able to use their better plans and superior pilots to accomplish a feat that carrier strategists would have deemed impossible only two years earlier. They allowed a substantial enemy carrier air force to throw the first blow in a battle, yet turned that blow into an unmitigated disaster for the attackers.

The battle of the Philippine Sea was similar: American naval aviators almost annihilated successive waves of Imperial planes while allowing almost no significant damage to the fleet they guarded. After the battle of the Philippine Sea, the reservoir of trained Imperial pilots had almost run dry, and there was simply no resiliency remaining in the force that had stunned two nations at Pearl Harbor.

If the Marianas sea battle was a defensive masterpiece, the struggle for the enemy-held islands was a generally first-rate offensive operation. It is sometimes easy to overlook the fact that the American soldiers and Marines were attacking from a fleet operating hundreds of miles from the nearest friendly land bases against an enemy that was not overwhelmingly outnumbered, was composed heavily of battle-tested units, and enjoyed some of the most advantageous terrain that a commander could hope to occupy in a battle. Yet, despite some false starts, the invaders were able to secure a total victory in which ten defenders were killed for every American fatality.

First, the ground victory in the Marianas demonstrated the enormous advantage that almost total control of the air and sea could confer on the attackers. Japanese commanders admitted in their reports to Tokyo that American shelling, bombing, and strafing wrecked their communications, interfered with concentrations for counterattackers and, perhaps most important, prevented the arrival of reinforcements external to the original garrison. Imperial officers had to fight with the men on hand; when they were dead or wounded there was absolutely no one to replace them. This is the nightmarish scenario for a besieged garrison from Carthage to the Alamo; indeed, it made time the ally of the invaders and the enemy of the defenders.

Second, the Americans were able to employ their supporting ground weapons with a limited, though critical, level of superiority over their adversaries' counterparts. Japanese artillery, especially on Saipan and Guam, provided outstanding support to Imperial infantry and actually inflicted the majority of American casualties. Every American eyewitness account emphasizes the Nipponese artillery as turning the battlefield into a giant shooting gallery reminiscent of the Western Front in World War I. Given the already noted Japanese advantage in terrain, the invaders could not tolerate even a draw in the struggle for support-weapon superiority; somehow, the Americans simply had to outgun the enemy or risk being locked in a stalemate that would bleed the invasion force white. Fortunately for the invaders, once beachheads had been reasonably secured, the Americans could use a devastating combination of superior numbers of cannon, superior-quality tanks, and huge numbers of bazookas and flamethrowers to eventually eradicate the initial relative immunity of Imperial artillery batteries that had caused such havoc in the early stages of the landings.

Third, although the Japanese forces generally exhibited an almost manic obsession to die for the emperor, most American soldiers and Marines exhibited the far more pragmatic determination to send as many adversaries to their eternal reward without any great desire to join them in celestial company. Imperial soldiers swore "seven lives to repay the Emperor," but it was the Americans who usually inflicted this loss ratio, especially against the terrifying yet largely ineffective banzai attacks. As a relative newcomer to authorship of books on the Pacific War, this writer still marvels at the almost childlike obsession of Japanese leaders in throwing away their best men in a seemingly never ending succession of absolutely worthless suicide charges. American films of the 1940s and early 1950s frequently depicted American Indians endlessly circling a besieged wagon train as settlers or soldiers calmly picked them off with only minimal losses to defenders. We now know that most tribes of Native Americans were far too intelligent and sophisticated ever to tolerate so profligate a loss of their irreplaceable fighting men for so little gain. Yet the astounding truth of the equally popular depiction of their World War II equivalent, the Japanese banzai attack on the sometimes surrounded Americans proved to be far more accurate! It appears to this author that just as the Imperial defenders were succeeding in inflicting potentially devastating losses to the Americans as they blasted away from concealment, they would almost irrationally surrender their primary advantage and charge, waving swords and sticks with bayonets, leaving hundreds of dead comrades when they finally retreated back to concealment. Just as the Viet Cong threw away the inherent advantages of guerilla war in the disastrous frontal assault that was the Tet offensive, the Japanese troops in the Marianas seemed to stage a succession of mini-Tets that invariably accelerated the progress of American advances.

The final apparent cause of American victory and Japanese defeat seems to lie in the emergence of competent, albeit not necessarily brilliant, American ground-force leadership. The whole controversy of "Smith v. Smith" and "Marines v. Army" seems to distract attention from a more serious, even-handed evaluation of the American command performance in the land battle for the Marianas. The nature of the Marianas campaign allowed little opportunity for the spectacular, brilliant leadership of a George Washington surprising the Hessians at Trenton, a Robert E. Lee flanking Fighting Joe Hooker's much larger army at Chancellorsville, or a George Patton thrusting tanks through France. Clever, unexpected flanking movements and rapid advances though a startled enemy simply were not going to happen on islands where each side essentially always knew where the enemy was and where they were heading and where an implacable object called an ocean effectively blocked any sweeping movement more than a few hundred yards wide. However, within these severe limitations, the men responsible for defeating the Japanese defenders generally served with commendable intelligence and energy. Generals Roy Geiger and Harry Schmidt orchestrated effective, efficient maneuvers on Guam and Tinian that consistently gave the invaders the initiative and forced the defenders simply to respond to each successive move on the chessboard of battle.

Of course, the saga of the two Smiths garners the most attention in any discussion of Marianas campaign command issues. After carefully reviewing a wide spectrum of available evidence, the author believes that neither Holland Smith nor Ralph Smith was in any respect incompetent in his actions and that both men should be rated as above-average, although hardly brilliant, commanders.

Ralph Smith's positive attributes of high intelligence, superior linguistic ability, and excellent knowledge of the European battle theatre would most likely have afforded him the opportunity to emerge as an excellent divisional commander in the drive across France and Germany, and it would not have been inconceivable for him to have risen to leadership of a corps some time before the German surrender. However, in the sometimes bizarre circumstances of command assignments in the aftermath of Pearl Harbor, Ralph Smith was essentially placed in the wrong theatre in regard to his particular talents. Then, in an equally bizarre time frame of the battle for Saipan, the general was fully involved in commanding a major combat action for exactly one full day in June 1944, and, even in this situation, was missing a third of his command.

Quite simply, the two regiments of the 27th Division that Smith led in the field ran into a buzz saw of Japanese fire at Death Valley and

Purple Heart Ridge. Given the fact that in some respects they were reenacting the Charge of the Light Brigade at Balaclava nine decades earlier, it is reasonable to assume that no two regiments of any army in the world in 1944 would have smashed through the Japanese positions in one or two days of battle. Ralph Smith could not come up with a plan to gain a major advance simply because there was no plan that would work until the Imperial flanks crumbled and the Nipponese troopers could be threatened from the rear. It is worth noting that the two regiments of this division that were accused by Holland Smith of "failing to advance" suffered proportionately more casualties than the two Marine divisions, which faced slightly better, although hardly easy, terrain to their front.

This assertion that Holland Smith should have known better does not place the commander of V Amphibious Corps in the ranks of incompetent generals. The Marine general was personally courageous, idolized by his men, and had a laudable instinct for the welfare of his common soldiers. However, even though he was generally correct in his assumption that a corps commander should spend much of his time in a central headquarters orchestrating the complex ballet that was a multidimensional offensive, this author also believes that he made a major error in judgment by failing to inspect in person the ground on which he accused the 27th Division units of mounting an improper advance. Holland Smith was very correct when he warned correspondent Robert Sherrod that he was igniting a firestorm by firing Ralph Smith. If the Marine general knew what he was starting, why didn't he at least take the time to see the situation for himself? When senior army officials retaliated for Ralph Smith's dismissal by essentially refusing to place army units under Marine command for the rest of the war, they were essentially making the commander of V Amphibious Corps the personification of Marine Corps leadership as they saw it.

For example, during the battle for Guam, Roy Geiger carried out the responsibilities of corps commander for a mixed U.S. Army-Marine force with nothing but high praise from subordinates in both services, and Harry Schmidt's record on Tinian demonstrated his ability to effectively command a major mixed-service campaign. The U.S. Army and Marine Corps did have somewhat different operational philosophies in the conduct of land battles, but the differences were probably not as extreme in practice as apologists for the two services have emphasized. The very nature of amphibious landings against heavily defended enemy beaches implied some element of a frontal charge that could roll up extensive initial casualties for the Marines. Yet senior Marines worked day and night to perfect the use of rocket boats, heavily gunned Amtracs, coordination with Marine air units, and early introduction of armor to the battlefield to shield the average rifleman from at least some of the firepower of the defenders. The assault on the Marianas was definitely not a replay of Tarawa because amphibious tactics were almost constantly evolving.

On the other hand, the charge by some Marine apologists that army units simply huddled under cover until supporting arms did their work for them is not only harsh but also unsubstantiated. The men hitting Omaha Beach in Normandy were soldiers, not Marines, and they did not and could not huddle on the beach and wait for support forces to clear the German defenses before they moved inland. Under the circumstances, the only logical choice was to surge forward and take heavy losses, as opposed to remaining in place and being annihilated. The 40 percent casualty rates for front-line soldiers clearing Omaha Beach and Marines clearing the beaches fronting Charan Kanoa are nearly identical and imply a level of sheer bravery and self-sacrifice that had little to do with service affiliation and much to do with membership in an American "Greatest Generation."

The second relevant topic in a concluding chapter on any great campaign is the range of consequences to the victor and the vanquished after the battle is over. In a general sense, similar to the successful invasion of northwest Europe during this same summer, American victory in the Marianas breached an enormous psychological barrier for both the United States and Japan. Hitler and Tojo spent much of the early part of 1944 boasting that their "Festung Europa" and "Castle Nippon" were guarded by walls that were simply unassailable no matter how much enemy power was thrust at them. It is difficult to determine just how much the German fuhrer and the Japanese premier, their senior military commanders, or the common people who bore the brunt of the war really believed these assertions, but it certainly shattered a major element of the credulity of the Nazis or the Nipponese militarists when these psychological walls came tumbling down rather quickly. This was not quite the scale of Saddam Hussein's prediction of a Mother of All Battles, which turned into a one-hundred-hour rout of a supposedly invincible army, but it is reasonable to suppose that most Germans were shocked to see Allied solders march through the Arc de Triomphe less than three months after D-Day, and most Japanese went from reading about the slaughter of the American invaders to reading about the "glorious suicide" of their own soldiers and civilians in an even shorter time.

The decisive victory in the Marianas encouraged American citizens and Japanese subjects to realize that the climax in the Pacific War was approaching far more rapidly than previously believed, as it became apparent on both sides that the United States could marshal enough power to penetrate any barrier the Japanese high command could throw in their path and that relatively soon the home islands would be subject to some combination of air, sea, and land attack. The Japanese defeat in the Marianas severely reduced the Imperial ability to defeat this growing threat in two related arenas.

First, the loss of the Marianas was in many respects the strategic equivalent of Ulysses S. Grant's capture of Vicksburg in the summer of 1863. That river city was the nexus between the more populated eastern half of the Confederacy and the resource-rich western half. Once the last link on the vital communications line on the opposite sides of the Mississippi River had been lost, the war would be irreversibly compartmentalized, with Richmond almost unable to dispatch reinforcements to help defend the trans-Mississippi region, and, in turn, losing the ability to tap into the resources of that region to supply the eastern armies. Similarly, American capture of the Marianas essentially split the Greater East Asia Co-Prosperity Sphere into regions: a southern sphere that was still relatively rich in resources but was unable to safely deliver most of those resources to the home islands; and a northern sphere that was still relatively rich in trained manpower, but was unable to safely deliver most of those men to places in imminent danger of American invasion.

Second, defeat in the Marianas for the first time placed the major industrial cities of Japan within operational range of the formidable destructive power of the new B-29 Superfortresses. Once the new strategic bombers could solve their teething problems and General Curtis Le May was able to convince the U.S. Army Air Force high command to utilize the aircraft for low-level incendiary attacks, the factories and homes of Japan would begin to burn out of control and the ability of the empire to wage war would slide even lower.

Until the Americans captured the Marianas, the people of the home islands had been largely immune to the immediate terror of the war their government had initiated. Only the minor damage inflicted by the sixteen Mitchells of the Doolittle raid had disturbed the tranquility of Nipponese life. Now the home islands were about to enter the front lines, and it would actually become more dangerous to be a child in a residential neighborhood of Tokyo than to be a soldier serving in Manchuria. Then, in a final carnival of death, a single Superfortress would take off from an airfield in Tinian that had been captured from the Japanese almost exactly a year earlier. In the same August humidity that had pervaded the Marianas battlefield in the summer of 1944, Colonel Paul Tibbets piloted the *Enola Gay* over aquamarine lagoons surrounded by achingly white coral reefs. Tinian had now become the springboard for atomic bombardment and the Hell that Admiral Miwa had warned was upon the Japanese people was now concentrated in one oddly shaped device that plummeted earthward over the sleepy summer skies of Hiroshima.

NOTES

Chapter 1

1. Kenneth Davis, *F.D.R.: The War President* (New York: Random House, 2000), 757.

2. Frank Freidel, *Franklin Roosevelt: A Rendezvous with Destiny* (Boston: Little, Brown, 1990), 459.

3. Harold Macmillan, *The Blast of War 1939–1945* (New York: Carroll and Graf, 1983), 192.

4. Ibid., 193.

5. Eric Larrabee, *Commander-in-Chief: Franklin Delano Roosevelt, His Lieutenants and Their War* (New York: Touchstone, 1987), 183.

6. Grace Hayes, *The History of the Joint Chiefs of Staff in World War II* (Annapolis, Md.: Naval Institute Press, 1987), 279.

7. Larrabee, *Commander-in-Chief*, 185.

8. Ernest King, *Fleet Admiral King, A Naval Record* (Annapolis, Md.: Naval Institute Press, 1982), 417.

9. Hayes, *History*, 278.

10. Larrabee, *Commander-in-Chief*, 186.

11. Hayes, *History*, 289.

Chapter 2

1. Agawa Hiroyuki, *The Reluctant Admiral: Yamamoto and the Imperial Navy* (Tokyo: Kodansha Int., 1979), 334.

2. John Toland, *The Rising Sun: The Decline and Fall of the Japanese Empire* (New York: Random House, 1970), 485.

3. Hiroyuki, *The Reluctant Admiral*, 290.

Chapter 3

1. Agawa Hiroyuki, *The Reluctant Admiral: Yamamoto and the Imperial Navy* (Tokyo: Kodansha Int., 1979), 350.

2. John Toland, *The Rising Sun: The Decline and Fall of the Japanese Empire* (New York: Random House, 1970), 503.

3. Stetson Conn, Rose Engeman, and Byron Fairchild, *Guarding the United States and Its Outposts* (Washington, D.C.: Office of Military History, 1964), 264.

4. Samuel Morison, *Aleutians, Gilberts and Marshalls*, vol. 7 of *History of Naval Operations in World War II* (Boston: Little, Brown, 1951), 40.

5. *United States Army Northern Area Operations* (Washington, D.C.: Office of Military History, 1964), 264.

6. Ibid.

7. Morison, *Aleutians, Gilberts and Marshalls*, 50.

8. *Time* magazine, July 5, 1943.

9. Ronal Spector, *Eagle Against the Sun: The American War with Japan* (New York: Random House, 1985), 226.

10. Dan Vandervat, *The Pacific Campaign: The U.S.-Japanese Naval War 1941–1945* (New York: Touchstone, 1991), 282.

Chapter 4

1. Ernest King, *Fleet Admiral King, A Naval Record* (Annapolis, Md.: Naval Institute Press, 1982), 427.

2. Ibid., 430.

3. Grace Hayes, *The History of the Joint Chiefs of Staff in World War II* (Annapolis, Md.: Naval Institute Press, 1987), 403.

4. Ronal Spector, *Eagle Against the Sun: The American War with Japan* (New York: Random House, 1985), 254.

5. E. B. Potter, *Nimitz* (Baltimore: Naval Institute Press, 1976), 241.

6. King, *Fleet Admiral King*, 489.

7. Charles Lockwood and Hans Christian Adamson, *Battles of the Philippine Seas* (New York: Thomas Crowell, 1967), 2.

8. Ibid., 4.

Chapter 5

1. Ernest King, *Fleet Admiral King, A Naval Record* (Annapolis, Md.: Naval Institute Press, 1982), 491.

2. E. P. Forrestel and Raymond Spruance, *A Study in Command* (Washington, D.C.: U.S. Government Printing Office, 1966), 69.

3. E. B. Potter, *Nimitz* (Baltimore: Naval Institute Press, 1976), 255.

4. Samuel Morison, *Aleutians, Gilberts and Marshalls*, vol. 7 of *History of Naval Operations in World War II* (Boston: Little, Brown, 1951), 149.

5. Ibid., 151.

6. Robert Sherrod, *Tarawa: The Story of a Battle* (New York: Duell, Sloan, and Pearce, 1944), 24.

7. Ibid., 26.

8. Holland Smith, *Coral and Brass* (New York: Scribner, 1949), 124.

9. Edmond Love, *The 27th Infantry Division in World War II* (Washington, D.C.: Infantry Journal Press, 1949), 51.

10. Smith, *Coral and Brass*, 125.

11. Ibid., 126.

12. Morison, *Aleutians, Gilberts and Marshalls*, 12–13.

Chapter 6

1. E. B. Potter, *Nimitz* (Baltimore: Naval Institute Press, 1976), 265.

2. Ibid.

3. Ernest King, *Fleet Admiral King, A Naval Record* (Annapolis, Md.: Naval Institute Press, 1982), 266.

4. Ibid., 267.

5. Samuel Morison, *Aleutians, Gilberts and Marshalls*, vol. 7 of *History of Naval Operations in World War II* (Boston: Little, Brown, 1951), 219.

6. Ibid., 220.

7. Oscar Gilbert, *Marine Tank Battles in the Pacific* (Conshohocken, Pa.: Combined Publishing, 2001), 125.

8. Ibid., 124.

9. Robert Heinl, *Soldiers of the Sea: The United States Marine Corps* (Baltimore: Nautical and Aviation Press, 1991), 423.

10. Gilbert, *Marine Tank Battles*, 133.

Chapter 7

1. E. B. Potter, *Nimitz* (Baltimore: Naval Institute Press, 1976), 279.
2. Ibid., 280.
3. Ibid., 281.
4. Ernest King, *Fleet Admiral King, A Naval Record* (Annapolis, Md.: Naval Institute Press, 1982), 534.
5. Potter, *Nimitz,* 281.
6. Eric Larrabee, *Commander-in-Chief: Franklin Delano Roosevelt, His Lieutenants and Their War* (New York: Touchstone, 1987), 254.
7. William Y'Blood, *Red Sun Setting* (Annapolis, Md.: Naval Institute Press, 1981), 8.
8. Larrabee, *Commander-in-Chief,* 254.

Chapter 8

1. Samuel Morison, *New Guinea and Marianas,* vol. 8 of *History of Naval Operations in World War II* (Boston: Little, Brown, 1951), 166.
2. Edwin Hoyt, *To the Marianas* (New York: Van Nostrano, 1980), 108.
3. Charles Lockwood and Hans Christian Adamson, *Battles of the Philippine Seas* (New York: Thomas Crowell, 1967), 46.
4. William Y'Blood, *Red Sun Setting* (Annapolis, Md.: Naval Institute Press, 1981), 15.
5. Lockwood and Adamson, *Battles of the Philippine Seas,* 47.
6. E. B. Potter, *Nimitz* (Baltimore: Naval Institute Press, 1976), 288.
7. Hoyt, *To the Marianas,* 558.
8. Potter, *Nimitz,* 294.
9. Ibid.
10. Ibid.

Chapter 9

1. Robert Sherrod, *On to Westward: The Battles of Saipan and Iwo Jima* (New York: Duell, Sloane, and Pearce, 1945), 32.
2. Ibid.

3. Philip Crowl, *United States Army in World War II: Campaign in the Marianas* (Washington, D.C.: Office of Military History, 1960), 58.

4. Ibid.

5. Ibid., 67.

6. Ibid., 69.

7. Samuel Morison, *New Guinea and Marianas,* vol. 8 of *History of Naval Operations in World War II* (Boston: Little, Brown, 1951), 175.

8. Ibid., 177.

9. Haruko Taya Cook and Theodore Cook, *Japan at War: An Oral History* (New York: New Press, 1992), 283.

10. Morison, *New Guinea and Marianas,* 183.

Chapter 10

1. Haruko Taya Cook and Theodore Cook, *Japan at War: An Oral History* (New York: New Press, 1992), 283.

2. Robert Sherrod, *On to Westward: The Battles of Saipan and Iwo Jima* (New York: Duell, Sloane, and Pierce, 1945), 45.

3. Cook and Cook, *Japan at War,* 283.

4. John Toland, *The Rising Sun: The Decline and Fall of the Japanese Empire* (New York: Random House, 1970), 264.

5. Cook and Cook, *Japan at War,* 285.

6. Carl Hoffman, *Saipan: The Beginning of the End* (Washington, D.C.: U.S. Marine Corps, 1980), 57.

7. Philip Crowl, *United States Army in World War II: Campaign in the Marianas* (Washington, D.C.: Office of Military History, 1960), 87.

8. Sherrod, *On to Westward,* 74.

9. Hoffman, *Saipan,* 60.

10. Crowl, *United States Army in World War II,* 95.

11. Cook and Cook, *Japan at War,* 286.

12. Crowl, *United States Army in World War II,* 96.

13. Cook and Cook, *Japan at War,* 286.

14. Ibid., 286.

Chapter 11

1. Samuel Morison, *New Guinea and Marianas,* vol. 8 of *History of Naval Operations in World War II* (Boston: Little, Brown, 1951), 215.

2. E. B. Potter, *Nimitz* (Baltimore: Naval Institute Press, 1976), 302.

3. William Y'Blood, *Red Sun Setting* (Annapolis, Md.: Naval Institute Press, 1981), 65.

4. E. P. Forrestal, *Admiral Raymond Spruance, U.S.N.: A Study in Command* (Washington, D.C.: Department of the Navy, 1968), 132.

5. Ibid., 136.

6. Morison, *New Guinea and Marianas,* 243.

7. Y'Blood, *Red Sun Setting,* 71.

8. Ibid., 84.

9. Ibid., 85.

Chapter 12

1. William Y'Blood, *Red Sun Setting* (Annapolis, Md.: Naval Institute Press, 1981), 102.

2. Samuel Morison, *New Guinea and Marianas,* vol. 8 of *History of Naval Operations in World War II* (Boston: Little, Brown, 1951), 274.

3. Edwin Hoyt, *To the Marianas: War in the Center Pacific 1944* (New York: Avon, 1983), 143.

4. Charles Lockwood and Hans Christian Adamson, *Battles of the Philippine Seas* (New York: Thomas Crowell, 1967), 101.

5. Ibid., 102.

6. Hoyt, *To the Marianas,* 146.

7. Y'Blood, *Red Sun Setting,* 116.

8. Ibid., 123.

9. Morison, *New Guinea and Marianas,* 272.

10. Ibid., 273.

11. Ibid., 277.

12. E. P. Forrestal, *Admiral Raymond Spruance, U.S.N.: A Study in Command* (Washington, D.C.: Department of the Navy, 1968), 140.

Chapter 13

1. Thomas Buell, *The Quiet Warrior: A Biography of Admiral Raymond Spruance* (Boston, Little Brown, 1974), 209.

2. William Y'Blood, *Red Sun Setting* (Annapolis, Md.: Naval Institute Press, 1981), 146.

3. Charles Lockwood and Hans Christian Adamson, *Battles of the Philippine Seas* (New York: Thomas Crowell, 1967), 109.

4. Y'Blood, *Red Sun Setting*, 150.

5. Ibid., 160.

6. Samuel Morison, *New Guinea and Marianas*, vol. 8 of *History of Naval Operations in World War II* (Boston: Little, Brown, 1951), 297.

7. Ibid., 298.

8. Ibid., 302.

9. Y'Blood, *Red Sun Setting*, 187.

10. Ibid., 199.

11. E. P. Forrestal, *Admiral Raymond Spruance, U.S.N.: A Study in Command* (Washington, D.C.: Department of the Navy, 1968), 141.

Chapter 14

1. Holland Smith, *Coral and Brass* (New York: Scribner, 1949), 30.

2. Ibid., 182.

3. Robert Sherrod, *On to Westward: The Battles of Saipan and Iwo Jima* (New York: Duell, Sloan, and Pierce, 1945), 60.

4. Carl Hoffman, *Saipan: The Beginning of the End* (Washington, D.C.: U.S. Marine Corps, 1980).

5. Oscar Gilbert, *Marine Tank Battles in the Pacific* (Conshohocken, Pa.: Combined Publishing, 2001), 183.

6. Smith, *Coral and Brass*, 192.

7. Guy Gabaldon, *Saipan: Suicide Island* (Saipan Island: privately printed, 1990), 83.

8. Ibid., 84.

9. Edwin Hoyt, *To the Marianas, War in the Central Pacific, 1944* (New York: Avon, 1983), 183.

10. Smith, *Coral and Brass*, 164.

Chapter 15

1. Harry Gailey, *"Howlin' Mad" vs. the Army* (Novato, Calif.: Presidio Press, 1986), 41.

2. Holland Smith, *Coral and Brass* (New York: Scribner, 1949), 189.

3. Ibid., 169.

4. Carl Hoffman, *Saipan: The Beginning of the End* (Washington, D.C.: U.S. Marine Corps, 1980), 142.

5. Smith, *Coral and Brass*, 711.

6. Gailey, *"Howlin' Mad,"* 176.

7. Robert Sherrod, *On to Westward: The Battles of Saipan and Iwo Jima* (New York: Duell, Sloan, and Pierce, 1945), 89.

8. Gailey, *"Howlin' Mad,"* 127.

9. Bernard Riggs, *Saipan* (Vicksburg, Miss.: privately printed, 1995), 81.

10. Ibid.

11. Sherrod, *On to Westward*, 90.

12. Carl Proehl, *The Fourth Marine Division in World War II* (Nashville, Tenn.: Battery Press, 1988), 66.

13. Guy Gabaldon, *Saipan: Suicide Island* (Saipan Island: privately printed, 1990), 90.

14. Sherrod, *On to Westward*, 137.

Chapter 16

1. John Toland, *The Rising Sun: The Decline and Fall of the Japanese Empire* (New York: Random House, 1970), 581

2. Carl Hoffman, *Saipan: The Beginning of the End* (Washington, D.C.: U.S. Marine Corps, 1980), 222.

3. Francis O'Brien, *Battling for Saipan* (Novato, Calif.: Presidio Press, 2003), 221.

4. Toland, *The Rising Sun*, 582.

5. O'Brien, *Battling for Saipan*, 232.

6. Hoffman, *Saipan*, 223.

7. O'Brien, *Battling for Saipan*, 278.

8. Brad Gates, *The Last Great Bonzai* (Washington, D.C.: privately printed, 1992), 24.

9. O'Brien, *Battling for Saipan,* 310.

10. Bernard Riggs, *Saipan* (Vicksburg, Miss.: privately printed, 1995), 84.

11. Guy Gabaldon, *Saipan: Suicide Island* (Saipan Island: privately printed, 1990), 104.

Chapter 17

1. Carl Hoffman, *The Seizure of Tinian* (Washington, D.C.: U.S. Marine Corps, 1981), 7.

2. Ibid., 17.

3. George Dyer, *The Amphibians Came to Conquer: The Story of Admiral Richmond Kelly Turner* (Washington, D.C.: Naval Historical Division, 1969), 952.

4. Samuel Morison, *New Guinea and Marianas,* vol. 8 of *History of Naval Operations in World War II* (Boston: Little, Brown, 1951), 361.

5. Henry Berry, *Semper Fi-Mac: Living Memories of the United States Marines* (New York: Arbor House, 1982), 226.

6. Hoffman, *Seizure of Tinian,* 62.

7. Ibid., 63.

8. Ibid., 64.

9. Ibid., 66.

Chapter 18

1. Carl Hoffman, *The Seizure of Tinian* (Washington, D.C.: U.S. Marine Corps, 1981), 79.

2. Carl Proehl, *The Fourth Marine Division in World War II* (Nashville, Tenn.: Battery Press, 1988), 105.

3. Edwin Hoyt, *To the Marianas: War in the Central Pacific, 1944* (New York, Avon, 1983), 234.

4. Oscar Gilbert, *Marine Tank Battles in the Pacific* (Conshohocken, Pa.: Combined Publishing, 2001), 174.

5. Ibid., 175.

6. Samuel Morison, *New Guinea and Marianas,* vol. 8 of *History of Naval Operations in World War II* (Boston: Little, Brown, 1951), 368.

7. Gilbert, *Marine Tank Battles,* 178.

8. Hoffman, *Seizure of Tinian,* 112.

Chapter 19

1. Philip Crowl, *United States Army in World War II: Campaign in the Marianas* (Washington, D.C.: Office of Military History, 1960), 333.

2. Samuel Morison, *New Guinea and Marianas,* vol. 8 of *History of Naval Operations in World War II* (Boston: Little, Brown, 1951), 378.

3. Ibid., 382.

4. Crowl, *United States Army in World War II,* 360.

5. Holland Smith, *Coral and Brass* (New York: Scribner, 1949), 409.

6. Henry Shaw, *History of Marine Corps Operations in World War II* (Washington, D.C.: U.S. Marine Corps, 1950), 337.

7. Henry Berry, *Semper Fi-Mac: Living Memories of the United States Marines* (New York: Arbor House, 1982), 174.

8. Oscar Gilbert, *Marine Tank Battles in the Pacific* (Conshohocken, Pa.: Combined Publishing, 2001), 189.

9. Shaw, *History of Marine Corps Operations,* 462.

10. Berry, *Semper Fi-Mac,* 175.

11. Gilbert, *Marine Tank Battles,* 190.

12. Crowl, *United States Army in World War II,* 336.

Chapter 20

1. Philip Crowl, *United States Army in World War II: Campaign in the Marianas* (Washington, D.C.: Office of Military History, 1960), 336.

2. Henry Shaw, *History of Marine Corps Operations in World War II* (Washington, D.C.: U.S. Marine Corps, 1950), 509.

3. Ibid., 510.

4. Ibid.

5. Lieutenant General Edward Craig to Commandant Marine Corps (CMC), 30 September, 1952.

6. Henry Berry, *Semper Fi-Mac: Living Memories of the United States Marines* (New York: Arbor House, 1982), 176.

7. O. R. Lodge, *The Recapture of Guam* (Washington, D.C.: Historical Division, United States Marine Corps, 1954), 78.

8. Shaw, *History of Marine Corps Operations,* 511.

9. Milland Kaufman, "Attack on Guam," *Marine Corps Gazette* 29, no. 2.

Chapter 21

1. Harry Gailey, *"Howlin' Mad" vs. the Army* (Novato, Calif.: Presidio Press, 1986), 219.

2. Ibid., 224.

3. Holland Smith, *Coral and Brass* (New York: Scribner, 1949), 127.

4. Ibid., 178.

5. Gailey, *"Howlin' Mad,"* 5.

6. Robert Sherrod, *Time,* September 18, 1944.

7. Gailey, *"Howlin' Mad,"* 240.

8. Robert Sherrod, "The Nature of the Enemy," *Time,* August 7, 1944.

9. Courtney Brown, *Tojo: The Last Banzai* (New York: Holt, Rinehart and Winston, 1967), 178.

10. Ibid., 180.

BIBLIOGRAPHY

Beltoe, James, and William Belote. *Titans of the Seas: The Development and Operations of American Carrier Task Force During World War II.* New York: Harper and Row, 1975.

Berry, Henry. *Semper Fi-Mac: Living Memories of the U.S. Mariners.* New York: Arbor House, 1982.

Bix, Herbert. *Hirohito and the Making of Modern Japan.* New York: HarperCollins, 2000.

Blair, Clay. *Silent Victory: The United States Submarine War Against Japan.* New York: J. B. Lippincott, 1975.

Brown, Courtney. *Tojo: The Last Banzai.* New York: Holt, Rinehart and Winston, 1967.

Buell, Thomas. *The Quiet Warrior: A Biography of Admiral Raymond Spruance.* Boston: Little, Brown, 1980.

Cook, Haruko Taya, and Theodore Cook. *Japan at War: An Oral History.* New York: New Press, 1992.

Craven, Wesley, and James Cate. *The Army Air Forces in World War II.* Chicago: University of Chicago Press, 1948.

Crowl, Philip. *Campaign in the Marianas.* Washington, D.C.: Department of the Navy, 1960.

Crowl, Philip, and Edmond Love. *Seizure of the Gilberts and Marshalls.* Washington, D.C.: Department of the Army, 1955.

Davis, Kenneth. *F.D.R.: The War President.* New York: Random House, 2000.

Dull, Paul. *A Battle History of the Imperial Japanese Navy.* Annapolis, Md.: Naval Institute Press, 1978.

Dyer, George. *The Amphibians Came to Conquer: The Story of Admiral Richmond Kelly Turner.* Washington, D.C.: Department of the Navy, 1969.

Forrestal, E. P. *Admiral Raymond Spruance, USN: A Study in Command.* Washington, D.C.: Department of Navy, 1968.

Freidel, Frank. *Franklin Roosevelt: A Rendezvous with Destiny.* Boston: Little Brown, 1990.

Gabaldon, Guy. *Saipan: Suicide Island.* Saipan Island: privately printed, 1990.

Gailey, Harry. *"Howlin' Mad" vs. the Army.* Novato, Calif.: Presidio Press, 1986.

Gates, Brad. *The Last Great Bonzai.* Washington, D.C.: privately published, 1992.

Gilbert, Oscar. *Mariner Tank Battles in the Pacific.* Consohohocken, Pa.: Combined Publishing, 2001.

Hayes, Grace. *The History of the Joint Chiefs of Staff in World War II: The War Against Japan.* Annapolis, Md.: Naval Institute Press, 1982.

Heinl, Robert. *Soldiers of the Sea: The United States Marine Corps.* Baltimore: Nautical and Aviation Publishing, 1991.

Hiroyuki, Agawa. *The Reluctant Admiral: Yamamoto and the Imperial Navy.* Tokyo: Kodansha International, 1979.

Hoffman, Carl. *Saipan: The Beginning of the End.* Washington, D.C.: Historical Division: United States Marine Corps, 1980.

_____. *The Seizure of Tinian.* Washington, D.C.: Historical Division, United States Marine Corps, 1981.

Hoyt, Edwin. *Storm over the Gilberts.* New York: Mason-Charter, 1978.

_____. *To the Marianas: War in the Central Pacific, 1944.* New York: Avon, 1983.

Isley, James, and Philip Crowl. *The U.S. Marines and Amphibious War.* Princeton: Princeton University Press, 1951.

King, Ernest. *Fleet Admiral King: A Naval Record.* Annapolis, Md.: Naval Institute Press, 1982.

Larrabee, Eric. *Commander in Chief: Franklin Delano Roosevelt: His Lieutenants and Their War.* New York, Touchstone, 1987.

Leahy, William. *I Was There.* New York: Whittlesey House, 1950.

Lockwood, Charles, and Hans Christian Adamson. *Battles of the Philippine Sea.* New York: Thomas Crowell, 1967.

Lodge, O. R. *The Recapture of Guam.* Washington, D.C.: Historical Division, United States Marine Corps, 1954.

Love, Edmund. *The 27th Infantry Division in World War II.* Washington, D.C.: Infantry Journal Press, 1949.

MacArthur, Douglas. *Reminiscences.* New York: McGraw Hill, 1984.

Macmillan, Harold. *The Blast of War 1939–1945.* New York: Carroll and Graf, 1983.

Morison, Samuel. *Aleutians, Gilberts and Marshalls.* Vol. 7 of *History of the Naval Operations in World War II.* Boston: Little, Brown, 1951.

———. *New Guinea and The Marianas.* Vol. 8 of *History of the Naval Operations in World War II.* Boston: Little, Brown, 1951.

O'Brien, Francis. *Battling for Saipan.* New York: Ballantine, 2003.

Potter, E. B. *Nimitz.* Baltimore: Naval Institute Press, 1976.

Poyer, Lin, Suzanne Falgout, and Lawerence Carucci. *The Typhoon of War: Micronesian Experiences of the Pacific War.* Honolulu: University of Hawaii Press, 2001.

Proehl, Carl. *The Fourth Marine Division in World War II.* Nashville, Tenn.: Battery Press, 1988.

Riggs, Bernard. *Saipan.* Vicksburg, Miss.: privately printed, 1995.

Roosevelt, Elliot. *As He Saw It: The World Conferences of F.D.R.* New York: Duell, Sloan, and Pearce, 1946.

Shaw, Henry. *History of Marine Corps Operations in World War II.* Washington, D.C.: U.S. Marine Corps, 1950.

Sherrod, Robert. *Tarawa: The Story of a Battle.* New York: Duell, Sloan, and Pearce, 1944.

———. *On to Westward: The Battles of Saipan and Iwo Jima.* New York: Duell, Sloan, and Pearce, 1945.

Smith, Holland. *Coral and Brass.* New York: Scribner, 1950.

Spector, Ronald. *Eagle Against the Sun: The American War with Japan.* New York: Random House, 1985.

Toland, John. *The Rising Sun: The Decline and Fall of the Japanese Empire, 1936–1945.* New York: Random House, 1970.

Van der Vat, Dan. *The Pacific Campaign: The U.S.-Japanese Naval War, 1941–1945.* New York: Touchstone, 1991.

Y'Blood, William. *Red Sun Setting: The Battle of the Philippine Sea.* Annapolis, Md.: Naval Institute Press, 1980.

INDEX